Learning SQL on SQL Server 2005

Other resources from O'Reilly

Learning SQL on SQL Server 2005

Sikha Saha Bagui and Richard Walsh Earp

O'REILLY®

Beijing · Cambridge · Farnham · Köln · Paris · Sebastopol · Taipei · Tokyo

Learning SQL on SQL Server 2005
by Sikha Saha Bagui and Richard Walsh Earp

Published by O'Reilly Media, Inc., 1005 Gravenstein Highway North, Sebastopol, CA 95472.

O'Reilly books may be purchased for educational, business, or sales promotional use. Online editions are also available for most titles (*safari.oreilly.com*). For more information, contact our corporate/institutional sales department: (800) 998-9938 or *corporate@oreilly.com*.

Editor: Jeff Pepper	**Cover Designer:** Karen Montgomery
Production Editor: Philip Dangler	**Interior Designer:** David Futato
Copyeditor: Nancy Wolfe Kotary	**Cover Illustration:** Dover Pictorial Archive
Indexer: Johnna VanHoose Dinse	**Illustrators:** Robert Romano and Jessamyn Read

Printing History:

April 2006:   First Edition.

 This book uses RepKover™, a durable and flexible lay-flat binding.

ISBN-10: 0-596-10215-1
ISBN-13: 978-0-596-10215-9
[M]

Dedicated to my father, Santosh Saha, and
mother, Ranu Saha
and
my husband, Subhash Bagui
and
my sons, Sumon and Sudip
and
Pradeep, Priyashi, and Piyali Saha
—S.B.

To my wife, Brenda,
and
my children: Beryl, Rich, Gen, and Mary Jo
—R.E.

Table of Contents

Preface

SQL Server is one of the most powerful database engines used today. Microsoft's latest release of SQL Server, SQL Server 2005, is a comprehensive database platform that provides secure and reliable storage for both relational and structured data, enabling one to build and manage high-performance data applications. SQL Server 2005's close integration with Microsoft Visual Studio, the Microsoft Office System, and a suite of new development tools set SQL Server 2005 apart from previous versions and from other database engines. This system allows developers to build, debug, and operate applications faster then ever before.

SQL Server 2005 can be installed on small machines using Microsoft Windows as well as on large servers. In recent years, the computer industry has seen a dramatic increase in the popularity of relational databases and multiuser databases, and the computer industry needs application developers and people who can write SQL code efficiently and correctly for relational and multiuser databases.

Why This Book?

This book is mainly intended to be a systematic guide to learning SQL using SQL Server 2005—a relational and multiuser database. The book is aimed at students who wish to learn SQL using Microsoft's SQL Server 2005. The book is expected to be used by schools and SQL training organizations as well as by database and IT professionals who are actively working with SQL Server 2005.

The book starts with very simple SQL concepts, and slowly builds into more complex query development. The purpose of this book is to present every topic, concept, and idea with examples of code and output. Exercises have also been included to gain SQL proficiency using SQL Server. The best approach to using this book efficiently is to read through the book with SQL Server open and active. As the book is read, it will be advantageous for you to work with and understand the examples.

If the book is used for a beginning database course, the exercises are presented to be done by the students over the course of one semester at a pace of one chapter per week. The exercises are found at the end of each chapter.

Due to the dramatic increase in the popularity of relational and multiuser databases, many schools and training organizations are using SQL Server in their database courses to teach database principles and concepts. This development has generated a need for a concise book on SQL Server programming, tied in with database principles and concepts—hence this book.

SQL and SQL Server

SQL (Structured Query Language) is a standard language used for querying, updating, and managing relational databases, and lately SQL has become the de facto standard "language" for accessing relational databases. SQL is not really as much of a language as it is a database query tool. In this book, we concentrate on learning SQL using SQL Server 2005.

SQL allows us to define a relational database—create and modify tables (in this sense, SQL is a *data definition language*, or DDL). SQL also allows us to tell SQL Server which information we want to select (retrieve), insert, update, or delete. That is, SQL also allows us to query the relational database in a most flexible way, as well as to change the stored data (and in this sense, SQL is a *data manipulation language*, or DML).

The book is targeted at SQL Server users on the Windows operating system, but is easily adaptable to other platforms.

Audience and Coverage

A book like this can be used in an "Introduction to Databases" course or a second database course along with textbooks like *Fundamentals of Database Systems*, 4th Edition, Addison Wesley, 2003 (Elmasri and Navathe), and *Database Processing, Fundamentals, Design & Implementation*, 9th Edition, Prentice Hall, 2003 (David Kroenke). Students could learn the database theory from the texts, and apply the theory using this book (using SQL Server) as they learn SQL.

This book can also be used as a standalone text in a course on learning SQL using SQL Server 2005. This book does not assume any prior computer knowledge.

This book consists of 11 chapters. Chapter 1 introduces the user to SQL Server 2005. In Chapter 1, you will learn how to open SQL Server 2005 using SQL Server Management Studio, load the database, and view and perform simple table manipulations. Chapter 1 also introduces the user to the query editor; shows you how to view, save, and print queries and output; and how to customize SQL Server 2005's settings. Chapter 2 introduces the user/learner to some basic SQL commands in SQL Server. Chapter 3 discusses creating, populating, altering, and deleting tables; an example relational database is built on the idea of tabular data. Chapter 4 introduces and covers different types of joins—a common database mechanism for combining tables. Chapter 5 covers SQL Server 2005's functions. Chapter 6 discusses query development as well as the use of views and other derived structures. Chapter 7 covers simple set operations. Chapters 8, 9, and 10 cover subqueries, aggregate functions, and correlated subqueries; and Chapter 11 presents indexes and constraints that can be added to tables in SQL Server 2005.

Appendix A describes the Student_course database and other databases that have been used throughout the book. Appendix B provides the actual script used to create the Student_course database. Glossaries defining terms and important functions are provided, as well as indexes of terms and functions in the book.

The book is sufficient for beginning SQL users to get an overview of what SQL Server entails and how to use SQL. Many SQL programmers have based their employment on this material. The book gives a very good feel for what SQL is, and how SQL is used in SQL Server.

A Few Notes About SQL Server 2005 Installation

For best results, one should install SQL Server 2005 on a computer that does not have a prerelease version of SQL Server 2005, Visual Studio 2005, or the .NET Framework 2.0 installed on it. If your computer has any of the prerelease versions on it, they *must* be removed in the correct order *before* you can successfully manually install the actual version of SQL Server 2005 software. For the correct order of these required uninstallations before you can install SQL Server 2005, visit:

http://msdn.microsoft.com/vstudio/express/support/uninstall/#Uninstall

We strongly recommend that you instead run the autoinstall tool (found at the same site), rather than attempting a manual install.

Once the uninstall has been correctly done, you may successfully load SQL Server 2005 and begin learning SQL.

Conventions Used in This Book

The following conventions are used in this book:

Italic

> Used for URLs and for emphasis when introducing a new term.

Constant width

> Used for MySQL and SQL keywords and for code examples.

Constant width bold
> In some code examples, highlights the statements being discussed.

Constant width italic
> In some code examples, indicates an element (e.g., a filename) that you supply.

UPPERCASE
> In code examples, generally indicates MySQL keywords.

lowercase
> In code examples, generally indicates user-defined items such as variables, parameters, etc.

punctuation
> In code examples, enter exactly as shown.

indentation
> In code examples, helps to show structure but is not required.

`--`
> In code examples, begins a single-line comment that extends to the end of a line.

/* and */
> In code examples, delimit a multiline comment that can extend from one line to another.

.
> In code examples and related discussions, qualifies a reference by separating an object name from a component name.

[ ] In syntax descriptions, enclose optional items.

{ } In syntax descriptions, enclose a set of items from which you must choose only one.

|
> In syntax descriptions, separates the items enclosed in curly brackets, as in {TRUE | FALSE}.

. . .
> In syntax descriptions, indicates repeating elements. An ellipsis also shows that statements or clauses irrelevant to the discussion were left out.

> Indicates a tip, suggestion, or general note. For example, we'll tell you if a certain setting is version-specific.

> Indicates a warning or caution. For example, we'll tell you if a certain setting has some kind of negative impact on the system.

Using Code Examples

This book is here to help you get your job done. In general, you may use the code in this book in your programs and documentation. You do not need to contact us for permission unless you're reproducing a significant portion of the code. For example, writing a program that uses several chunks of code from this book does not require permission. Selling or distributing a CD-ROM of examples from O'Reilly books *does* require permission. Answering a question by citing this book and quoting example code does not require permission. Incorporating a significant amount of example code from this book into your product's documentation *does* require permission.

We appreciate, but do not require, attribution. An attribution usually includes the title, author, publisher, and ISBN. For example: "*Learning SQL on SQL Server 2005* by Sikha Saha Bagui and Richard Walsh Earp. Copyright 2006 O'Reilly Media, Inc., 0-596-10215-1."

If you feel that your use of code examples falls outside fair use or the permission given here, feel free to contact us at *permissions@oreilly.com*.

How to Contact Us

We have tested and verified the information in this book and in the source code to the best of our ability, but given the amount of text and the rapid evolution of technology, you may find that features have changed or that we have made mistakes. If so, please notify us by writing to:

> O'Reilly Media, Inc.
> 1005 Gravenstein Highway North
> Sebastopol, CA 95472
> 800-998-9938 (in the United States or Canada)
> 707-829-0515 (international or local)
> 707-829-0104 (fax)

You can also send messages electronically. To be put on the mailing list or request a catalog, send email to:

> *info@oreilly.com*

To ask technical questions or comment on the book, send email to:

> *bookquestions@oreilly.com*

As mentioned in the earlier section, we have a web site for this book where you can find code, errata (previously reported errors and corrections available for public view), and other book information. You can access this web site at:

> *http://www.oreilly.com/catalog/learnsqlsvr05*

For more information about this book and others, see the O'Reilly web site:

> *http://www.oreilly.com*

Acknowledgments

Our special thanks are due to our editor, Jeff Pepper, and the production crew at O'Reilly for putting up with all the changes.

We would also like to thank President John Cavanaugh, Dean Jane Halonen, and Provost Sandra Flake of the University of West Florida for their inspiration, encouragement, support, and true leadership quality. We would also like to express our gratitude to Dr. Wes Little on the same endeavor.

Our sincere thanks also go to Dr. Ed Rodgers for his continuing support and encouragement throughout past years. We also appreciate Dr. Leo Terhaar, chair, Computer Science Department, for his advice, guidance, and support, and encouraging us to complete this book. Last, but not least, we would like to thank our fellow faculty members, Dr. Jim Bezdek and Dr. Norman Wilde for their continuous support and encouragement.

CHAPTER 1

Starting Microsoft SQL Server 2005

This chapter introduces SQL Server 2005 and SQL Server 2005's Management Studio and its basic workings. You will learn how to create a database, view the objects and default tables in a database, use a query editor, activate the database in different ways, and create tables in the database using a load script. The load script is available at *http://www.cs.uwf.edu/~sbagui*. The load script will create the Student_course database for you. This database will be used throughout the rest of the book to learn SQL. At this point, you may want to copy the load script, *SQLServer2005_load.sql*, to your working directory on your computer, before you start working on the next section. Right-click on the script on the web site, select Save Target As, and save it to your working directory.

In this chapter, you will also learn how to view and modify table definitions; delete a table and a database; type, parse, execute and save a query; display the results in different forms; stop execution of a query; and print the query and results. The final section of this chapter discusses customizing SQL Server 2005's settings.

Starting Microsoft SQL Server 2005 and SQL Server 2005's Management Studio

To start Microsoft SQL Server 2005 and open up SQL Server 2005's Management Studio, follow these steps:

From the Start menu, go to All Programs, select Microsoft SQL Server 2005, and then SQL Server Management Studio (as shown in the Figure 1-1).

You will get the screen shown in Figure 1-2. This screen allows you to connect to Microsoft SQL Server 2005. If the server type and server name are different from the defaults that came up, enter the appropriate server type and server name, and select Windows Authentication. Then, click Connect.

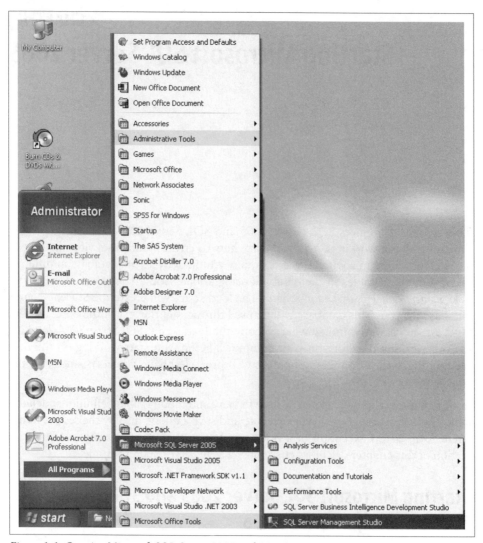

Figure 1-1. Opening Microsoft SQL Server 2005 and SQL Server Management Studio

 Your system may require a username and password for each SQL Server instance.

Once connected to the server that you typed in, you will get the Microsoft SQL Server Management Studio screen (Figure 1-3) that we will be using throughout the rest of the book.

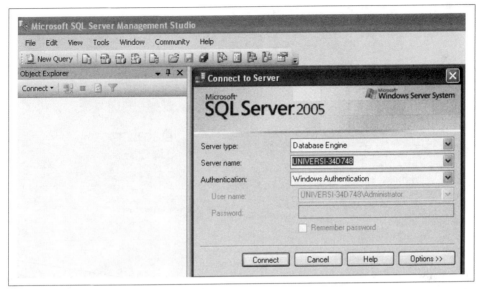

Figure 1-2. Connecting to Microsoft SQL Server 2005

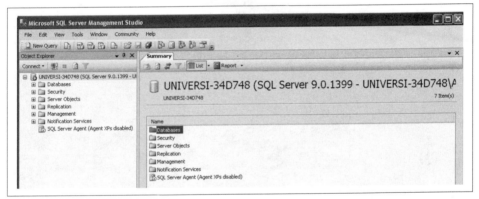

Figure 1-3. Connected to Microsoft SQL Server 2005's Server

The Microsoft SQL Server Management Studio screen contains the Object Explorer on the left portion of the screen and, to start with, a Summary tab on the right portion of the screen. The Object Explorer provides a hierarchical view of objects. For example, you can navigate through a database, table, column, or other types of objects, as we will soon show you.

Creating a Database in Microsoft SQL Server 2005

Before we begin to work with Microsoft SQL Server 2005, we will create a database. To create a database, as shown in Figure 1-4, right click on Databases in the Object Explorer and select New Database... from the context menu.

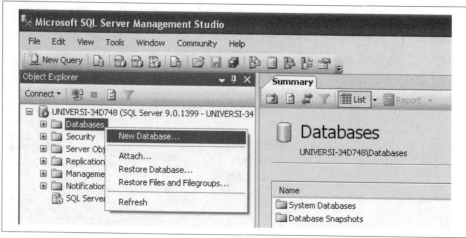

Figure 1-4. Creating a New Database

You will get the New Database dialog box, as shown in Figure 1-5. We will create a database called Student_course.

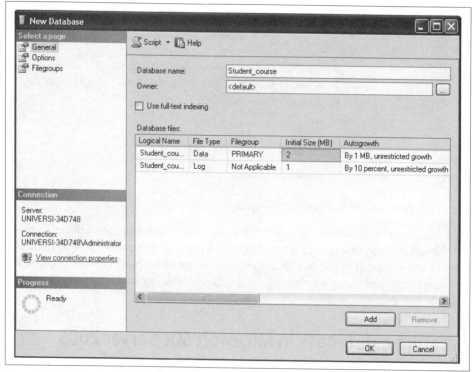

Figure 1-5. Typing in the database name

Type in your database name as Student_course. You may leave the Owner as
<default> for now, as shown in Figure 1-5. Click OK. You will get the screen shown
in Figure 1-6.

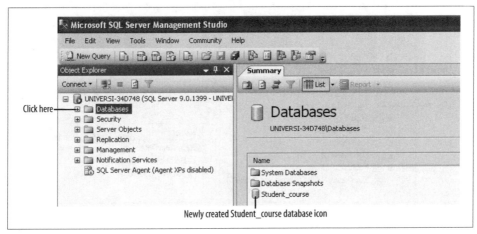

Figure 1-6. The Student_course database

The Student_course database has now been created. Note the newly created Student_
course database icon under the Summary tab on the righthand side of the screen
below Databases (see Figure 1-6).

In order to view the Student_course database under the Object Explorer (on the left
side of your screen) right away, you may have to first right-click on the Databases
node and then select Refresh.

Then, as shown in Figure 1-6, you may now expand the Databases node by clicking
on the + sign beside Databases under the Object Explorer, and you also will see the
Student_course database node under and Databases (under the Object Explorer on
the left portion of your screen), as shown in Figure 1-7.

Objects in the Student_course Database

A SQL Server database is a collection of many objects, such as tables, views, and synonyms, defined to support activities performed with data.

From Figure 1-7, expand the Student_course database node by clicking on the + sign
beside the Student_course node, and you will get the screen shown in Figure 1-8,
which shows the default objects that are in the Student_course database.

Default Tables in the Student_course Database

A database is a collection of related tables. So far we have created the Student_course
database, but we have not created any tables.

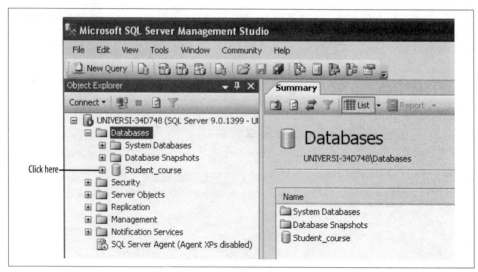

Figure 1-7. The Student_course database under the Object Explorer

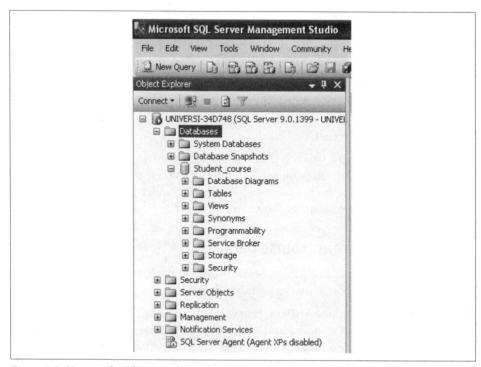

Figure 1-8. Viewing the Objects in the Student_course database

To view the default tables in the Student_course database, expand the Tables node (as shown in Figure 1-9), and the only default table in the Student_course database, System Tables, will be displayed.

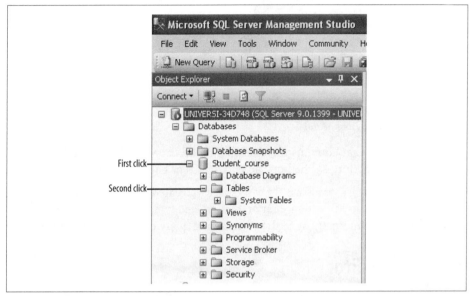

Figure 1-9. System tables in the Student_coursedatabase

At this point you may click on the – sign beside the Tables node, and then on the – sign beside the Student_course node to close those up, and you will get back to Figure 1-7.

Default System Databases

SQL Server 2005 comes with some default System databases—master, model, msdb, and tempdb. To view these default database nodes, expand the Database node and then System Databases node, as shown in Figure 1-10, and you will be able to see the default System databases.

master is a database composed of system tables that keeps track of server installation as a whole and all other databases that are subsequently created. The SQL Server Management Studio query window defaults to the master database context. Any queries executed from the query window will execute in the master database unless you change the context.

model is a template database. Every time a new database is created, SQL Server makes a copy of the model database (and all of the objects in it) to form the basis of the new database. If you want all your new databases to inherit certain properties, you could include these properties and objects in your model database.

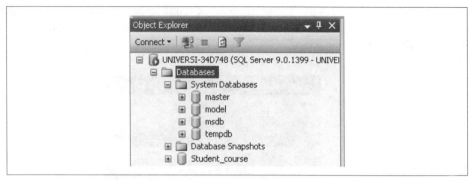

Figure 1-10. Default System Databases

msdb is a database that contains the metadata and database objects used by the SQL Server agent that performs scheduled activities such as backups and replication tasks.

tempdb is a temporary database or workspace recreated every time SQL Server is restarted. tempdb is used for temporary tables created by users and to hold intermediate results created internally by SQL Server during query processing and sorting.

The Query Editor

The most important thing you do in SQL Server 2005, or in any other database for that matter, is query the database. Queries in SQL Server 2005 are typed in the query editor. The query editor can be opened in two ways, as discussed in the following subsections: (a) by right-clicking, and (b) by using the New Query button.

Opening the Query Editor by Right-Clicking

Select the Student_course database and right-click, as shown in Figure 1-11. Select New Query.

Figure 1-12 shows the query editor, which can be used to create queries and other SQL scripts and execute them against SQL Server databases.

The first query will be called SQLQuery1.sql by default. Later we will show you how to change the name of the query when saving it.

If the query editor is opened in this way, the Student_course database automatically becomes the database against which the queries are executed, because you initially selected Student_course and then right-clicked. If we want to work in our Student_course database, we have to make sure that the Student_course database is active. If the Student_course database is not active, we have to activate it—we show you how to do this in different ways in the following sections.

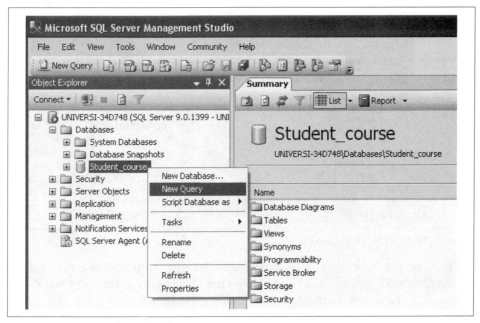

Figure 1-11. Opening the query editor

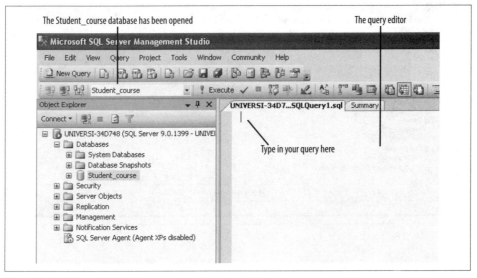

Figure 1-12. The query editor

Opening the Query Editor Using the New Query Button

You can also open the query editor by selecting the New Query button from the top menu (leftmost icon), as shown in Figure 1-13.

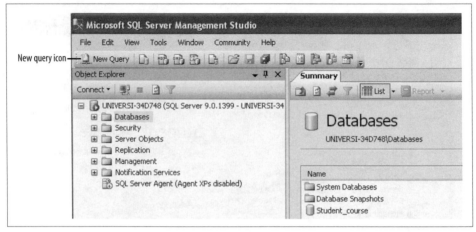

Figure 1-13. Using the New Query icon

If you used the New Query icon from Figure 1-13 (without selecting the Student_course database), you will get Figure 1-14. Here, note that the Student_course database is not the active database; master is the active database, because SQL Server 2005 defaults to master.

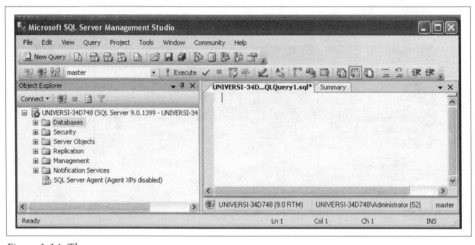

Figure 1-14. The query screen

But we want to use the Student_course database that we just created, so we have to activate the Student_course database. Click on the drop-down icon of the Combo box beside master and select Student_course, as shown in Figure 1-15. This step activates or opens the Student_course database.

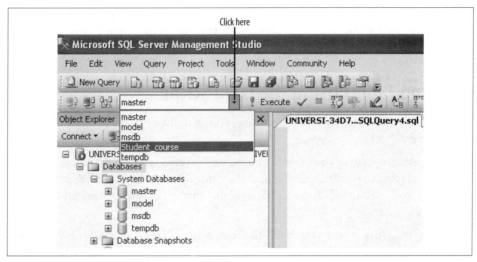

Figure 1-15. Selecting the Student_course database

Opening or Activating the Database Using USE

You can also activate or open the Student_course database by typing in the following in the query editor (as shown in Figure 1-16):

```
USE Student_course
```

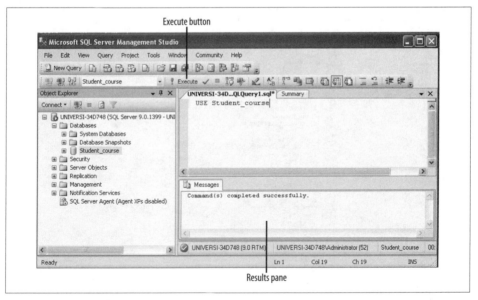

Figure 1-16. Using USE

Then, click the Execute button (it is on the menu bar above the query editor screen). You will get the following message in the results pane (as shown in Figure 1-16):

```
Command(s) completed successfully
```

Creating Tables Using the Load Script

A table is used to store data in a database, and, a database is typically composed of many tables.

After the Student_course database is opened or activated, you need to create tables in the Student_course database and insert data into the tables. To do this, run (execute) the load script, *SQLServer2005_load.sql*, that you downloaded and saved to your working directory.

Go to the directory where you saved the load script, *SQLServer2005_load.sql*. Double-click *SQLServer2005_load.sql*. Then, select the whole script and copy it. This script will be pasted into SQL Server 2005's query editor. Open SQL Server 2005's query editor as shown in Figure 1-12. Make sure that the Student_course database is active. Paste the load script into the query editor, as shown in the Figure 1-17.

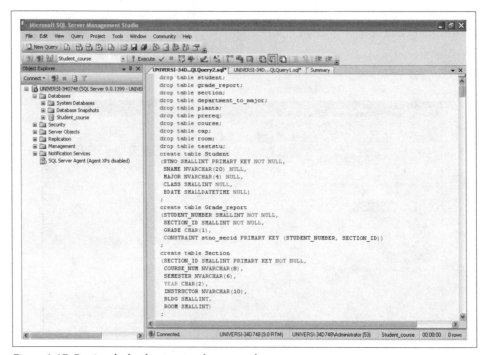

Figure 1-17. Pasting the load script into the query editor

Once the script has been pasted into the query editor, execute this script by clicking the Execute button or the F5 shortcut key. This script takes only a few seconds to execute. You will get the results shown in Figure 1-18—on the bottom part of the screen under the Messages tab.

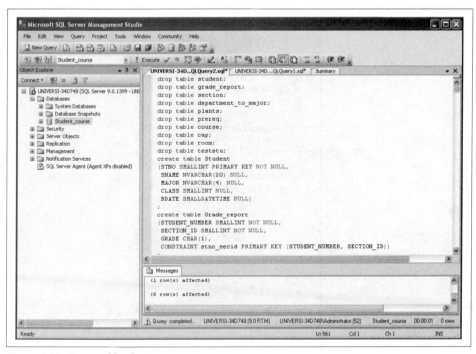

Figure 1-18. Executed load script

This script creates the tables Cap, Course, Department_to_major, Dependent, Grade_report, Plants, Prereq, Room, Section, Student, and teststu, in the Student_course database and inserts data into them. The tables in the Student_course database are laid out in Appendix A. We also present the T-SQL for the load script in Appendix B.

To view the tables that were created by the load script, expand the Student_course node and then expand the Tables node. You will get the screen shown in Figure 1-19. Every table shows up as a node under Student_course.

Viewing Table Definitions

Every table in SQL Server 2005 has a table definition. The table definition gives us information about a table such as the column names in the table, the data types of the columns in the table and whether the columns allow null (missing) values.

To view the definition of the Student table for example, expand the Student node by clicking on the + sign beside it, and then expand the Columns node, by clicking on the + sign beside it, as shown in Figure 1-20. You will be able to view the columns in the Student table. The columns in the Student table are stno, sname, major, class, and bdate.

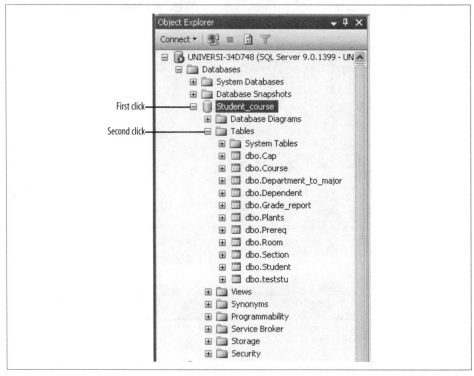

Figure 1-19. Viewing the tables in the Student_coursedatabase

Modifying Table Definitions

If you wish to modify any of the column specifications—for example, if you want to insert or delete columns, rename a column, change the data type of a column, or allow or disallow null fields—you need to modify the table definition. The table definition can be modified by modifying the column definition or by modifying the table definition.

Modifying Column Definitions

To modify the column definition, right-click the column that you wish to modify. For example, if you wish to modify the column definition of the SNAME field of the Student table, as seen in Figure 1-20, right-click the SNAME field of the Student table (as shown in Figure 1-21), and select one of the following options—New Column, Modify, Rename, Delete, Refresh or Properties.

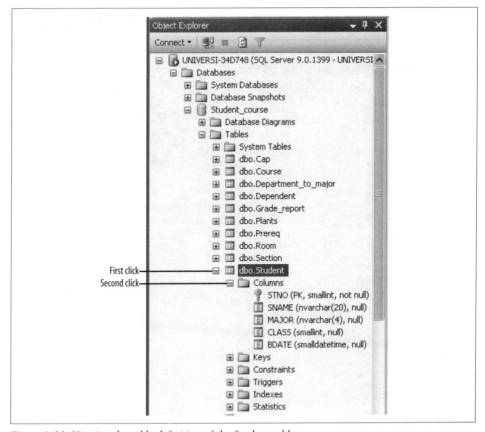

First click
Second click

Figure 1-20. Viewing the table definition of the Student table

Modifying the Table Definition Directly

Another way to view or modify the table definition is to right-click the table—for example, Student—and then select Modify, as shown in Figure 1-22.

The table definition of the Student table is now displayed, as shown in Figure 1-23.

You can delete or insert columns from here, change the data types, allow or disallow null values, and more. Once you have finished making your changes (or just viewing the table definition, if that is what you intended to do), you can close this window. You will be asked if you wish to save the changes and you may select Yes or No, depending on whether you made changes to the table definition and you want to save the changes.

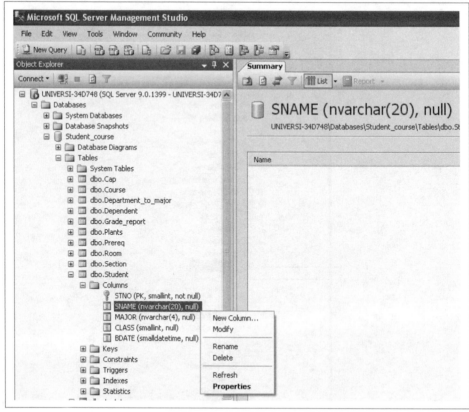

Figure 1-21. Modifying the column definition

Viewing Table Data

To view the data in a table, right click on the table, as shown in Figure 1-22, and select Open Table. For example, to view the data of the Student table, right-click on the Student table, and select Open Table. This will show all 48 rows of the Student table, of which we show the first 14 rows here:

```
STNO    SNAME     MAJOR   CLASS   BDATE
-----   -------   ------  -----   ----------------------
2       Lineas    ENGL    1       4/15/1980 12:00:00 AM
3       Mary      COSC    4       7/16/1978 12:00:00 AM
8       Brenda    COSC    2       8/13/1977 12:00:00 AM
10      Richard   ENGL    1       5/13/1980 12:00:00 AM
13      Kelly     MATH    4       8/12/1980 12:00:00 AM
14      Lujack    COSC    1       2/12/1977 12:00:00 AM
15      Reva      MATH    2       6/10/1980 12:00:00 AM
17      Elainie   COSC    1       8/12/1976 12:00:00 AM
```

19	Harley	POLY	2	4/16/1981 12:00:00 AM
20	Donald	ACCT	4	10/15/1977 12:00:00 AM
24	Chris	ACCT	4	2/12/1978 12:00:00 AM
34	Lynette	POLY	1	7/16/1981 12:00:00 AM
49	Susan	ENGL	3	3/11/1980 12:00:00 AM
62	Monica	MATH	3	10/14/1980 12:00:00 AM

.
.
.

This screen also allows you to insert data, make changes to the data, and save this changed data.

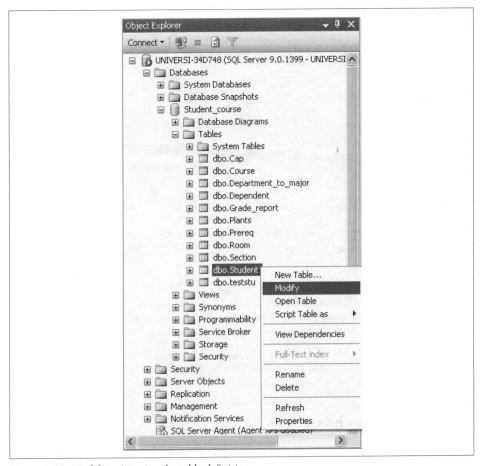

Figure 1-22. Modifying/viewing the table definition

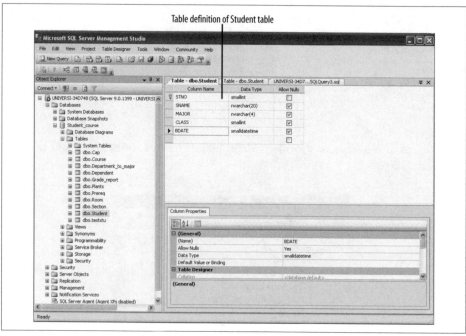

Table definition of Student table

Figure 1-23. Viewing the table definition of the Student table using the Modify option

Deleting a Table

To delete a table, right-click on the table that you wish to delete (as shown in Figure 1-22), and then select Delete. Deleting a table will delete the table, table definition, and all of the data in the table.

> Once you delete a table, there will be no way to get the table or its data back except by restoring from a backup. Be very careful that you indeed intend to permanently dispose of data before selecting Delete.

Do not delete any tables right now. We provide this information for later reference, should you have to delete tables.

Deleting a Database

To delete a database, right-click on the database that you would like to delete, and select Delete, as shown in Figure 1-24.

> But please do not delete the database right now.

Figure 1-24. Deleting a database

Entering a SQL Query or Statement

Like every computer language, a SQL query or statement is used to give instructions to the computer. A query is a request for data stored in SQL Server. The computer analyzes each instruction and interprets it. If the instruction is "understandable" to the computer, the computer produces a result. If the computer cannot figure out what the instruction means, it displays an error message.

In this book, we focus on Transact-SQL (T-SQL), SQL Server's variant of SQL. In SQL Server 2005, the SQL query is typed in the query editor screen, as shown in Figure 1-12. But, before you type in your query, make sure the database that you wish to work with is active or open. To type in or work on the queries in this book, the Student_course database should be active or open.

Right click on Student_course and then select New Query. Type the following SQL query in the resulting screen:

```
USE Student
SELECT *
FROM Student
```

USE Student opens the Student_course database, as shown in Figure 1-12. SELECT is the SQL keyword that means "select data" or "retrieve the following data from the database." The * is interpreted to mean "show all columns in the result." FROM is the keyword that names the source of the data, and Student is the name of a table. So this is a simple SQL query that tells SQL Server to display all the rows and columns (all the data) in the Student table.

Parsing a Query

Before you execute your query, you may parse your query. The Parse Query button is shown in Figure 1-25. By parsing the query you can make sure that your query is correctly written, before you execute your query.

Executing a Query

To execute a query, click the Execute button, shown in Figure 1-25. If there are no errors in the query, the Execute button will execute (run) the query and the results will show on the results pane (bottom partition) of the screen.

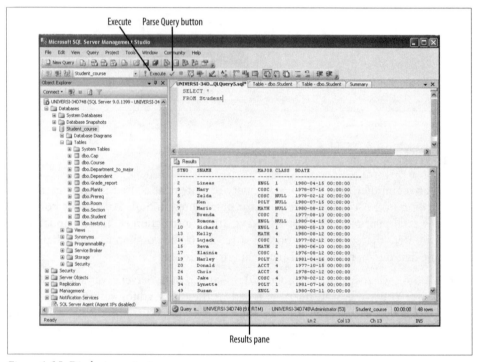

Figure 1-25. Displaying output

Color Coding

The automatic color coding of SQL code in the query editor will help you type in your SQL query correctly. It will help you prevent and resolve errors. If you are using the default color codes, for example, and you type in a keyword that is not displayed in blue, the keyword is probably misspelled. If your code is displayed in red, you might have omitted a closing quotation mark for a character string.

Saving a Query

To save a query, while the query is on the query editor screen, from the top menu, select File and Save SQLQuery1.sql As.... A dialog box will open up and you will be able to type the name under which you want to save your query, and you will also be able to navigate to the directory to which you want to save your query.

Displaying the Results

Results in SQL Server 2005 are displayed in the Results pane. The Results pane is shown in Figure 1-25. SQL queries can be executed to view results in grid form or text form, or the results can be saved to a file, as discussed in the following subsections.

Viewing Results in Grid Form

The grid form displays the results in spreadsheet-like grids. To execute a query and view query results in grid form, first click the "Results to grid" icon (this icon is shown in Figure 1-26) and then click the Execute button.

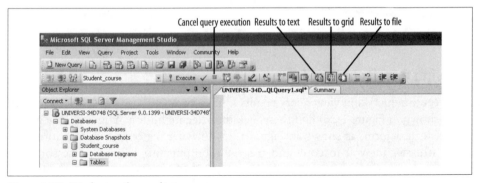

Figure 1-26. Displaying the results icons

 You may also click <F5> on the keyboard to execute queries.

You will now get the results in grid form, as shown in Figure 1-27.

On Figure 1-27, on the bottom panel of the screen, the name of the database and the number of rows in the result set are displayed.

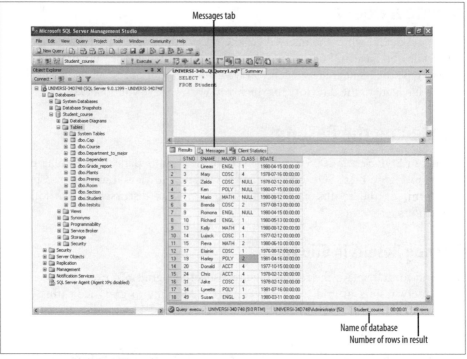

Figure 1-27. Viewing results in grid form

Viewing Results in Text Form

To execute a query and view query results in text form, click on the "Results to text" icon (shown in Figure 1-26) and then click the Execute button. You will now get the results in text form, as shown in Figure 1-25. Viewing the output in text form may make it easier for you to copy and paste the output into a word processor, from where you can print the output easily. Figure 1-25 also displays, on the bottom panel of the screen, the name of the database and the number of rows in the result set.

Saving Results to File

To save your query results to a file, from Figure 1-26, select Results to File icon (this icon is shown in Figure 1-26), and then click the Execute button. The Save Results window will come up and you will be able to select the appropriate directory and enter the appropriate filename and save the results to file for later use. The Results to File option produces output formatted for Crystal Reports. Crystal Reports is the best-selling database reporting tool and is included with SQL Server. It is beyond our scope to discuss Crystal Reports here.

To open this Crystal Report (the saved file), select File from the top menu, Open, and then File (as shown in Figure 1-28). Then, navigate to the directory where you saved your file, select your file, and your results will be displayed on the screen.

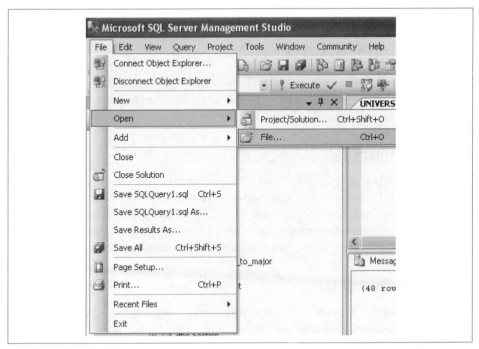

Figure 1-28. Opening Crystal Reports

Stopping Execution of a Long Query

If you want to stop the execution of a long-running query, you may click on the Cancel Query Execution button (shown in Figure 1-26), or you may press Alt-Break.

Viewing Error Messages

To view error messages, click on the Message tab (shown in Figure 1-27). This displays the messages (as well as error messages) of the SQL query output.

Printing the Query and Results

Once the SQL query is on the query editor screen, you can print the query by selecting File->Print from the top menu.

To print the results, the query should be executed in the Results in Text mode. Then, when the results are displayed in the bottom window partition (the results pane), place your cursor in the results pane by clicking anywhere in the results pane (see Figure 1-25 for the results pane), and then select File → Print from the top menu.

When the results are saved to file, they can, of course, be retrieved and printed from the file.

Customizing SQL Server 2005

You can customize some options in SQL Server 2005 by selecting Tools → Options from the top menu. You will get the following tabs: Environment, Source Control, Text Editor, Query Execution, Query Results, Designers.

The Environment tab

The Environment tab has the General, Fonts and Colors, Keyboards and Help options. Among other options, the General tab allows you to change the default start-up window options of SQL Server 2005. The Fonts and Colors option allows you to change, among other things, an items foreground and background color. The Keyboard option allows you to change keyboarding options like Shortcuts.

The Source Control Tab

The Source Control tab specifies the source control plug-in to use with Microsoft SQL Server Management Studio and allows changes to plug-in specific options.

The Text Editor Tab

The Text Editor tab allows you to change the default editor and change other language and text options.

The Query Execution Tab

The Query Execution tab allows you to change the default ROWCOUNT options, TEXTSIZE options, execution time-out length, and other settings.

The Query Results Tab

The Query Results tab allows you to change the default type for results, the default location for results to be saved, and other settings.

The Designer Tab

The Designer tab allows you to change the default table and database designer settings.

Summary

In this chapter, we have shown you how to start Microsoft SQL Server 2005 and SQL Server 2005's Management Studio. We have also shown you how to create the Student_course database that we will be using throughout the rest of this book. In addition, we have demonstrated how to work with tables. We have shown you how to type, parse, execute and save a simple query. In the process, we have also familiarized you with the main screens and workings of SQL Server 2005's Management Studio. Towards the end of the chapter, we showed you how to change (or customize) some of SQL Server 2005's default settings to suit your needs.

Review Questions

1. If I want to see what fields a table is made of, and what the sizes of the fields are, what option do I have to look for?
2. What is a query?
3. A SQL query is typed in the _____ .
4. What is the purpose of the model database?
5. What is the purpose of the master database?
6. What is the purpose of the tempdb database?
7. What is the purpose of the USE command?
8. If you delete a table in the database, will the data in the table be deleted too?
9. What is the Parse Query button used for? How does this help you?
10. Tables are created in a _____ in SQL Server 2005.

Exercises

The tables available in the Student_course database are shown in Appendix A.

1. The Student_course database contains the following tables: Student, Dependent, Grade_report, Section, Department, Course, Prereq, Room, Cap, Plants.
    a. View the table definition of each of these tables.
    b. View the data of each of these tables. Save your results to a file and print them out.
2. Write a SQL query to view all the columns and rows in the Student table. (Hint: To retrieve all columns, use SELECT * in your query; the * means "all columns"). Save and execute the query. Save the results to a file and print out the results.

CHAPTER 2

Beginning SQL Commands in SQL Server

In this chapter, we discuss how to write (build) simple SQL query statements in SQL Server 2005 using the SELECT statement. We examine how to retrieve data from a table by the use of SELECT statements, how to SELECT fields (columns) and rows from tables, how to use the ORDER BY and WHERE clauses, and how to use the AND, OR, and BETWEEN operators. The concept of COUNT and null values is also to be established. Then, to make writing queries simpler, we discuss how to use table and column aliases, table qualifiers, synonyms, and finally we present a convention for writing SQL statements.

Displaying Data with the SELECT Statement

One of the very first things that you would usually want to do with a set of tables (or a database) is to see what information the tables contain. To display the information in a table using a query, you use a SELECT command on the table. SELECT is *usually* the first word in a SQL statement or query. The SELECT statement returns information from a table (or a set of tables, the database) as a set of records, or a *result set*. The result set is a tabular arrangement of data, composed of rows and columns. The SELECT statement shows the output on the computer screen (as shown in Figures 1-26 and 1-28 of Chapter 1). It does not save the results. The simplest and most commonly used form of the SELECT syntax is:

```
SELECT fields (a.k.a. columns or attributes)
FROM Table
```

Here, Table is the name of the table from which the data will be displayed, and fields are the columns (attributes) that you chose to display from the named table. If you did not know the name of the columns in the table, or you wanted to display all the columns in the table, you would use an asterisk (*) in place of fields; substituting an asterisk (*) in place of fields would list all the columns in the table.

So, the SELECT statement gives us a result set that is composed of the data from columns of a table.

SQL commands in SQL Server 2005 do not have to be terminated by a semicolon, as is true in several other SQL languages.

But, before we use the SELECT statement, we have to make sure that the right database is open. To open a database that you want to use, type the following in the query editor screen (the query editor screen is shown in Figure 1-12 of Chapter 1):

```
USE Student_course
```

and then click the Execute button.

Student_course is the name of the database that we would like to open. The Student_course database should now be active.

Once the Student_course database is active, to display all the data from a table called Dependent from our database (Student_course database), type the following in the query editor screen:

```
SELECT *
FROM       Dependent
```

The * means all columns of the Dependent table. Now click the Execute button to execute this query. Your results will display in the result pane.

SELECT without the FROM

Most SQL languages require a FROM in a query. But, SELECT statements in SQL Server do not need to be from a table. SQL Server allows us to write some special queries without FROM. For example, using a special function, GETDATE, we may type this:

```
SELECT GETDATE( )
```

and the query will return the date and time as defined by the host computer:

```
-----------------------
2006-01-12 21:55:30.107

(1 row(s) affected)
```

Note that these columns do not have any headings.

In SQL Server 2005, a SELECT statement can also be used to make an assignment. For example, the following example assigns 100 to col1, and 200 to col2:

```
SELECT col1=100, col2=200
```

with the results:

```
col1        col2
----------- -----------
100         200

(1 row(s) affected)
```

"col1" and "col2" are column aliases. Column aliases are discussed in detail later in this chapter.

```
SELECT 'A', 'B'
```
produces:

```
---- ----
A    B
```

```
(1 row(s) affected)
```

Note that this output has no headings either.

```
SELECT 4+3, 4-3, 4*3, 4/3
```
produces:

```
----------- ----------- ----------- -----------
7           1           12          1
```

```
(1 row(s) affected)
```

To include meaningful column headings here, we can type:

```
SELECT Additions=4+3, Subtractions=4-3, Multiplications=4*3, Divisions=4/3
```
which results in:

```
Additions   Subtractions Multiplications Divisions
----------- ------------ --------------- -----------
7           1            12              1
```

```
(1 row(s) affected)
```

 "/" gives the whole-number quotient of a division.

Displaying or Selecting Columns from a Table

Using a SELECT statement, you do not have to display or return all the columns from a table. You may choose to display only certain relevant columns from a table, provided you know the names of the columns in the table. In this section, we show you how to display or return one column from a table, more than one column from a table, and then how to display or return all columns from a table. Then we introduce the ORDER BY clause and also show you how to order the output in ascending or descending order by adding the ASC or DESC commands, respectively, to the ORDER BY clause.

Displaying or SELECTing One Column from a Table

To be able to display or return particular fields or columns from a table, you need to know the column names in the table. To view the column names that a table contains, you will have to go to the Table Definition of a table. Chapter 1 (Figure 1-20) shows you how to view the table definitions of tables.

You may find it odd that a someone working with a database might not know the column names. However, when creating a table, one has great latitude with naming columns. If you knew, for example, that a table called Customer contained a name and address, you'd have to know the exact name of the column. If the table creator called the customer's name CustName, then to retrieve the data from that column, you'd have to use CustName and not any variation of it (like CustomerName or Name or anything else).

Select the table for which you want to see the definition by right clicking on the table from the Object Explorer, and then clicking on Columns. Now, right-click on the Dependent table and click Columns, and you will see the table definition of the Dependent table.

Figure 2-1 shows the definition of the Dependent table. The table definition provides the exact column names, the data types of the columns, the field sizes and information on whether the fields can hold nulls. The data type allows you to enter only a particular kind of data in the columns. The field sizes allow you to enter only up to a certain number of characters in a field. null or not null tells you whether the field will allow for nulls.

The Dependent table in Figure 2-1 has columns PNO (short for parent_number) of data type SMALLINT (small integers), DNAME (short for dependent name) of data type NVARCHAR (a varying number of characters), RELATIONSHIP (for relationship to parent or Student) of data type NVARCHAR, SEX of data type CHAR (one character), and AGE of data type SMALLINT. The only field in the Dependent table that cannot be null is STNO.

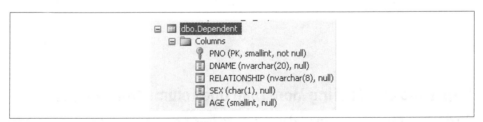

Figure 2-1. Definition of the Dependent table

Data types are discussed in detail in the next chapter.

Once you know what columns a table contains, you may choose to view or display particular columns of the table. Following is the general syntax to display or SELECT the data from one field or column of a table:

```
SELECT field_name
FROM table
```

Refer to Appendix A for a complete list of tables and columns in the Student_course database.

For example, to display or SELECT data for a column called dname from the Dependent table, you type the following query in the query editor:

```
SELECT dname
FROM    Dependent
```

This query returns a result set containing 39 records or rows (of which the first 10 rows are shown):

```
dname
--------------------
Matt
Mary
Beena
Amit
Shantu
Raju
Rani
Susan
Sam
Donald II
  .
  .
  .
(39 row(s) affected)
```

Displaying or SELECTing More than One Column from a Table

To display or SELECT (or return) data for more than one column of the table, the column names have to be separated by commas. For example, to display the data from the dname and relationship columns in the Dependent table, type the following query:

```
SELECT dname, relationship
FROM    Dependent
```

This query also produces 39 rows of output (we show the first 12 rows here):

```
dname                relationship
-------------------- ------------
Matt                 Son
Mary                 Daughter
Beena                Spouse
Amit                 Son
Shantu               Daughter
Raju                 Son
Rani
Susan                Daughter
Sam                  Son
Donald II            Son
Chris                Son
Susan                Daughter
  .
  .
  .

(39 row(s) affected)
```

In this example, we see a row where dname (dependent name) is Rani, but no relationship has been assigned or entered. This is a very typical problem in any database—data is missing or unknown, also known as NULL. Therefore, preferably, when data is entered into a table, all columns should be valued. In this case probably an empty string was entered, otherwise SQL Server 2005 assigns a NULL value.

 The concept of NULLs is introduced later in this chapter.

Displaying or SELECTing All Columns of a Table

There are times when you will want to display or select all the columns of a table. To do so, as illustrated previously, you use a * in place of the column names. For example, the following produces an output of 39 rows and all the columns in the Dependent table:

```
SELECT *
FROM   Dependent
```

This query also produces 39 rows of output (of which we show the first 15 rows here):

PNO	DNAME	RELATIONSHIP	SEX	AGE
2	Matt	Son	M	8
2	Mary	Daughter	F	9
2	Beena	Spouse	F	31
10	Amit	Son	M	3
10	Shantu	Daughter	F	5

```
14      Raju            Son         M   1
14      Rani                        F   3
17      Susan           Daughter    F   4
17      Sam             Son         M   1
20      Donald II       Son         M   NULL
20      Chris           Son         M   6
34      Susan           Daughter    F   5
34      Monica          Daughter    F   1
62      Tom             Husband     M   45
62      James           Son         M   14
 .
 .
 .

(39 row(s) affected)
```

ORDER BY

A table maintains the data in the order that the system stores it in, which is unpredictable. Remember that a relational database contains sets of rows of data and sets are not ordered. If you wish to display the contents of a table in a predictable manner, you may use the ORDER BY clause in the SELECT statement. For example, to order the Dependent table by field age, you would type the following:

```
SELECT dname, age
FROM   Dependent
ORDER  BY age
```

This produces the following 39 rows of output, ordered by age (of which the first 20 rows are shown below):

```
dname                   age
--------------------    ------
Donald II               NULL
Mita                    NULL
Losmith                 NULL
Prakash                 1
Mithu                   1
Raju                    1
Sam                     1
Monica                  1
Jon                     2
Rakhi                   2
Jake                    2
Nita                    2
Mahesh                  2
Rani                    3
Amit                    3
Susan                   4
Sebastian               4
Mamta                   4
Madhu                   5
Shantu                  5
```

```
.
.
.
```

```
(39 row(s) affected)
```

The ORDER BY does not actually change the order of the data in the table. It only displays or returns the data (output) in a particular order.

When using an ORDER BY in a SELECT statement, you do not have to have the column that you are ordering by in the SELECT statement. For example, you may display only the dependent name and age while ordering by sex, as follows:

```
SELECT dname, age
FROM   Dependent
ORDER  BY sex
```

This would produce 39 rows of output, of which we are showing the first 5 rows (the females are shown first, because it is ordered alphabetically):

```
dname                age
-------------------- ------
Mary                 9
Beena                31
Shantu               5
Rani                 3
Susan                4
.
.
.
```

```
(39 row(s) affected)
```

Although the previous output is not wrong, it is may appear to be randomly ordered by someone who does not know what was used in the ORDER BY statement. Therefore, it is generally better to display the column that you are ordering by also, as follows:

```
SELECT dname, age, sex
FROM   Dependent
ORDER  BY sex
```

This query would once again produce 39 rows, of which we are showing the first 5 rows:

```
dname                age    sex
-------------------- ------ ----
Mary                 9      F
Beena                31     F
Shantu               5      F
Rani                 3      F
Susan                4      F
.
.
.
```

```
(39 row(s) affected)
```

ORDER BY and NULLs

When data has not been entered for a particular column of a particular row, this cell gets a NULL value. Null means that data is missing or unavailable, so the cell has no value.

If the field that you choose to ORDER BY contains nulls, the fields that have null values assigned to them are placed at the top of the displayed list of output. This is because of the way SQL Server stores null values internally. Look at the output of the following query:

```
SELECT dname, age
FROM    Dependent
ORDER  BY age
```

which produces 39 rows of output, of which we are showing the first 16 rows:

```
dname                    age
--------------------     ------
Donald II                NULL
Mita                     NULL
Losmith                  NULL
Prakash                  1
Mithu                    1
Raju                     1
Sam                      1
Monica                   1
Jon                      2
Rakhi                    2
Jake                     2
Nita                     2
Mahesh                   2
Rani                     3
Amit                     3
Susan                    4
 .
 .
 .

(39 row(s) affected)
```

If nothing was entered in a column (an empty string was entered), the column behaves just like a NULL field when using the ORDER BY clause. For example, if we type in the following query:

```
SELECT dname, relationship
FROM    Dependent
ORDER  BY relationship
```

we get 39 rows of output, of which we are showing the first 8 rows:

```
dname                    relationship
--------------------     -----------
Rani
Susan                    Daughter
Mary                     Daughter
```

```
Susan           Daughter
Monica          Daughter
Hillary         Daughter
Phoebe          Daughter
Shantu          Daughter
  .
  .
  .

(39 row(s) affected)
```

In this table, nothing (an empty string) was entered in the relationship column for the dependent Rani.

Ascending and Descending Order

In SQL Server, the default order of an ORDER BY is ascending. To display or order output in descending order, the keyword DESC has to be appended to the ORDER BY clause. And, in order to display or order output in ascending order, the keyword ASC can be appended to the ORDER BY clause.

So, unless you specify otherwise, the following two queries will give you the same output:

```
SELECT dname, age
FROM   Dependent
ORDER  BY age
```

and:

```
SELECT dname, age
FROM   Dependent
ORDER  BY age ASC
```

The top query returns a result set ordered in ascending order by age by default. The second query has the keyword ASC appended to the ORDER BY clause, so it also orders in ascending order by age (the output for these queries has been shown previously).

In order to display or order output in descending order, the keyword DESC can be appended to the ORDER BY clause, as follows:

```
SELECT dname, age
FROM   Dependent
ORDER  BY age DESC
```

This produces 39 rows of output in descending order of age (of which the first 10 rows are shown here):

```
dname                age
-------------------- ------
Tom                  45
Beena                31
Barbara              26
Barbara              23
```

```
Susan          22
Susie          22
Xi du          22
Sally          22
Hillary        16
James          14
  .
  .
  .

(39 row(s) affected)
```

Ordering Within an Order

There will be times when you will want to sort groups within an order by another
order. SQL Server syntax allows you to do this. For example, using the Dependent
table, if you want to order all the dependents by sex, and within sex you want to
order by age in descending order, would you type the following query:

```
SELECT dname, sex, age
FROM   Dependent
ORDER  BY sex, age DESC
```

This query would produce the following 39 rows of output:

```
dname                sex  age
-------------------- ---- ------
Beena                F    31
Barbara              F    26
Barbara              F    23
Susan                F    22
Susie                F    22
Xi du                F    22
Sally                F    22
Hillary              F    16
Phoebe               F    12
Mary                 F    9
Mona                 F    7
Rekha                F    6
Madhu                F    5
Shantu               F    5
Susan                F    5
Susan                F    4
Mamta                F    4
Rani                 F    3
Rakhi                F    2
Nita                 F    2
Monica               F    1
Mita                 F    NULL
Tom                  M    45
James                M    14
Matt                 M    8
Chris                M    6
```

```
Om            M    6
James         M    5
Sebastian     M    4
Amit          M    3
Jon           M    2
Jake          M    2
Mahesh        M    2
Prakash       M    1
Mithu         M    1
Sam           M    1
Raju          M    1
Donald II     M    NULL
Losmith       M    NULL

(39 row(s) affected)
```

You could also order by descending order of sex, and descending order of age, as follows:

```
SELECT dname, sex, age
FROM   Dependent
ORDER  BY sex DESC, age DESC
```

This query would give the following 39 rows of output:

```
dname                 sex   age
--------------------  ----  ------
Tom                   M     45
James                 M     14
Matt                  M     8
Chris                 M     6
Om                    M     6
James                 M     5
Sebastian             M     4
Amit                  M     3
Jake                  M     2
Jon                   M     2
Mahesh                M     2
Prakash               M     1
Mithu                 M     1
Raju                  M     1
Sam                   M     1
Donald II             M     NULL
Losmith               M     NULL
Beena                 F     31
Barbara               F     26
Barbara               F     23
Sally                 F     22
Susan                 F     22
Susie                 F     22
Xi du                 F     22
Hillary               F     16
Phoebe                F     12
Mary                  F     9
Mona                  F     7
```

```
Rekha          F    6
Madhu          F    5
Shantu         F    5
Susan          F    5
Susan          F    4
Mamta          F    4
Rani           F    3
Nita           F    2
Rakhi          F    2
Monica         F    1
Mita           F    NULL
```

(39 row(s) affected)

Displaying or SELECTing Rows or Tuples from a Table

In relational database terminology, a table is called a *relation*, and is denoted by the name of the relation followed by the columns (or attributes), as shown here:

```
Dependent(pno, dname, relationship, sex, age)
```

An instance of a relation is a row of a relation (table) with values. We will use the term "row" to refer to a line of output. Although database literature also uses the term "tuple" or "record" in place of row, we will most often use the word "row," because "row" is more commonly used in relational databases (and SQL Server 2005 is a relational database).

In the previous section, we showed you how to select or display particular columns from a table, but we did not explain how to select or display specific rows. Usually you would want to select or display only particular rows from a table. For example, you may want to list all the dependents who are older than five, or list all the dependents who are female. In such a case, you want only the rows WHERE the dependents are older than five, or, only the rows WHERE the dependents are female. That is, you want to display only the rows that meet a certain condition or criteria.

By using a WHERE clause in a SELECT statement, you can selectively choose rows that you wish to display based on a criterion. For additional filtering, the WHERE clause can be used with logical operators like AND and OR, and the BETWEEN operator and its negation, NOT BETWEEN.

Filtering with WHERE

The WHERE clause is a row filter that is used to restrict the output of rows (or tuples) in a result set. When the WHERE clause is used, the SQL Server database engine selects the rows from the table for the result set that meet the conditions listed in the WHERE clause. So, as we have previously illustrated, if no WHERE clause is used in a query, the query will return all rows from the table.

Following is the general syntax of a SELECT statement with a WHERE clause:

```
SELECT column-names
FROM   Table
WHERE  criteria
```

For example, consider the following query:

```
SELECT *
FROM   Dependent
WHERE  sex = 'F'
```

This query produces 22 rows of output (of which we show the first 10 rows):

```
PNO     DNAME                RELATIONSHIP SEX  AGE
------  -------------------- ------------ ---- ------
2       Mary                 Daughter     F    9
2       Beena                Spouse       F    31
10      Shantu               Daughter     F    5
14      Rani                              F    3
17      Susan                Daughter     F    4
34      Susan                Daughter     F    5
34      Monica               Daughter     F    1
62      Hillary              Daughter     F    16
62      Phoebe               Daughter     F    12
128     Mita                 Daughter     F    NULL
.
.
.

(22 row(s) affected)
```

The output for this query lists all the columns of the Dependent table, but only the rows WHERE the sex attribute has been assigned a value of F.

The WHERE clause can be used with several comparison operators:

- > (greater than)
- <> not equal
- = equal
- >= greater than or equal to
- <= less than or equal to

WHERE may be used in a query in addition to ORDER BY. Following is an example of a query that displays the dname and age from the Dependent table where the age of the dependent is less than or equal to 5, ordered by age:

```
SELECT   dname, age
FROM     Dependent
WHERE    age <= 5
ORDER BY age
```

This query produces 19 rows of output (of which we show the first 11 rows):

```
dname                age
-------------------- ------
Raju                 1
Sam                  1
Monica               1
Prakash              1
Mithu                1
Nita                 2
Rakhi                2
Jake                 2
Jon                  2
Mahesh               2
Rani                 3
.
.
.

(19 row(s) affected)
```

So far we have shown you how to include only one condition in your WHERE clause. If you want to include multiple conditions in your WHERE clause, you can use logical operators like AND and OR, and other operators like BETWEEN and its negation, NOT BETWEEN. The following sections discuss and illustrate the use of the AND, OR, and BETWEEN operators, and also the NOT BETWEEN in the WHERE clause.

The AND Operator

The AND is a way of combining conditions in a WHERE clause. An AND operator is used in a WHERE clause if more that one condition is required. Using the AND further restricts the output of rows (tuples) in the result set. For example, consider the following query:

```
SELECT  *
FROM    Dependent
WHERE   age <= 5
AND     sex = 'F'
```

which produces the following nine rows of output:

```
PNO    DNAME                RELATIONSHIP SEX  AGE
------ -------------------- ------------ ---- ------
10     Shantu               Daughter     F    5
14     Rani                              F    3
17     Susan                Daughter     F    4
34     Susan                Daughter     F    5
34     Monica               Daughter     F    1
128    Nita                 Daughter     F    2
142    Rakhi                Daughter     F    2
153    Madhu                Daughter     F    5
153    Mamta                Daughter     F    4

(9 row(s) affected)
```

The output for this query lists all the columns of the Dependent table, but only the rows WHERE the value of the age attribute is less than or equal to 5 *and* the sex is female. The AND means that *both* the criteria, age <= 5 and sex = 'F', have to be met for the row to be included in the result set. 'F' is in single quotes in this query because sex was defined as character data (CHAR) when the table was created. Text or character data has to be in single quotes in SQL Server 2005. Double quotes would not be acceptable in SQL Server 2005. Numeric data (e.g., age <= 5) should not be in quotes.

An extensive discussion of data types is presented in the next chapter.

The OR Operator

The OR operator is another way of combining conditions in a WHERE clause. Unlike the AND operator, the OR operator allows the database engine to select the row to be included in the result set if *either* of the conditions in the WHERE clause are met. So, although you could also use the OR operator with your WHERE clause if you wanted to include more that one condition in your WHERE clause, either of the conditions in the WHERE clause can be met for a row to be included in the result set.

Consider the following query:

```
SELECT  *
FROM    Dependent
WHERE   age >20
OR      sex = 'F'
```

which produces 23 rows of output (of which we are showing the first 10):

PNO	DNAME	RELATIONSHIP	SEX	AGE
2	Mary	Daughter	F	9
2	Beena	Spouse	F	31
10	Shantu	Daughter	F	5
14	Rani		F	3
17	Susan	Daughter	F	4
34	Susan	Daughter	F	5
34	Monica	Daughter	F	1
62	Tom	Husband	M	45
62	Hillary	Daughter	F	16
62	Phoebe	Daughter	F	12
.				
.				
.				

(23 row(s) affected)

This output lists of all dependents who are either greater than 20 years of age *or* are female. The OR means that either of the criteria, age > 20 or sex = 'F', has to be met for the row to be included in the output.

The BETWEEN Operator

The BETWEEN operator is yet another way of combining filtering conditions in a WHERE clause. In SQL Server 2005, the BETWEEN operator allows you to determine whether a value falls within a given range of values (inclusive). The general syntax of the BETWEEN operator is:

```
SELECT...
FROM
WHERE
BETWEEN value1 AND value2
```

For example, if we want to find all the dependents between the ages of 3 and 5, we would type the following:

```
SELECT   dname, age
FROM     Dependent
WHERE    age
BETWEEN 3 AND 5
```

This query produces the following nine rows of output:

```
dname                 age
--------------------  ------
Amit                  3
Shantu                5
Rani                  3
Susan                 4
Susan                 5
James                 5
Sebastian             4
Madhu                 5
Mamta                 4

(9 row(s) affected)
```

 In SQL Server 2005, *value1* in the BETWEEN clause has to be less than *value2*. In some SQL languages (for example, in Access SQL), *value1* does not have to be less than *value2*.

Because the operator is inclusive, the end points of the comparison have been included in the output; that is, the BETWEEN clause takes the values from *value1* and *value2*.

As we will often point out, SQL statements may be written in several ways. For example, the BETWEEN that we illustrated earlier may also be written as follows:

```
SELECT dname, age
FROM    Dependent
WHERE   age >=3
AND     age <=5
```

This query produces the same output as the previous query. So, BETWEEN can be considered shorthand for "greater-than-or-equal-to AND less-than-or-equal-to some value."

Negating the BETWEEN Operator

The BETWEEN operator can be negated by using the keyword NOT before the BETWEEN operator. NOT BETWEEN allows you to determine whether a value does not occur within a given range of values. The general syntax of the NOT BETWEEN is:

```
SELECT...
FROM
WHERE
NOT BETWEEN value1 AND value2
```

For example, if we want to find all the dependents who are not between the ages of 3 and 15, we would type the following:

```
SELECT dname, age
FROM    Dependent
WHERE   age
NOT BETWEEN 3 AND 15
```

which would give us the following 19 rows:

dname	age
Beena	31
Raju	1
Sam	1
Monica	1
Tom	45
Hillary	16
Jon	2
Prakash	1
Mithu	1
Nita	2
Barbara	26
Rakhi	2
Susan	22
Susie	22
Xi du	22
Barbara	23
Jake	2
Mahesh	2
Sally	22

(19 row(s) affected)

Here the end points of the comparison are *not* included in the result set. The previous NOT BETWEEN query could also be written as follows:

```
SELECT sname, class
FROM   Student
WHERE  class <1
OR     class >3
```

NOT BETWEEN could be considered shorthand for "less-than OR greater-than some value."

The COUNT Function

The COUNT function is used to return a count of the number of rows that the output will produce, without actually displaying all of the output (rows) themselves. This function often comes in handy when you have large tables, or you expect a large output. In such situations, it is desirable to determine the number of rows of output that you will be getting before actually displaying the output. In this section, we introduce the COUNT function and we also take another look at the concept of null values.

If you type the following command:

```
SELECT *
FROM   Dependent
```

you will get an output that includes all the rows of the Dependent table plus all the values for all columns in those rows. If you want to know only the *number* of rows in the output (rather than view the actual rows themselves), type the following:

```
SELECT COUNT(*)
FROM   Dependent
```

This query produces the following output:

```
-----------
39

(1 row(s) affected)
```

This output says that there are 39 rows in the Dependent table. Note that the actual rows themselves are not displayed.

It is often useful to count the occurrence of column values that have a value. For example, suppose we want to find how many nonnull rows are in a particular column. With this query:

```
SELECT COUNT(age)
FROM   Dependent
```

we get:

```
-----------
36

Warning: Null value is eliminated by an aggregate or other SET operation.

(1 row(s) affected)
```

COUNT(age) counts only the rows in which age is not null, meaning that it counts only the rows that have a defined value. Therefore, the preceding output is 36 rows rather than 39 rows because the age column in the Dependent table includes 3 null values. If you want COUNT to count rows and include rows that have fields with null values, you would use COUNT(*). In the next section, we discuss null values in more detail.

IS NULL

Null values are used to designate missing data in columns. The IS NULL condition is the only condition that directly tests for nulls. Null values are unmatched by all other conditions in WHERE clauses. Rows with null values cannot be retrieved by using = NULL in a WHERE clause, because NULL signifies a missing value. No value is considered to be equal to, greater than, or less than NULL. Even a space is not considered to be a NULL, and a null is not considered to be a space. Nulls are not considered like any other value in a table either, since nulls do not have data types. Also, because nulls do not have data types, there is no distinction between nulls in numeric columns and nulls in text columns or date columns.

The following query provides dependent names and the ages of dependents (from the Dependent table) that have null values for their age columns:

```
SELECT dname, age
FROM   Dependent
WHERE  age IS NULL
```

This produces the following three rows of output:

```
dname                age
-------------------- ------
Donald II            NULL
Mita                 NULL
Losmith              NULL

(3 row(s) affected)
```

IS NOT NULL

To retrieve all rows that are not nulls, IS NOT NULL can be used. The following query will give all the rows that are not nulls—the remaining 36 rows of the table (of which we show the first 10 rows):

```
SELECT dname, age
FROM   Dependent
WHERE  age IS NOT NULL
```

which produces 36 rows of output (of which the first 10 rows are shown):

```
dname                age
-------------------- ------
Matt                 8
Mary                 9
Beena                31
```

```
Amit              3
Shantu            5
Raju              1
Rani              3
Susan             4
Sam               1
Chris             6
.
.
.

(36 row(s) affected)
```

The ROWCOUNT Function

In an earlier section, we discussed how to limit the number of rows that are returned by a SELECT statement with the use of a WHERE clause and logical operators. In this section, we introduce the ROWCOUNT function, another way of limiting the number of rows that can be the returned by a SELECT statement.

The WHERE clause assumes that you have knowledge of the actual data values present in a data set. But what if you want to see only a sample of a result set, and you have no idea which range of values are present in the table? In this case, the ROWCOUNT function can come in handy.

For example, to see the first 10 rows of the Dependent table, you can type:

```
SET ROWCOUNT 10
SELECT *
FROM    Dependent
```

This query returns the following 10 rows of output:

```
PNO    DNAME                RELATIONSHIP SEX  AGE
------ -------------------- ------------ ---- ------
2      Matt                 Son          M    8
2      Mary                 Daughter     F    9
2      Beena                Spouse       F    31
10     Amit                 Son          M    3
10     Shantu               Daughter     F    5
14     Raju                 Son          M    1
14     Rani                              F    3
17     Susan                Daughter     F    4
17     Sam                  Son          M    1
20     Donald II            Son          M    NULL

(10 row(s) affected)
```

After using ROWCOUNT, you should reset the ROWCOUNT property by:

```
SET ROWCOUNT 0
```

If you do not reset the ROWCOUNT property, you will keep getting whatever you set your ROWCOUNT to for the remainder of this session (that is, until you log off).

If you set ROWCOUNT and issue multiple queries in the same batch, the rows are limited for all queries within the batch.

Other important functions are discussed in Chapter 5.

Using Aliases

Column aliases and table aliases are temporary names assigned within a query to columns and tables respectively. They are created on the fly in a query, and do not exist after the query is run. In this section, we discuss column aliases and table aliases.

Column Aliases

Column aliases are used to improve the readability of a query and its output. In SQL Server 2005, a column alias can be declared either before or after the column designation in the SELECT statement.

We will first display a query *without* a column alias:

```
SELECT dname, age, sex
FROM   Dependent
WHERE  age > 5
```

This query produces 17 rows of output (of which we show the first 10 rows):

```
dname                   age    sex
--------------------    ------  ----
Matt                    8      M
Mary                    9      F
Beena                   31     F
Chris                   6      M
Tom                     45     M
James                   14     M
Hillary                 16     F
Phoebe                  12     F
Om                      6      M
Barbara                 26     F
.
.
.

(17 row(s) affected)
```

Notice that SQL Server 2005 (by default) uses the column names from the Dependent table for the column headings. These column names may not be so explicit or descriptive. For example, what is dname? We would probably assume it's a name of something, but what does the "d" in front of name stand for? Using more descriptive headings in the output would considerably increase readability. To use more descriptive column headings, you can include column aliases just before or after the column name by using AS in the SELECT statement, as shown next (in the first few examples, we place the descriptive column headings after the column names):

```
SELECT dname AS Dependent_name, age AS Dependent_age, sex AS Dependent_sex
FROM    Dependent
WHERE   age > 5
```

This query produces 17 rows of output (of which we show the first 10 rows):

```
Dependent_name        Dependent_age Dependent_sex
--------------------  ------------- -------------
Matt                  8             M
Mary                  9             F
Beena                 31            F
Chris                 6             M
Tom                   45            M
James                 14            M
Hillary               16            F
Phoebe                12            F
Om                    6             M
Barbara               26            F
  .
  .
  .


(17 row(s) affected)
```

That output has more descriptive headings.

To embed a blank in the column alias, you have to put the column alias in single or double quotes, as shown in the following example:

```
SELECT dname AS "Dependent Name", age AS "Dependent Age", sex AS "Dependent Sex"
FROM    Dependent
WHERE   age > 5
```

This query produces 17 rows of output (of which we show the first 10 rows):

```
Dependent Name        Dependent Age Dependent Sex
--------------------  ------------- -------------
Matt                  8             M
Mary                  9             F
Beena                 31            F
Chris                 6             M
Tom                   45            M
James                 14            M
Hillary               16            F
Phoebe                12            F
Om                    6             M
Barbara               26            F
  .
  .
  .


(17 row(s) affected)
```

In fact, if you use single quotes in the previous query, you can also omit the AS. That is, typing in the following query gives you the same output as does the previous query:

```
SELECT dname 'Dependent Name', age 'Dependent Age', sex 'Dependent Sex'
FROM    Dependent
WHERE   age > 5
```

Column aliases can also be placed in square brackets, as shown in the following query:

```
SELECT dname AS [Dependent Name], age AS [Dependent Age], sex AS [Dependent Sex]
FROM    Dependent
WHERE   age > 5
```

Finally, column aliases can be placed in square brackets before = column name, as shown here:

```
SELECT [Dependent Name] = dname, [Dependent Age] = age, [Dependent Sex] = sex
FROM    Dependent
WHERE   age > 5
```

These previous two queries produce the same output (and headings) as the query before them.

If we wish to eliminate the brackets in the previous query, we can use only a one-word alias before the = column name, as shown:

```
SELECT Name = dname, Age = age, Sex = sex
FROM    Dependent
WHERE   age > 5
```

This query produces 17 rows of output (of which we show the first 10 rows):

```
Name                   Age    Sex
--------------------   ------ ----
Matt                    8      M
Mary                    9      F
Beena                   31     F
Chris                   6      M
Tom                     45     M
James                   14     M
Hillary                 16     F
Phoebe                  12     F
Om                      6      M
Barbara                 26     F
.
.
.

(17 row(s) affected)
```

Table Aliases

A table alias, usually used in multi-table queries (we discuss multi-table queries in Chapter 4 onwards), allows us to use a shorter name for a table when we reference the table in the query. A table alias is temporary, and does not exist after the query is run. We will explore multi-table queries in future chapters. Following is an example of the previous query written with a one-letter table alias:

```
SELECT  d.dname
FROM    Dependent d
WHERE   d.age > 5
```

This query produces 17 rows of output (of which we show the first 10 rows):

```
dname
--------------------
Matt
Mary
Beena
Chris
Tom
James
Hillary
Phoebe
Om
Barbara
.
.
.

(17 row(s) affected)
```

In this query, the table alias is the letter d *after* the table name, Dependent. A table alias can also be defined by a short, meaningful word or expression after the table name, rather than a one-letter table alias, but the one-letter table alias is commonly used by SQL programmers. Once a table alias has been defined in a query, it can be used in place of the table name. So, d could be used in place of Dependent if the table name needed to be used again in this particular query, but it is not reusable in multiple queries within the same batch. Again note that the table alias is not valid outside this query (or, after this query is executed). That is, if you type SELECT * from d , you will get an error message. There is no such table as d (d was locally defined as the table alias for that particular query, and is valid only in that particular query).

Table Aliases Used as Table Qualifiers

In the previous example, the construction d.dname contains a table qualifier (the d. part). Table qualifiers are needed when the same column name has been used in more than one table. Table qualifiers before the column names determine which table the column is from. For example, if TableA has a column called Field1 and TableB also has a column Field1, if we do not use a table qualifier in a multi-table query, there is no way that the query engine can know which Field1 the query is referring to. To correctly handle this situation, we would have to use a table qualifier in the form `Table1.FieldA`, where `Table1` is the table qualifier (this is also an alias, in a way).

 Once again, multi-table queries will be discussed from Chapter 4 onward.

Following is an example of a query with a table qualifier used for the age column:

```
SELECT *
FROM    Dependent
WHERE   Dependent.age > 5
```

This query produces 17 rows of output (of which we show the first 10 rows):

```
PNO     DNAME                 RELATIONSHIP SEX  AGE
------  --------------------  ------------ ---- ------
2       Matt                  Son          M    8
2       Mary                  Daughter     F    9
2       Beena                 Spouse       F    31
20      Chris                 Son          M    6
62      Tom                   Husband      M    45
62      James                 Son          M    14
62      Hillary               Daughter     F    16
62      Phoebe                Daughter     F    12
126     Om                    Son          M    6
128     Barbara               Wife         F    26
.
.
.

(17 row(s) affected)
```

It is also very common in SQL to alias a table and then also use the table alias as a table qualifier, as illustrated here:

```
SELECT *
FROM    Dependent d
WHERE   d.age > 5
```

The output of this query will be the same as the output of the previous query.

In this query, d (the table alias) is also the table qualifier. Not only is a construction like this very common, but it also helps to circumvent typing errors when writing commands.

The advantages of using table qualifiers and table aliases may not be so apparent in the examples presented in this chapter, because we are working only with single tables here. As we start working with multiple tables (from Chapter 4 onwards), their advantages will become more obvious.

Synonyms

In the last section, we discussed one way of referring to a table—through the use of table aliases. Table aliases are not permanent, in the sense that they do not exist after the query has been executed. In this section, we show you another way of referring to a table—*synonyms*. Synonyms are more permanent; they are available for use until they are deleted. In this section, we show you how to create, use, and delete synonyms.

SQL Server 2005 allows you to create synonyms for your tables. Synonyms are usually shorter names that can be used in place of the table name. If a change is made in the original table or its data, this change will be reflected when the synonym is used. And, if a change is made in the data of the table using a synonym, this change will be reflected in the original table. But, you cannot alter the table's definition using the synonym. Alter table commands (covered in Chapter 3) can be used only on the actual tables.

The general syntax to create a synonym is:

```
CREATE SYNONYM synonym_name
FOR Table_name
```

For example, to create a synonym for the Student table called s1, type:

```
CREATE SYNONYM s1
FOR Student
```

To view the synonym that you just created, from the Object Explorer, expand Student_course database and then Synonyms (as shown in Figure 2-2), and you will see the synonym, s1.

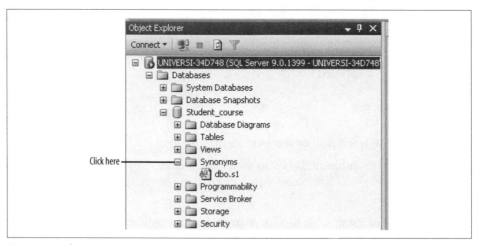

Figure 2-2. The synonym

You can now type:

```
SELECT *
FROM s1
```

And you will get the same output as if you typed:

```
SELECT *
FROM Student
```

A synonym will exist until you delete it. The general syntax to delete a synonym is:

```
DROP SYNONYM synonym_name
```

So, if you want to delete the synonym s1, type:

```
DROP SYNONYM s1
```

You can also delete the synonym by right-clicking on the synonym and selecting Delete.

If you forget which synonym has been created for which table, right-click on the synonym and select Properties.

Adding Comments to SQL Statements

Comments are nonexecutable words or phrases included in SQL queries to make the queries easier to understand (particularly by other people). Comments are ignored by the SQL engine, but they are very useful to programmers in determining what the statement does, when it was written, who wrote it, and so on. There are two ways of including comments in SQL Server 2005. The first way is by the use of dashes, as shown here:

```
SELECT *            -- displays "all" attributes
FROM    Dependent d -- of the Dependent table
WHERE   d.age > 5   -- where the age of the dependent is greater than 5.
```

The second way of including comments in Server SQL 2005 is by the use of /*...*/ construction. Following is an example of a commented statement that uses this format:

```
SELECT dname, age     /* displays the dependent name and age  */
FROM    Dependent d    /* from the Dependent table       */
WHERE   d.age > 5       /* where the age of the dependent is greater than 5 */
```

 SQL Server 2005 allows you to include comments even before the first line in a query and after the last line in a query.

We wish to encourage the use of comments in writing SQL queries, particularly for complex queries, and when queries will be debugged or enhanced by others.

SQL Server 2005 also has icons to turn lines into comment lines. For example, if you type in the query as shown in Figure 2-3, and then you wish to make the last line a comment line, highlight the last line and click the Make Comment button and the last line will become a comment line. If you wish to remove the comment, click the button beside it, the Remove Comment button, and the comment will be removed, turning the line into a regular line.

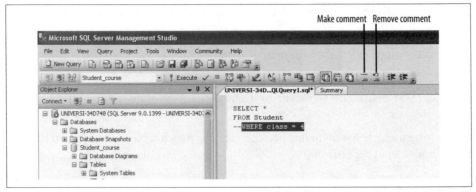

Figure 2-3. Icons for adding/removing comments

Some Conventions for Writing SQL Statements

Although SQL statements often contain multiple commands and multiple lines, there are no fixed rules for writing SQL statements; SQL is a "free-form" language. We suggest that you use the following conventions to increase the readability of your queries, especially as your statements or queries become more complex:

- Use uppercase letters for the keywords, which inclues SELECT, FROM, and WHERE. Use lowercase letters for the user-supplied words (SQL Server 2005 is not case-sensitive for commands).

- Align the keywords SELECT, FROM, and WHERE on separate lines, like this:
```
SELECT *
FROM    Dependent
WHERE   age > 5
```

A Few Notes About SQL Server 2005 Syntax

A few things that you need to know about syntax in SQL Server 2005:

- SQL Server 2005 allows blank lines in the SQL window.

- Queries in SQL Server 2005 do not have to end in a semicolon.

- SQL Server 2005 allows you to include comments anywhere in a SQL script or query. Many other SQL languages will not let you include a comment as the first line of a script or query (other SQL languages will look for a SQL statement beginning with a command like SELECT on the first line of a script or query), but SQL Server 2005 will allow you to include a comment on the first line of a script or query. SQL Server 2005 also allows comments after the semi-colon (which may have been used to end a query). Many SQL languages will not accept anything typed after the semi-colon.

- SQL Server 2005 will allow you to type in multiple queries on the query editor screen at one time, and you may only execute the ones that you wish to execute. For example, if you type in the following three queries on the query editor screen:

```
SELECT *
FROM    Dependent

SELECT *
FROM    Student

SELECT *
FROM    Course
```

To first execute the middle query, SELECT * FROM Student, you may highlight this query and click the Execute button. If you then wish to execute the first query, SELECT * FROM Dependent, you may highlight this query and click on the Execute button. You can, of course, do this as many times as you wish, and in any combination that you wish.

Summary

In this chapter, we have shown you how to use the basic SELECT statement and how to extract columns and rows using SELECT. We introduced the COUNT and ROWCOUNT functions, the AND, OR, and BETWEEN operators, table and column aliases, and synonyms. We also touched on the concept of nulls and have shown you how to include comments. Towards the end of the chapter, we presented some conventions for writing SQL statements and a few notes about SQL Server syntax. You will need this basic knowledge and understanding to work the forthcoming chapters.

Review Questions

1. What is usually the first word in a SQL query?
2. Does a SQL Server 2005 SELECT statement require a FROM?
3. Can a SELECT statement in SQL Server 2005 be used to make an assignment? Explain with examples.
4. What is the ORDER BY used for?
5. Does ORDER BY actually change the order of the data in the tables or does it just change the output?
6. What is the default order of an ORDER BY clause?

7. What kind of comparison operators can be used in a WHERE clause?

8. What are four major operators that can be used to combine conditions on a WHERE clause? Explain the operators with examples.

9. What are the logical operators?

10. In a WHERE clause, do you need to enclose a text column in quotes? Do you need to enclose a numeric column in quotes?

11. Is a null value equal to anything? Can a space in a column be considered a null value? Why or why not?

12. Will COUNT(column) include columns with null values in its count?

13. What are column aliases? Why would you want to use column aliases? How can you embed blanks in column aliases?

14. What are table aliases?

15. What are table qualifiers? When should table qualifiers be used?

16. Are semicolons required at the end of SQL statements in SQL Server 2005?

17. Do comments need to go in a special place in SQL Server 2005?

18. When would you use the ROWCOUNT function versus using the WHERE clause?

19. Is SQL case-sensitive? Is SQL Server 2005 case-sensitive?

20. What is a synonym? Why would you want to create a synonym?

21. Can a synonym name of a table be used instead of a table name in a SELECT statement?

22. Can a synonym of a table be used when you are trying to alter the definition of a table?

23. Can you type more than one query in the query editor screen at the same time?

Exercises

Unless specified otherwise, use the Student_course database to answer the following questions.

In writing out all the following queries, use table and column aliases wherever you feel that it would improve the readability of your output. Follow the conventions for writing SQL statements. Also, for future reference, you may want to get into the practice of saving your queries by question number. For example, save the query you write for Question 2-2a as *query2-2a*. Print the query and your results.

 Refer to Appendix A for a complete listing of all tables (and their columns) available in the Student_course database.

1. The Student_course database used in this book has the following tables: Student, Dependent, Course, Section, Prereq (for prerequisite), Grade_report, Department_to_major, and Room.

   a. Display the data from each of these tables by using the simple form of the SELECT * statement.

   b. Display the first five rows from each of these tables.

2. Display the student name and student number of all students who are juniors (hint: class = 3).

   a. Display the student names and numbers (from question 2) in descending order by name.

3. Display the course name and number of all courses that are three credit hours.

   a. Display all the course names and course numbers (from question 3) in ascending order by course name.

4. Display the building number, room number, and room capacity of all rooms in descending order by room capacity. Use appropriate column aliases to make your output more readable.

5. Display the course number, instructor, and building number of all courses that were offered in the Fall semester of 1998. Use appropriate column aliases to make your output more readable.

6. List the student number of all students who have grades of C or D.

7. List the offering_dept of all courses that are more than three credit hours.

8. Display the student name of all students who have a major of COSC.

9. Find the capacity of room 120 in Bldg 36.

10. Display a list of all student names ordered by major.

11. Display a list of all student names ordered by major, and by class within major. Use appropriate table and column aliases.

12. Count the number of departments in the Department_to_major table.

13. Count the number of buildings in the Room table.

14. What output will the following query produce?

```
SELECT COUNT(class)
FROM Student
WHERE class IS NULL
```

    Why do you get this output?

15. Use the BETWEEN operator to list all the sophomores, juniors, and seniors from the Student table.

16. Use the NOT BETWEEN operator to list all the sophomores and juniors from the Student table.

17. Create synonyms for each of the tables available in the Student_course database. View your synonyms in the Object Explorer.

CHAPTER 3

Creating, Populating, Altering, and Deleting Tables

In the SQL Server 2005 database, data is stored in tables (also known as *relations* in relational database theory). In Chapter 2, we discussed how to write queries to retrieve data from *existing* tables by using the SELECT statement. In this chapter, we will discuss how to create tables and insert data into them, and how to alter, update, and delete tables and their data using SQL. We start the chapter with a discussion of data types. You need to know the different data types before you can use the CREATE TABLE command to create tables. In the CREATE TABLE command, in addition to the column names, the data types and sizes of the columns have to be included.

Data Types in SQL Server 2005

Every column in a table has a data type. The data type of a column specifies what kind of information or values can be stored in the column, and what kind of operations can be performed on those values. It is a matter of mapping the domain values you need to store to the corresponding data type. In selecting a data type, you should avoid wasting storage space, while allowing enough space for a sufficient range of possible values over the life of your application. SQL Server 2005 supports 30 different data types. We will discuss the most commonly used data types by dividing the data types into four major categories: numeric, character, date and time, and miscellaneous.

 Domain values are the set of all possible values that a column can have. For example, the domain values for a GPA column may be 0 to 4.

Several of the primary data types also have valid synonyms that can be used instead of the regular data types. The synonyms are external names that are intended to make one SQL product compatible with another.

The more specific you are when selecting a data type for a column, the more accurate the information in your database will be. The following sections briefly describe each data type and its valid synonyms.

Numeric Data Types

Numeric data types should be used for storing numeric data, for data on which you want to perform numeric comparisons or arithmetic operations. Numeric data types can be divided into two groups: integers and decimals.

Integer data types

Integer data types have no digits after the decimal point, and range in size from 1 to 8 bytes of internal storage. Integer data types in SQL Server 2005 include:

- BIGINT, which uses 8 bytes of storage and can be used to store numbers from -2^{63} to $2^{63} -1$. Avoid using the BIGINT data type unless you really need its additional storage capacity.
- INT, which uses 4 bytes of storage and can be used to store numbers from -2^{31} to $2^{31} -1$.
- SMALLINT, which uses 2 bytes of storage and can be used to store numbers from -2^{15} to $2^{15} -1$.
- TINYINT, which uses 1 byte of storage and can be used to store numbers from 0 to 255.
- MONEY, which uses 8 bytes of storage.
- SMALLMONEY, which uses 4 bytes of storage.

MONEY and SMALLMONEY are included among integer types because they are internally stored the same way as integers.

 The synonym for INT is INTEGER.

Decimal data types

Decimal data types allow a larger range of values as well as a higher degree of accuracy than integer data types. For decimal data types, you can specify a precision and a scale. *Precision* is the total number of digits stored, and *scale* is the maximum number of digits to the right of the decimal point. The storage space of decimal data varies according to the precision. Decimals with a precision of 1 to 9 would take up 5 bytes of storage space; decimals with a precision of 10 to 19 would take up 9 bytes of storage, and so on.

Decimal data types include:

- REAL, which uses 4 bytes for storage and has a precision of 7 digits. The synonym for REAL is FLOAT[(n)] for n = 1 to 7.

- FLOAT, which uses 8 bytes for storage and has a precision of 15 digits. The synonym for FLOAT is DOUBLE PRECISION and FLOAT[(n)] for n = 8 to 15.

- DECIMAL, whose storage size varies based on the specified precision and uses 2 – 17 bytes for storage. The synonyms for DECIMAL are DEC and NUMERIC.

Rounding errors can occur when using the FLOAT or REAL data types. NUMERIC or DECIMAL are better in such cases, because they give the precision and scale, without the problems of FLOAT or REAL.

When you are trying to select the numeric data type to use, your decision should be based on the maximum range of possible values that you want to store, and the precision and scale that you need. But, at the same time, you have to realize that data types that can store a greater range of values take up more space.

 NUMERIC most closely resembles Oracle's NUMBER data type.

Character Data Types

Character data types are used to store any combination of letters, numbers and symbols. Single quotes have to be used when entering character data. SQL Server 2005 has five types of character data types: CHAR, VARCHAR, TEXT, NCHAR, NVARCHAR.

The CHAR data type

CHAR(n)s are fixed-length single-byte character strings that can be used to store up to 8,000 bytes of data. CHAR data is used when the column length is known and unvarying; for example, a Social Security number could be of CHAR(9) data type. Because CHARs use a fixed storage length, CHARs are accessed faster than VARCHARs (varying length character strings). You can and should specify the maximum byte length of a CHAR(n) data type with a value for n; otherwise, the default size will be used and the default size may be set to a size much higher than what you need. The synonym for CHAR is CHARACTER.

The VARCHAR data type

VARCHAR(n)s are variable length single-byte character strings that can also be used to store up to 8000 bytes of data. You can and should also specify the maximum byte length of VARCHARs with n, too; otherwise, as with the CHAR data type, the default size will be used, and the default size may be set to a size much higher than what you need. Variable length means that if less data than the specified n bytes is used, the storage size will be the actual length of the data entered. The synonym for VARCHAR is CHAR VARYING. VARCHAR is the most commonly used character (string) type.

VARCHAR2 is the Oracle equivalent of VARCHAR.

The TEXT data type

TEXTs are also variable-length single-byte character strings, but may be used to store more than 8,000 bytes. The TEXT data type, in SQL Server 2005, is a large object data type, better used if you need to store large strings of data. TEXT has extra overhead that drags down performance. Therefore, the use of the TEXT data type is not encouraged.

LONG is the Oracle equivalent of TEXT.

The NCHAR data type

NCHARs are fixed-length Unicode character strings. You can also specify the maximum byte length of NCHAR with *n*. The synonym for NCHAR is NATIONAL CHAR.

The NVARCHAR data type

NVARCHARs are variable-length Unicode character strings. You can specify the maximum byte of NVARCHAR length with *n*. The synonym for NVARCHAR is NATIONAL CHARACTER VARYING.

Unicode character strings

Unicode character strings need two bytes for each stored character. Most English and European alphabets can, however, be stored in single-byte characters. Single-byte character strings can store up to 8,000 characters, and Unicode character strings can store up to 4,000 characters.

Selecting the character data types

Some general rules that you can follow to determine which character data type to use:

- Use the variable-length data types (VARCHAR) over fixed-length data types (CHAR) when you expect a lot of null values or a lot of variation in the size of data.
- If a column's data does not vary widely in number of characters, consider using CHAR instead of VARCHAR.
- NVARCHAR or NCHAR data types should not be used unless you need to store 16-bit character (Unicode) data. NVARCHARs and NCHARs take up twice as much space as VARCHAR or CHAR data types, reducing I/O performance.

Date and Time Data Types

SQL Server 2005 has two data types for storing date and time information: DATETIME and SMALLDATETIME. DATETIME uses 8 bytes. SMALLDATETIME uses 4 bytes of storage. Internally, the DATETIME and SMALLDATETIME values are stored completely differently from how you enter them or how they are displayed. They are stored as two separate components, a date component and a time component.

 DATE is the Oracle equivalent of DATETIME.

When creating primary keys, do not consider using the DATETIME and SMALLDATETIME data types. From a performance standpoint, it is better to use a data type that uses less space for a primary key. The less the space used for a primary key, the smaller the table and index, and the less I/O overhead will be required to access the primary key.

 Creation of primary keys will be discussed in Chapter 11.

Miscellaneous Data Types

Among other data types available in SQL Server 2005 are BINARY, IMAGE, BIT, TABLE, SQL_VARIANT, UNIQUEIDENTIFIER, and the XML data type (one of SQL Server 2005's newest enhancements).

The BINARY data type

The BINARY data types are BINARY and VARBINARY.

BINARY data types are used to store strings of bits, and values are entered and displayed using their hexadecimal (hex) representation. The maximum length of the BINARY data type is 8,000 bytes. You can specify the maximum byte length of BINARY data with *n*.

The VARBINARY data type can store up to 8,000 bytes of variable-length binary data. Once again, you can also specify the maximum byte length with *n*. The VARBINARY data type should be used (instead of the BINARY data type) when you expect to have null values or a variation in data size.

 RAW is the Oracle equivalent of VARBINARY.

The IMAGE data type

The IMAGE data type is a large object binary data type that stores more than 8000 bytes. The IMAGE data type is used to store binary values and is also used to store pictures.

LONG RAW is the Oracle equivalent of IMAGE.

The BIT data type

The BIT data type is actually an integer data type that can store only a 0 or a 1 and can consume only a single bit of storage space. However, if there is only a one bit column in a table, it will actually take up a whole byte. Up to 8-bit columns are stored in a single byte. The BIT data type is usually used for true/false or yes/no types of data. BIT columns cannot be NULL and cannot have indexes on them.

The monetary data types

Monetary data types are generally used to store monetary values. SQL Server 2005 has two monetary data types:

- MONEY, which uses 8 bytes of storage
- SMALLMONEY, which uses 4 bytes of storage

The TABLE data type

The TABLE data type can be used to store the result of a function and can be used as the data type of local variables. Columns in tables, however, cannot be of type TABLE. Table variables are sometimes preferable to temporary tables, because table variables are cleaned up automatically at the end of a function or stored procedure.

Temporary tables are covered in Chapter 6. Discussing functions and stored procedures is beyond the scope of this book.

The SQL_VARIANT data type

Values stored in a SQL_VARIANT column can be any data type except TEXT or IMAGE. The usage of the SQL_VARIANT data type should be avoided for several reasons: (a) a SQL_VARIANT column cannot be part of a primary or foreign key; (b) a SQL_VARIANT column cannot be part of a computed column; (c) a SQL_VARIANT column can be used in indexes or as other unique keys only if they are shorter than 900 bytes; (d) a SQL_VARIANT column must convert the data to another data type when moving data to objects with other data types.

Foreign keys are discussed in Chapter 11.

The UNIQUEIDENTIFIER data type

The UNIQUEIDENTIFIER data type, also referred to as globally unique identifier (GUID) or universal unique identifier (UUID), is a 128-bit generated value that guarantees uniqueness worldwide, even among unconnected computers.

The XML data type

The XML data type is a new data type that has been added to SQL Server 2005 to handle XML data. XML can model complex data. The XML column can be typed or untyped. Like other data types, the XML data type must meet specific formatting criteria. It must conform to well-formatted XML criteria (which is untyped) and you can optionally add additional conformance criteria by specifying a Schema collection (typed). SQL Server will also allow you to store XML documents associated with multiple schema definitions. The XML data type will allow you to store complete XML documents or fragments of XML documents. XML documents are limited to two gigabytes of data.

Selecting Data Types

Here we present some general rules that you can follow to determine which data type to use to define a column:

- Use the smallest possible column sizes. The smaller the column size, the lesser the amount of data that SQL Server has to store and process, and the faster SQL Server will be able to read and write the data. In addition, the narrower the column, the faster a sort will be performed on a column.

- Use the smallest possible data type for a column that will hold your data. For example, if you are going to be storing numbers from 1 to 99 in a column, you would be better off selecting the TINYINT data type instead of the INT data type.

- For numeric data, it is better to use a numeric data type such as INTEGER, instead of using VARCHAR or CHAR, because numeric data types generally require less space to hold numeric values then character data types. This saves space, and smaller columns can improve performance when the columns are searched, joined with other columns, or sorted.

Joins are discussed in Chapter 4.

- FLOATs or REALs should not be used to define primary keys. Integer data types can be used for primary keys.

- Avoid selecting the fixed length columns—CHAR or NCHAR—if your column will have a lot of nulls. The NULL in a CHAR or NCHAR field will take up the entire fixed length of 255 characters. This wastes much space and reduces SQL Server's overall performance.

- If you are going to be using a column for frequent sorts, consider an integer-based column rather than a character-based column. SQL Server sorts integer data faster than character data. [1]

Creating a Table

In SQL Server 2005, a relational database, data is loaded into tables that are created in a database. In Chapter 1, we showed you how to create a database. In this section we will concentrate on creating a table within an existing database.

In SQL, the CREATE TABLE command is used to create a table. In SQL Server 2005, the CREATE TABLE command has to be typed in the query editor screen.

The general syntax of the CREATE TABLE statement is:

```
CREATE TABLE Tablename
   (column_name type,  column_name, type, .....)
```

To demonstrate how this CREATE TABLE command works, we provide two examples.

For the first example, we will create a table called Employee that has four columns (attributes). First, type the following in the query editor screen (make sure that you have selected the Student_course database before typing this; if you do not remember how to select the Student_Course database, refer to Figure 1-16 of Chapter 1):

```
CREATE TABLE  Employee (names          VARCHAR(20),
                        address         VARCHAR(20),
                        employee_number INT,
                        salary          SMALLMONEY)
```

Execute the query.

You will get:

```
Command(s) completed successfully.
```

This CREATE TABLE query created a table called Employee with four columns (in the Student_course database): names, address, employee_number, and salary. The data type of names is VARCHAR (variable-length character), with a maximum length of 20 characters. The data type of address is VARCHAR, with a maximum length of 20 characters. The data type of employee_number is INT and the data type of salary is SMALLMONEY.

To view the Employee table in the Student_course database, expand the Student_course node (under the Object Explorer) and the Tables node, and you should be able to see the Employee table, as shown in Figure 3-1.

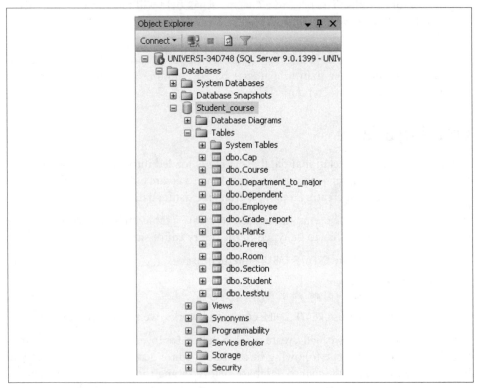

Figure 3-1. Viewing the Employee table

To look at the table definition of the table you just created, right-click on the table, Employee, and select Modify. Figure 3-2 shows the table definition of the Employee table.

Column Name	Data Type	Allow Nulls
names	varchar(20)	☑
address	varchar(20)	☑
employee_number	int	☑
salary	smallmoney	☑
		☐

Figure 3-2. Table Definition of Employee table

For the second example to demonstrate the use of the CREATE TABLE command, we will create a table called Names (type the following query):

```
CREATE TABLE Names
   (fullname VARCHAR(20))
```

This table has only one column, fullname. Its data type is VARCHAR and the maximum length of a name in this table is 20 characters.

Inserting Values into a Table

There are several ways to insert values into a table using SQL in SQL Server 2005. We will illustrate the two most commonly used ways: using INSERT INTO .. VALUES and using INSERT INTO .. SELECT.

Using INSERT INTO .. VALUES

One way to insert values into *one* row of a table is to use the INSERT INTO command with the VALUES option. The INSERT INTO .. VALUES option needs the column list and all the columns in the correct order.

The general syntax for the INSERT INTO .. VALUES option is:

```
INSERT INTO TableName
VALUES ('character_attribute_value', numeric_attribute_value, ...)
```

We will first illustrate inserting data with the INSERT INTO .. VALUES option using the Names table we created in the preceding section. So, type the following in the query editor:

```
INSERT INTO Names
VALUES ('Joe Smith')
```

where:

- INSERT is the SQL command to insert data
- INTO is a necessary keyword
- Names is the name of an existing table
- VALUES is another necessary keyword
- 'Joe Smith' is a string of letters corresponding to the VARCHAR data type

Then click the Execute button. You will get a message that will tell you how many rows were inserted by the query:

```
(1 row(s) affected)
```

Now, if you type the following SQL query:

```
SELECT *
FROM    Names
```

You will get:

```
fullname
--------------------
Joe Smith

(1 row(s) affected)
```

The INSERT INTO .. VALUES option appends rows to a table (that is, rows are added to the end of the table). So, if you use the INSERT INTO .. VALUES option again as follows:

```
INSERT INTO Names
VALUES ('Sudip Kumar')
```

And then type:

```
SELECT *
FROM    Names
```

You get this result:

```
fullname
--------------------
Joe Smith
Sudip Kumar

(2 row(s) affected)
```

If you created a table with *n* attributes (columns), you usually would have *n* values in the INSERT INTO .. VALUES statement, in the order of the definition of the columns in the table. For example, to insert into the Employee table that you created earlier, the INSERT INTO .. VALUES statement to insert a row would have to match column for column and would look like this:

```
INSERT INTO Employee
VALUES ('Joe Smith', '123 4th St.', 101, 2500)
```

Note that character data is entered with single quotes around it. Numeric data does not use quotes (as shown by 101 and 2500).

Now if you type:

```
SELECT *
FROM    Employee
```

You get the following:

```
names                address              employee_number salary
-------------------- -------------------- --------------- -----------
Joe Smith            123 4th St.          101             2500.00

(1 row(s) affected)
```

An INSERT that looks like the following is incorrect, because it does not include all four columns of the Employee table:

```
INSERT INTO Employee
VALUES ('Joe Smith', '123 4th St.')
```

You may INSERT a row with less than all the columns by naming the columns you want to insert into, like this:

```
INSERT INTO Employee (names, address)
VALUES ('Joe Smith', '123 4th St.')
```

In this case, the row will contain nulls or default values for the values left out, which you will see if you type:

```
SELECT *
FROM Employee
```

This will give:

```
names                address              employee_number salary
-------------------- -------------------- --------------- -----------
Joe Smith            123 4th St.          101             2500.00
Joe Smith            123 4th St.          NULL            NULL

(2 row(s) affected)
```

An INSERT that looks like the following is incorrect, because it does not have the values in the same order as the definition of the table:

```
INSERT INTO Employee
VALUES (2500, 'Joe Smith', 101, '123 4th St.')
```

If for some reason the data had to be entered in this order, the previous statement could be corrected by specifying the column names, as shown here:

```
INSERT INTO Employee (salary, names, employee_number, address)
VALUES (2500, 'Joe Smith', 101, '123 4th St.')
```

At this point, typing:

```
SELECT *
FROM Employee
```

would give us the following output:

```
names                address              employee_number salary
-------------------- -------------------- --------------- -----------
Joe Smith            123 4th St.          101             2500.00
Joe Smith            123 4th St.          NULL            NULL
Joe Smith            123 4th St.          101             2500.00

(3 row(s) affected)
```

You may actually include the keyword, null, if the address and the salary were unknown:

```
INSERT INTO Employee
VALUES ('Joe Smith', null, 101, null)
```

Now having added four rows to our table, type:

```
SELECT *
FROM Employee
```

This query will give the following output:

```
names                address              employee_number salary
-------------------- -------------------- --------------- -----------
Joe Smith            123 4th St.          101             2500.00
Joe Smith            123 4th St.          NULL            NULL
Joe Smith            123 4th St.          101             2500.00
Joe Smith            NULL                 101             NULL

(4 row(s) affected)
```

To delete all the rows in the Employee table as well as in the Names table, type:

```
DELETE FROM Employee
```

Then:

```
DELETE FROM Names
```

We will revisit the DELETE command later in the chapter.

For the rest of this chapter, we will set up our Employee table with more meaningful data. Suppose we deleted all the test rows from the previous examples with a DELETE statement and then suppose we used the INSERT INTO .. VALUES option to insert valid data into the Employee table, making it look like this:

```
names                address              employee_number salary
-------------------- -------------------- --------------- -----------
Joe Smith            123 4th St.          101             2500.00
Pradeep Saha         27 Shillingford      103             3300.00
Sumit Kumar          95 Oxford Rd         105             1200.00
Joya Das             23 Pesterfield Cr    114             2290.00
Terry Livingstone    465 Easter Ave       95              3309.00

(5 row(s) affected)
```

 More than one INSERT INTO .. VALUES command can be typed in on one screen in SQL Server 2005.

Using INSERT INTO .. SELECT

With the INSERT INTO .. VALUES option, you insert only one row at a time into a table. With the INSERT INTO .. SELECT option, you may (and usually do) insert *many* rows into a table at one time.

The general syntax for the INSERT INTO .. SELECT option is:

```
INSERT INTO target_table(column1, column2, column3, ...)
  "SELECT clause"
```

We will first illustrate inserting with the INSERT INTO .. SELECT by populating the Names table (the one that you created earlier in this chapter and then removed all rows from with a `DELETE FROM Names`). To copy all the names from the `Employee` table into the `Names` table, type the following:

```
INSERT INTO Names(fullname)
  SELECT  names
  FROM    Employee
```

And now if you type:

```
SELECT *
FROM    Names
```

you will get the following five rows of output:

```
fullname
--------------------
Joe Smith
Pradeep Saha
Sumit Kumar
Joya Das
Terry Livingstone

(5 row(s) affected)
```

We do not have to copy all the names from the `Employee` table to the `Names` table. For example, we could restrict the `INSERT .. SELECT` like this:

```
INSERT INTO Names(fullname)
  SELECT names
  FROM    Employee
  WHERE   salary > 2600
```

This would give us only the following two rows in `Names`:

```
fullname
--------------------
Pradeep Saha
Terry Livingstone

(2 row(s) affected)
```

As with the `INSERT INTO .. VALUES` option, if you create a table with *n* columns, you usually would have *n* values in the `INSERT INTO .. SELECT` option in the order of the table definition, or you would have to name the columns you are inserting. For example, suppose we have a table called `Emp1`, created with three columns:

```
Emp1 (addr, sal, empno)
```

The columns, `addr`, `sal`, `empno`, stand for address, salary, and employee number, respectively.

Now suppose that we want to load the existing empty table called `Emp1` from the `Employee` table with the appropriate columns.

 As with the `INSERT INTO .. VALUES` option, the `INSERT INTO .. SELECT` option has to match column for column.

An INSERT INTO .. SELECT statement would look like this:

```
INSERT INTO Emp1(addr, sal, empno)
  SELECT address, salary, employee_number
  FROM   Employee
```

The Emp1 table would now have the following five rows:

```
addr                    sal           empno
--------------------  ------------  -----------
123 4th St.             2500.00         101
27 Shillingford         3300.00         103
95 Oxford Rd            1200.00         105
23 Pesterfield Cr       2290.00         114
465 Easter Ave          3309.00         95

(5 row(s) affected)
```

If we created a table, Emp2, with identical columns (or attributes) as Emp1, we could use the following INSERT to load data from table Emp1 to Emp2:

```
INSERT INTO Emp2
  SELECT *
      FROM Emp1
```

The Emp2 table would now have the same data as the Emp1 table. This is one way of creating a backup table.

Again, note that the Emp2 table has to exist (be created with the same columns and types) before loading it with the INSERT INTO .. SELECT option.

One caution must be pointed out, however. An erroneous INSERT INTO .. SELECT could succeed if the data types of the SELECT match the data types of the columns in the table to which we are inserting. For example, say we execute the following statement (remember that both sal and empno are numeric types):

```
INSERT INTO Emp1 (addr, sal, empno)
  SELECT address, employee_number, salary
  FROM   Employee
```

This INSERT will succeed because the data types match. The following output results after executing the previous INSERT statement:

```
addr                    sal           empno
--------------------  ------------  -----------
123 4th St.             101.00          2500
27 Shillingford         103.00          3300
95 Oxford Rd            105.00          1200
23 Pesterfield Cr       114.00          2290
465 Easter Ave          95.00           3309

(5 row(s) affected)
```

The wrong information has been inserted in Emp1's columns. The employee_number from Employee has been inserted into the sal column in Emp1, and the salary of

Employee has been inserted into the empno column of Emp1. So, be careful and line up or match up the columns (attributes) in the INSERT INTO and SELECT statements when using an INSERT INTO .. SELECT.

As you might have already guessed from the INSERT INTO .. VALUES section, you do not have to insert the whole row with an INSERT INTO..SELECT. You may load fewer columns than a whole row of Employee with INSERT .. SELECT. Once again, if we delete all rows from Emp1, and then execute a statement like this:

```
INSERT INTO Emp1 (addr, sal)
  SELECT  address, salary
  FROM    Employee
```

This INSERT would leave the other column, empno (of the Emp1 table), with nulls as shown here:

```
SELECT *
FROM   Emp1
```

This query produces the following output:

```
addr                  sal           empno
--------------------  ------------  -----------
123 4th St.           2500.00       NULL
27 Shillingford       3300.00       NULL
95 Oxford Rd          1200.00       NULL
23 Pesterfield Cr     2290.00       NULL
465 Easter Ave        3309.00       NULL

(5 row(s) affected)
```

In conclusion, you must be careful with the INSERT INTO .. SELECT option, because, unlike the INSERT INTO .. VALUES option (which inserts one row at a time), you almost always insert multiple rows, and if types match, the insert will take place whether it makes sense or not.

The UPDATE Command

Another common command used for setting/changing data values in a table is the UPDATE command. As with INSERT INTO .. SELECT, you often UPDATE more than one row. To examine how the UPDATE command works, we will use the tables we created in the previous section.

The general format for the UPDATE command is:

```
UPDATE TableName
SET fieldname...
```

For example, if you want to set *all* salaries in the table Emp2 to zero, you may do so with one UPDATE command:

```
UPDATE Emp2
SET sal = 0
```

Now, if you type:

```
SELECT *
FROM Emp2
```

You will get:

```
addr                 sal          empno
-------------------- ------------ ----------
123 4th St.          0.00         101
27 Shillingford      0.00         103
95 Oxford Rd         0.00         105
23 Pesterfield Cr    0.00         114
465 Easter Ave       0.00          95

(5 row(s) affected)
```

This UPDATE command sets all salaries in all rows of the Emp2 table to zero, regardless of previous values. As with any statement that affects all rows, this may be viewed as a dangerous command and caution should be observed.

It is often useful to include a WHERE clause in the UPDATE command so that values are set selectively. For example, if we assume that employee numbers are unique, we can UPDATE a specific employee from the Employee table with the following statement:

```
UPDATE Employee
SET    salary = 0
WHERE  employee_number=101
```

This query produces the following output:

```
names                address              employee_number salary
-------------------- -------------------- --------------- ------------
Joe Smith            123 4th St.          101                     0.00
Pradeep Saha         27 Shillingford      103                  3300.00
Sumit Kumar          95 Oxford Rd         105                  1200.00
Joya Das             23 Pesterfield Cr    114                  2290.00
Terry Livingstone    465 Easter Ave       95                   3390.00

(5 row(s) affected)
```

Only employee number 101's row is updated. Once again, note that we do not use the quotes around 101, since employee_number is defined as an INT column (a numeric column). Quotes would have to be used around any character or string columns.

The ALTER TABLE Command

In the last few sections we looked at how to add, change, and update rows in a table with the INSERT and UPDATE commands. In this section, we discuss how you can add, change (modify), and delete *columns* in a table's definition by using SQL's ALTER TABLE command. ALTER TABLE commands are known as data definition (DDL) commands, because they change the definition of a table.

Adding a Column to a Table

You may add columns to a table with little difficulty. The general syntax for adding a column to a table is:

```
ALTER TABLE Tablename
ADD column-name type
```

For example, to add a column called bonus (a SMALLMONEY column) to the Employee table, you type in the following:

```
ALTER TABLE Employee
ADD bonus SMALLMONEY
```

This command alters the table definition of the Employee table, as shown in Figure 3-3 (to get Figure 3-3, click on the + beside the Employee table and then click on the + beside Columns—in the Object Explorer on the left side of your screen):

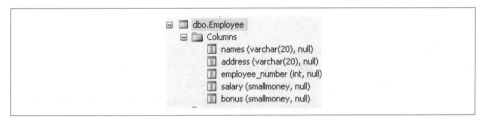

Figure 3-3. Column added to Employee table

When columns are added to existing tables, they will initially contain null values. Data may be added to the new column using an UPDATE command.

Changing a Column's Data Type in a Table

In SQL Server 2005, you can change a column's data type with existing data in it, provided that the new column data type will accommodate the existing data. The general syntax for changing a column's data type in a table is:

```
ALTER TABLE Tablename
ALTER COLUMN column-name new_type
```

For example, to change the data type of the bonus column from SMALLMONEY to FLOAT, you would type the following:

```
ALTER TABLE EMPLOYEE
ALTER COLUMN bonus FLOAT
```

This query would produce the table definition of the Employee table shown in Figure 3-4.

Column Name	Data Type	Allow Nulls
names	varchar(20)	☑
address	varchar(20)	☑
employee_number	int	☑
salary	smallmoney	☑
bonus	float	☑

dbo.Employee:...tudent_course) Query2: Query...dent_cou

Figure 3-4. Altered column's data type for bonus column in the Employee table

 You may have to refresh the Employee table before you can see this change made to the table definition. To refresh the Employee table, right click on the Employee table and then select Refresh. Then, select the Employee table and select Modify.

Changing a column's length in a table

You may want to change the size of a column in a table. You typically make a column larger, and SQL Server 2005 will not have a problem with that, because larger columns will accommodate existing data. But, if you want to make a column smaller (which is unusual), sometimes SQL Server 2005 will let you do it and other times it will not.

When will SQL Server 2005 allow you to reduce the length of your column without any problems?

- When you do not have any data in that column yet (it's all NULL).
- When all the data in that column is still less than the size you are changing the column to.

If you try to reduce the column size to a size where you would be cutting off some of the data, SQL Server 2005 will give you an error and will not let you do it.

For example, if you type in the following ALTER TABLE command, trying to change the names column of the Employee table to a size of 5 (where you would be losing some data):

```
ALTER TABLE Employee
ALTER COLUMN names VARCHAR(5)
```

You will get the following error message:

```
Msg 8152, Level 16, State 14, Line 1
String or binary data would be truncated.
The statement has been terminated.
```

And, upon viewing the table definition of the Employee table, you will find that the column size of the names column was not altered.

If, however, you type:

```
ALTER TABLE Employee
ALTER COLUMN names VARCHAR(19)
```

You will get the message:

```
Command(s) completed successfully.
```

Now if you look at the table definition of the Employee table, you will see that the names column has been changed to a size of 19 characters, as shown in Figure 3-5.

Column Name	Data Type	Allow Nulls
names	varchar(19)	☑
address	varchar(20)	☑
employee_number	int	☑
salary	smallmoney	☑
bonus	float	☑
		☐

Figure 3-5. Altering a column's length in the Employee table

But before you can view this change, you may have to refresh the Employee table.

SQL Server 2005 allowed this reduction in column size, as all the data in the names column was less than 19 characters in length.

Before you proceed to the following section, please change the size of the names column back to 20.

Deleting a Column from a Table

The following is the general syntax for deleting a column from a table:

```
ALTER TABLE Tablename
DROP column column-name
```

For example, to delete the column called bonus from the Employee table, type the following:

```
ALTER TABLE Employee
DROP column bonus
```

This query produces the definition of the Employee table shown in Figure 3-6, which matches the original design for the table shown in Figure 3-2.

The DROP column command will also delete a column even if there is data in it, so you have to be very careful when using it. This is another one of the commands that affects multiple rows and caution must be observed.

dbo.Employee:...tudent_course)	Query0: Query...dent_cou	
Column Name	Data Type	Allow Nulls
▶ names	varchar(20)	☑
address	varchar(20)	☑
employee_number	int	☑
salary	smallmoney	☑

Figure 3-6. Design of Employee table after dropping a column

We will discuss a few other uses of the ALTER TABLE command in subsequent chapters. For example, you can use it to define or change a default column value, enable or disable an integrity constraint, manage internal space, and so on.

The DELETE Command

Earlier in the chapter, we saw that the DELETE command can be used to remove all rows of a table. In this section we revisit the powerful DELETE. Keep in mind as you read this that the DELETE statement can affect multiple rows as we have seen and hence, one must be careful when using it. Following is the general syntax of the DELETE command used to delete rows from a table:

```
DELETE FROM Table
WHERE (condition)
```

(condition) determines which rows of the table will be deleted. As you saw earlier, if no WHERE condition is used, all the rows of the table will be deleted.

 Multiple rows can be affected by the DELETE command, so be careful when using it.

Here is an example of using the DELETE command on our original Employee table:

```
DELETE FROM Employee
WHERE salary < 1500
```

Now if you type:

```
SELECT *
FROM EMPLOYEE
```

You will get the following four rows of output:

```
names                address              employee_number salary
-------------------  -------------------  --------------- -----------
Joe Smith            123 4th St.          101             2500.00
Pradeep Saha         27 Shillingford      103             3300.00
Joya Das             23 Pesterfield Cr    114             2290.00
Terry Livingstone    465 Easter Ave       95              3390.00

(4 row(s) affected)
```

Deleting a Table

The general syntax to delete or remove an entire table and its contents is:

```
DROP TABLE Tablename
```

For example, to delete the table called Names from your database, you would type the following:

```
DROP TABLE Names
```

There are times when it is appropriate to delete all the data in a table and there are times when the entire table should be eradicated. When a table is dropped, it no longer exists; its definition is removed from the database. But, when data is deleted from a table with a DELETE statement (maybe with a WHERE condition), the table may be repopulated, because only the data from the table was removed, but the definition is intact.

Summary

In this chapter, we dealt with basic table manipulations. We showed you how to create tables, insert data into tables, update data in tables, add and delete columns from tables, alter column types and sizes, and delete entire tables. We also discussed the basic data types available in SQL Server 2005.

Review Questions

1. The INSERT INTO .. VALUES option will insert rows into the _____ of a table.

2. While you are inserting values into a table with the INSERT INTO .. VALUES option, does the order of the columns in the INSERT statement have to be the same as the order of the columns in the table?

3. While you are inserting values into a table with the INSERT INTO .. SELECT option, does the order of the columns in the INSERT statement have to be the same as the order of the columns in the table?

4. When would you use an INSERT INTO .. SELECT option versus an INSERT INTO .. VALUES option? Give an example of each.

5. What does the UPDATE command do?

6. Can you change the data type of a column in a table after the table has been created? If so, which command would you use?

7. Will SQL Server 2005 allow you to reduce the size of a column?

8. What integer data types are available in SQL Server 2005?

9. What is the default value of an integer data type in SQL Server 2005?

10. What decimal data types are available in SQL Server 2005?

11. What is the difference between a CHAR and a VARCHAR datatype?

12. Does Server SQL treat CHAR as a variable-length or fixed-length column? Do other SQL implementations treat it in the same way?

13. If you are going to have too many nulls in a column, what would be the best data type to use?

14. When columns are added to existing tables, what do they initially contain?

15. What command would you use to add a column to a table in SQL Server?

16. In SQL Server, which data type is used to store large object data types?

17. If I do not need to store decimal places, what would be a good numeric data type to use?

18. If I need to store decimal places, but am not worried about rounding errors, what would be a good data type to use?

19. Should a column be defined as a FLOAT if it is going to be used as a primary key?

Exercises

Unless specified otherwise, use the Student_course database to answer the following questions. Also, use appropriate column headings when displaying your output.

1. Create a table called Cust with a customer number as a fixed-length character string of 3, an address with a variable-length character string of up to 20, and a numeric balance.

   a. Insert values into the table with INSERT INTO .. VALUES option. Use the form of INSERT INTO .. VALUES option that requires you to have a value for each column; therefore, if you have a customer number, address, and balance, you must insert three values with INSERT INTO .. VALUES option.

   b. Create at least five tuples (rows in the table) with customer numbers 101 to 105 and balances between 200 to 2000.

   c. Display the table with a simple SELECT.

   d. Show the balances for customers with customer numbers 103 and 104.

   e. Add a customer number 90 to your Cust table.

   f. Show a listing of the customers in balance order (high to low), using ORDER BY in your SELECT. (Result: Five tuples, or however many you created.)

2. From the Student table (from our Student_course database), display the student names, classes, and majors for freshmen or sophomores (class <= 2) in descending order of class.

3. From your Cust table, show a listing of only the customer balances in ascending order where balance > 400. (You can choose some other constant or relation if you want, such as balance <= 600.) The results will depend on your data.

4. Create another two tables with the same data types as Cust but without the customer addresses. Call one table Cust1 and the other Cust2. Use column names cnum for customer number and bal for balance. Load the table with the data you have in the Cust table with one less tuple. Use an INSERT INTO .. SELECT with appropriate columns and an appropriate WHERE clause.

   a. Display the resulting tables.

5. Alter the Cust1 table by adding a date_opened column of type DATETIME. View the table definition of Cust1.

   a. Add some more data to the Cust1 table by using the INSERT INTO .. VALUES option.

   After each of the following, display the table.

   b. Set the date_opened value in all rows to '01-JAN-06'.

   c. Set all balances to zero.

   d. Set the date_opened value of one of your rows to '21-OCT-06'.

   e. Change the type of the balance column in the Cust1 table to FLOAT. Display the table definition. Set the balance for one row to 888.88 and display the table data.

   f. Try changing the type of balance to INTEGER. Does this work in SQL Server?

   g. Delete the date_opened column of the Cust1 table.

   h. When you are finished with the exercise (but be sure you are finished), delete the tables Cust, Cust1, and Cust2.

References

[1] Data Type Performance Tuning Tips for Microsoft SQL Server: *http://www.sql-server-performance.com/datatypes.asp*

CHAPTER 4

Joins

This chapter discusses *joins*—a common way to combine tables in SQL. In Chapter 2, you learned how to write simple query statements in SQL using just one table. In "real" databases, however, data is usually spread over many tables. This chapter shows you how to join tables in a database so that you can retrieve related data from more than one table. The join operation is used to combine related rows from two tables into a result set. Join is a binary operation. More than two tables can be combined using multiple join operations. Understanding the join function is fundamental to understanding relational databases, which are made up of many tables.

We start out the chapter by discussing the JOIN command. Then, we show how the same join could also be achieved with an INNER JOIN and using a WHERE clause. The concepts of the Cartesian product, equi-joins and non-equi joins, self joins, and natural joins are also introduced. We also show how multiple table joins can be performed with nested JOINs and with a WHERE clause. Finally, the concept of OUTER JOINs, with specific illustrations of the LEFT and RIGHT OUTER joins and the FULL OUTER JOIN, is also discussed.

The JOIN

In SQL Server 2005, the join is accomplished using the ANSI JOIN SQL syntax (based on ANSI Standard SQL-92), which uses the JOIN keyword and an ON clause. The ANSI JOIN syntax requires the use of an ON clause for specifying how the tables are related. One ON clause is used for each pair of tables being joined. The general form of the ANSI JOIN SQL syntax is:

```
SELECT columns
FROM table1 JOIN table2
ON table1.column1=table2.column1
```

The basic idea of a join is as follows: Suppose we have the following two tables, Table 4-1 and Table 4-2.

Table 4-1. The XYZ Table

columnA	columnB	columnC
X1	Y1	Z1
X2	Y2	Z2
X3	Y3	Z3

Table 4-2. The XDE Table

columnA	columnD	columnE
X1	D1	E1
X2	D2	E2
X3	D3	E3

The common column between the two tables (Table 4-1 and Table 4-2) is columnA. So the join would be performed on columnA. A SQL JOIN would give a table where columnA of Table1 = columnA of Table2. This would produce the new table, Table 4-3, the result of the join, as shown below:

Table 4-3. Joining XYZ with XDE

columnA	columnB	columnC	columnA	columnD	columnE
X1	Y1	Z1	X1	D1	E1
X2	Y2	Z2	X2	D2	E2
X3	Y3	Z3	X3	D3	E3

There are several types of joins in SQL. To be precise, the previous model refers to an *inner join*, where the two tables being joined must share at least one common column. The columns of the two tables being joined by the JOIN command are matched using an ON clause. SQL Server will actually translate the example JOIN statement to an unambiguous INNER JOIN form, as you shall see. When inner-joining two tables, the JOIN returns rows from both tables only if there is a corresponding value in both tables as described by the ON clause column. In other words, the JOIN disregards any rows in which the specific join condition, specified in the ON clause, is not met.

To illustrate the JOIN using our database (Student_course database), we present the following two examples.

Example 1

To find the student names and dependent names of all the students who have dependents, we need to join the Student table with the Dependent table, because the data that we want to display is spread across these two tables. Before we can formulate the JOIN query, we have to examine both tables and find out what relationship exists between the two tables. Usually this relationship is where one table has a column as a primary key and the other table has a column as a foreign key. A *primary key* is a unique identifier for a row in a table. A *foreign key* is so called because the key it references is "foreign" to the table where it exists.

Let us first look at the table descriptions of the Student and Dependent tables, shown in Figures 4-1 and 4-2, respectively.

Table - dbo.Student	Summary	
Column Name	Data Type	Allow Nulls
▶🔑 STNO	smallint	☐
SNAME	nvarchar(20)	☑
MAJOR	nvarchar(4)	☑
CLASS	smallint	☑
BDATE	smalldatetime	☑

Figure 4-1. Description of Student table

Table - dbo.Dependent	Summary	
Column Name	Data Type	Allow Nulls
▶ PNO|	smallint	☐
DNAME	nvarchar(20)	☑
RELATIONSHIP	nvarchar(8)	☑
SEX	char(1)	☑
AGE	smallint	☑

Figure 4-2. Description of Dependent table

In examining these two tables, we note that student number (stno in the Student table) is the primary key of the Student table. stno is the unique identifier for each student. The Dependent table, which was not created with a primary key of its own, contains a reference to the Student table in that for each dependent, a parent number (pno) is recorded. pno in the Dependent table is a foreign key—it represents a primary key from the table it is referencing, Student. pno in the Dependent table is not unique, because a student can have more than one dependent; that is, one stno can be linked to more than one pno.

From the table descriptions, we can see that the Student table (which has columns stno, sname, major, class, and bdate) can be joined with the Dependent table (which has columns pno, dname, relationship, sex, and age) by columns stno from the Student table and pno from the Dependent table. Following the ANSI JOIN syntax, we can join the two tables as follows:

```
SELECT stno, sname, relationship, age
FROM Student s JOIN Dependent d
ON s.stno=d.pno
```

In this construction, Student refers to the Student table and s is the table alias of the Student table. Likewise, Dependent refers to the Dependent table and d is the table alias of the Dependent table. The table alias simplifies writing queries or expressions using single-letter table aliases. We very strongly recommend using table aliases in all multi-table queries. This query requests the student number (stno) and student name (sname) from the Student table, and the relationship and age from the Dependent table when the student number in the Student table (stno) matches a parent number (pno) in the Dependent table.

 Table aliases were discussed in Chapter 2.

When the previous query is typed and executed, you will get the following output showing the dependents of the students:

stno	sname	relationship	age
2	Lineas	Son	8
2	Lineas	Daughter	9
2	Lineas	Spouse	31
10	Richard	Son	3
10	Richard	Daughter	5
14	Lujack	Son	1
14	Lujack		3
17	Elainie	Daughter	4
17	Elainie	Son	1
20	Donald	Son	NULL
20	Donald	Son	6
34	Lynette	Daughter	5
34	Lynette	Daughter	1
62	Monica	Husband	45
62	Monica	Son	14
62	Monica	Daughter	16
62	Monica	Daughter	12
123	Holly	Son	5
123	Holly	Son	2
126	Jessica	Son	6
126	Jessica	Son	1
128	Brad	Son	1
128	Brad	Daughter	NULL
128	Brad	Daughter	2
128	Brad	Wife	26
132	George	Daughter	6
142	Jerry	Daughter	2
143	Cramer	Daughter	7
144	Fraiser	Wife	22
145	Harrison	Wife	22
146	Francis	Wife	22
147	Smithly	Wife	23

147	Smithly	Son	4
147	Smithly	Son	2
147	Smithly	Son	NULL
153	Genevieve	Daughter	5
153	Genevieve	Daughter	4
153	Genevieve	Son	2
158	Thornton	wife	22

(39 row(s) affected)

Example 2

To find the course names and the prerequisites of all the courses that have prerequisites, we need to join the Prereq table with the Course table. Course names are in the Course table and the Prereq (prerequisites) table contains the relationship of each course to its prerequisite course. The descriptions of the Prereq table and Course tables are shown in Figures 4-3 and 4-4, respectively.

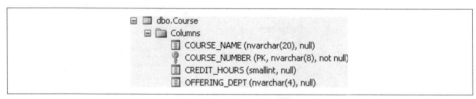

Figure 4-3. Description of Prereq table

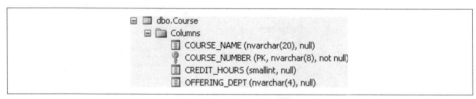

Figure 4-4. Description of Course table

From these descriptions, we first note that the Course table has course_number as its primary key—the unique identifier for each course. The Prereq table also contains a course number, but the course number in the Prereq table is not unique—there are often several prerequisites for any given course. The course number in the Prereq table is a foreign key referencing the primary key of the Course table. The Prereq table (which has columns course_number and prereq) can be joined with the Course table (which has columns course_name, course_number, credit_hours, and offering_dept) by the relationship column in both tables, course_number, as follows:

```
SELECT *
FROM Course c JOIN Prereq p
ON c.course_number=p.course_number
```

The same query could be written without the table alias (using a table qualifier) as follows:

```
SELECT *
FROM Course JOIN Prereq
ON Course.course_number=Prereq.course_number
```

However, the use of the table alias is so common that the table-alias form should be used. Also, aliases let you select columns that have the same names from the tables. This query will display those rows (12 rows) that have course_number in the Course table equal to course_number in the Prereq table, as follows:

COURSE_NAME	COURSE_NUMBER	CREDIT_HOURS	OFFERING_DEPT	COURSE_NUMBER	PREREQ
MANAGERIAL FINANCE	ACCT3333	3	ACCT	ACCT3333	ACCT2220
ORGANIC CHEMISTRY	CHEM3001	3	CHEM	CHEM3001	CHEM2001
DATA STRUCTURES	COSC3320	4	COSC	COSC3320	COSC1310
DATABASE	COSC3380	3	COSC	COSC3380	COSC3320
DATABASE	COSC3380	3	COSC	COSC3380	MATH2410
ADA - INTRODUCTION	COSC5234	4	COSC	COSC5234	COSC3320
ENGLISH COMP II	ENGL1011	3	ENGL	ENGL1011	ENGL1010
FUND. TECH. WRITING	ENGL3401	3	ENGL	ENGL3401	ENGL1011
WRITING FOR NON MAJO	ENGL3520	2	ENGL	ENGL3520	ENGL1011
MATH ANALYSIS	MATH5501	3	MATH	MATH5501	MATH2333
AMERICAN GOVERNMENT	POLY2103	2	POLY	POLY2103	POLY1201
POLITICS OF CUBA	POLY5501	4	POLY	POLY5501	POLY4103

```
(12 row(s) affected)
```

Rows from the Course table without a matching row in the Prereq table are not included from the JOIN result set. Courses that do not have prerequisites are not in the result set.

 A primary key is a column or a minimal set of columns whose values uniquely identify a row in a table. A primary key cannot have a null value. Creation of primary keys is discussed in Chapter 11.

The inner join uses equality in the ON clause (the join condition). When an equal sign is used as a join condition, the join is called an *equi-join*. The use of equi-joins is so common that many people use the phrase "join" synonymously with "equi-join"; when the term "join" is used without qualification, "equi-join" is inferred.

When dealing with table combinations, specifically joins, it is a good idea to estimate the number of rows one might expect in the result set. To find out how many rows will actually occur in the result set, the COUNT function is used. For example:

```
SELECT COUNT(*)
FROM Course c JOIN Prereq p
ON c.course_number=p.course_number
```

will tell us that there are 12 rows in the result set.

In any equi join, let us suppose that the two tables to be joined have X number of rows and Y number of rows respectively. How many rows does one expect in the join? A good guideline is in the order of MAX(X,Y). In our case, we have 12 rows in the Prereq table and 32 rows in the Course table. MAX(12,32) = 32, but we actually got 12 rows. MAX(X,Y) is just a guideline. The actual and expected number of rows need not match exactly. It is possible that some Course-Prereq combinations might be repeated.

The INNER JOIN

In SQL Server, the keyword combination INNER JOIN behaves just like the JOIN discussed in the previous section. The general syntax for the INNER JOIN is:

```
SELECT columns
FROM table1 INNER JOIN table2
ON table1.column1=table2.column1
```

Using the INNER JOIN, the JOIN query presented in the previous section also could be written as:

```
SELECT *
FROM Course INNER JOIN Prereq
ON Course.course_number=Prereq.course_number
```

And, this query too, would produce the same results as given in the previous section.

 As with the JOIN, the INNER JOIN cannot be used without the ON clause.

Using a WHERE Clause Instead of a JOIN

Another way of joining tables in SQL Server is to use a WHERE clause instead of using the JOIN or INNER JOIN command. According to the SQL-92 standard, the inner join can be specified either with the JOIN/INNER JOIN construction or with a WHERE clause. To perform a join with a WHERE clause, the tables to be joined are listed in the FROM clause of a SELECT statement, and the "join condition" between the tables to be joined is specified in the WHERE clause.

The JOIN from the preceding section could be written with a WHERE clause as follows:

```
SELECT *
FROM Course c, Prereq p
WHERE c.course_number= p.course_number
```

This command will display the same 12 rows as was previously shown (when the JOIN was used). You will soon see one of the reasons it is better not to use WHERE.

Associative Property of the JOIN

When two tables are being joined, it does not matter whether TableA is joined with TableB, or TableB is joined with TableA. For example, the following two queries would essentially give the same result set (output):

```
SELECT *
FROM Course c JOIN Prereq p
ON c.course_number=p.course_number
```

and:

```
SELECT *
FROM Prereq p JOIN Course c
ON p.course_number=c.course_number
```

The only difference in the two result sets would be the order of the columns. But the result set column order can be controlled by listing out the columns in the order that you want them after the SELECT instead of using the SELECT * syntax.

Column Types in Joins

Joins have to be performed on "compatible" columns; that is, a character column may be joined to another character column, a numeric column may be joined to another numeric column, and so forth. So, for example, a CHAR column can be joined to a VARCHAR column (both being character columns), or an INT column can be joined to a REAL column (both being numeric columns). Having made the point that compatible columns are required, and keeping in mind that SQL is not logical, it is up to the programmer to match semantics. In reality, why would you join two tables unless a relationship existed? If you ask SQL to join a job_title column with a last_name column, it will try to do so even though it makes no sense!

Some columns types—for example, IMAGE—cannot be joined, as these columns will generally not contain "like" columns. Joins cannot be operated on binary data types.

Performance Hint for Efficient Joins

Join on the narrowest columns possible. The narrower the column, the less storage space is used by SQL Server, and SQL Server can read and write the data faster.

The Cartesian Product

In a SQL statement, a Cartesian product is where every row of the first table in the FROM clause is joined with each and every row of the second table in the FROM clause. A Cartesian product is produced when the WHERE form of the JOIN is used without the WHERE. An example of a Cartesian product (join) would be:

```
SELECT *
FROM Course c, Prereq p
```

The preceding command combines all the data in both the tables and makes a new result set. All rows in the Course table are matched with all rows in the Prereq table (a Cartesian product). This produces 384 rows of output, of which we show the first 10 rows here:

```
COURSE_NAME          COURSE_NUMBER CREDIT_HOURS OFFERING_DEPT COURSE_NUMBER PREREQ
-------------------- ------------- ------------ ------------- ------------- -------
ACCOUNTING I         ACCT2020      3            ACCT          ACCT3333      ACCT2220
ACCOUNTING II        ACCT2220      3            ACCT          ACCT3333      ACCT2220
MANAGERIAL FINANCE   ACCT3333      3            ACCT          ACCT3333      ACCT2220
ACCOUNTING INFO SYST ACCT3464      3            ACCT          ACCT3333      ACCT2220
INTRO TO CHEMISTRY   CHEM2001      3            CHEM          ACCT3333      ACCT2220
ORGANIC CHEMISTRY    CHEM3001      3            CHEM          ACCT3333      ACCT2220
INTRO TO COMPUTER SC COSC1310      4            COSC          ACCT3333      ACCT2220
TURBO PASCAL         COSC2025      3            COSC          ACCT3333      ACCT2220
ADVANCED COBOL       COSC2303      3            COSC          ACCT3333      ACCT2220
DATA STRUCTURES      COSC3320      4            COSC          ACCT3333      ACCT2220
 .
 .
 .

(384 row(s) affected)
```

As we pointed out earlier, before combining tables, it is a good idea to get a count of the number of rows one might expect. This can be done by:

```
SELECT COUNT(*) AS [COUNT OF CARTESIAN]
FROM Course c, Prereq p
```

which produces the following output:

```
COUNT OF CARTESIAN
------------------
384

(1 row(s) affected)
```

From these results, we can see that the results of a Cartesian "join" will be a relation, say Q, which will have n^*m rows (where n is the number of rows from the first relation, and m is the number of rows from the second relation). In the preceding example, the result set has 384 rows (32 times 12), with all possible combinations of rows from the Course table and the Prereq table. If we compare these results with the results of the earlier query (with the WHERE clause), we can see that both the results have the same structure, but the earlier one has been row-filtered by the WHERE clause to include only those rows where there is equality between Course.course_number and Prereq.course_number. Put another way, the earlier results make more sense because they present only those rows that correspond to one another. In this example, the Cartesian product produces extra, meaningless rows.

Oftentimes, the Cartesian product is the result of a user having forgotten to use an appropriate WHERE clause in the SELECT statement when formulating a join using the WHERE format. Note that if the JOIN or INNER JOIN syntax (ANSI JOIN syntax) is used, one cannot avoid the ON clause (no ON clause produces a syntax error). Hence, producing a Cartesian product inadvertently in SQL Server 2005 using the JOIN/ INNER JOIN is much harder to do.

Uses of the Cartesian Product

Though the Cartesian product is generally regarded as not so useful in SQL per se, if harnessed properly, a Cartesian product can be used to produce exceptionally useful result sets, for example:

- The Cartesian product can be used to generate sample or test data.
- The simplest Cartesian product of two sets is a two-dimensional table or a cross-tabulation whose cells may be used to enter frequencies or to designate possibilities.
- The Cartesian product is needed if you want a collection of all ordered n-tuples (rows with n columns) that can be formed so that they contain one element of the first set, one element of the second set, . . . , and one element of the nth set. For example, if set (or table) X is the 13-element set { A, K, Q, J, 10, 9, 8, 7, 6, 5, 4, 3, 2} and set (or table) Y is the 4-element set {spades, hearts, diamonds, clubs}, then the Cartesian product of those two sets is the 52-element set { (A, spades), (K, spades), . . . , (2, spades), (A, hearts), . . . , (3, clubs), (2, clubs) }.

CROSS JOIN Used to Generate a Cartesian Product

In SQL Server, a CROSS JOIN can be used to return a Cartesian product of two tables. The form of the CROSS JOIN is:

```
SELECT *
FROM Table1 CROSS JOIN Table2
```

Using our database, Student_course, the following CROSS JOIN would produce the same result (Cartesian product) as the query (without the WHERE clause) used in the earlier section:

```
SELECT *
FROM Course CROSS JOIN Prereq p
```

Equi-Joins and Non-Equi-Joins

Joins with comparison (non-equal) operators—that is, =, >, >=, <, <=, and <>—on the WHERE or ON clauses are called *theta joins*, where *theta* represents the relational operator. Inner joins with an = operator are called *equi-joins* and joins with an operator other than an = sign are called *non-equi-joins*.

Equi-Joins

The most common join involves join conditions with equality comparisons. Such a join, where the comparison operator is = in the WHERE or ON clause, is called an equi-join. The following is an example:

```
SELECT *
FROM Course c JOIN Prereq p
ON c.course_number=p.course_number
```

Another way to look at a join of any kind is that it is the Cartesian product with an added condition. The output for this query has been shown earlier in this chapter. You will note that the result of the join is simply the Cartesian product with the rows where the course numbers are equal. Per the output, you will see that this query displays all rows that have course_number in the Course table equal to course_number in the Prereq table. All the join columns have been included in this result set. This means that course_number has been shown twice—once from the Course table, and once from the Prereq table—and, this duplicate column is of course redundant.

Non-Equi-Joins

Joins that do not test for equality are non-equi-joins. Non-equi-joins are rare. The following section on self joins provides an example of a theta join without an equality (=) operator (a non-equi join).

Self Joins

On some occasions, you will need to join a table with itself. Joining a table with itself is known as a *self join*.

In a regular join, a row of a table (Table A) is joined with a row of another table (Table B) if the column value used for the join in Table A matches the column value used for the join in Table B. One row of a table is processed at a time. But, if the information that you need is contained in several different rows of the same table, for example if you need to compare row1, column1, with row2, column1, you will need to join the table with itself.

Suppose that we want to find all the students who are more senior than other students. We have to join the Student table with itself. Logically, we need to take a row from the Student table and look through the rest of the Student table to see which rows fit the criterion ("more senior"). To accomplish this, we will use two versions of the Student table. Here is our query:

```
SELECT 'SENIORITY' = x.sname + ' is in a higher class than ' + y.sname
FROM Student AS x, Student AS y
WHERE y.class = 3
AND x.class > y.class
```

First we alias the Student table as x, and then we alias another instance of the Student table as y. Then we join where x.class is greater than y.class and we added the WHERE qualifier y.class = 3, so this effectively gives us only the seniors. We restricted the result to "just seniors" to keep the result set smaller). The use of the > sign is also an example of a non-equi-join.

 + is a string concatenation operator in SQL Server. String concatenation is discussed in detail in the next chapter.

This query produces the 70 rows of output (of which we show a sample):

```
SENIORITY
-----------------------------------------------------------
Mary is in a higher class than Susan
Kelly is in a higher class than Susan
Donald is in a higher class than Susan
Chris is in a higher class than Susan
Jake is in a higher class than Susan
Holly is in a higher class than Susan
Jerry is in a higher class than Susan
Harrison is in a higher class than Susan
Francis is in a higher class than Susan
Benny is in a higher class than Susan
Mary is in a higher class than Monica
Kelly is in a higher class than Monica
Donald is in a higher class than Monica
.
.
.
Mary is in a higher class than Phoebe
Kelly is in a higher class than Phoebe
Donald is in a higher class than Phoebe
.
.
.
Mary is in a higher class than Rachel
Kelly is in a higher class than Rachel
Donald is in a higher class than Rachel
.
.
.
Mary is in a higher class than Cramer
Kelly is in a higher class than Cramer
Donald is in a higher class than Cramer
.
.
.
(70 row(s) affected)
```

In this join, all the rows where x.class is greater than y.class (which is restricted to 3) are joined to the rows that have y.class = 3. So Mary, the first row that has x.class = 4, is joined to the first row where class = 3 (y.class = 3), which is Susan. Then, the next row in the Student table with x.class = 4 is Kelly, so Kelly is joined to Susan (y.class = 3), etc.

 To more fully understand how the self join is working, view the data in the Student table.

The alternative INNER JOIN syntax for this non-equi-join is:

```
SELECT 'SENIORITY' = x.sname + ' is more senior than ' + y.sname
FROM Student AS x INNER JOIN Student AS y
ON x.class > y.class
WHERE y.class = 3
```

Using ORDER BY with a Join

As with other SELECT statements, the ORDER BY clause can be used in joins to order the result set. For example, to order the result set (output) of one of the queries presented earlier in this chapter by the course_number column, we would type the following:

```
SELECT c.course_name, c.course_number, c.credit_hours, c.offering_dept, p.prereq
FROM Course c JOIN Prereq p
ON c.course_number=p.course_number
ORDER BY c.course_number
```

Or this alternative:

```
SELECT c.course_name, c.course_number, c.credit_hours, c.offering_dept, p.prereq
FROM Course c JOIN Prereq p
ON c.course_number=p.course_number
ORDER BY 2
```

ORDER BY 2 means to order by the second column of the result set. This query produces the same 12 rows as the previous query, but ordered alphabetically in the order of course_number:

COURSE_NAME	COURSE_NUMBER	CREDIT_HOURS	OFFERING_DEPT	PREREQ
MANAGERIAL FINANCE	ACCT3333	3	ACCT	ACCT2220
ORGANIC CHEMISTRY	CHEM3001	3	CHEM	CHEM2001
DATA STRUCTURES	COSC3320	4	COSC	COSC1310
DATABASE	COSC3380	3	COSC	COSC3320
DATABASE	COSC3380	3	COSC	MATH2410
ADA - INTRODUCTION	COSC5234	4	COSC	COSC3320
ENGLISH COMP II	ENGL1011	3	ENGL	ENGL1010
FUND. TECH. WRITING	ENGL3401	3	ENGL	ENGL1011
WRITING FOR NON MAJO	ENGL3520	2	ENGL	ENGL1011

MATH ANALYSIS	MATH5501	3	MATH	MATH2333
AMERICAN GOVERNMENT	POLY2103	2	POLY	POLY1201
POLITICS OF CUBA	POLY5501	4	POLY	POLY4103

```
(12 row(s) affected)
```

Joining More Than Two Tables

You will frequently need to perform a join in which you have to get data from more than two tables. A join is a pair-wise, binary operation. In SQL Server, you can join more than two tables in either of two ways: by using a nested JOIN, or by using a WHERE clause. Joins are always done pair-wise.

Joining Multiple Tables Using a Nested JOIN

The simplest form of the nested JOIN is as follows:

```
SELECT columns
FROM table1 JOIN
(table2 JOIN table3
ON table3.column3=table2.column2)
ON table1.column1=table2.column2
```

Here Tables 2 and 3 are joined to form a virtual table that is then joined to Table 1 to create your result set. Note that the join in parentheses is completed first.

As an example of a nested join, if we want to see the courses (course names and numbers) that have prerequisites and the departments (department names) offering those courses, we will have to join three tables—Course, Prereq, and Department_to_major, because the data that we want to display is spread among these three tables. We could choose to first join the Course table with the Prereq table, and then join that result to the Department_to_major table. The Department_to_major table contains the names of the departments. To determine which columns of the Department_to_major table can be used in the join, we have to also look at the description of the Department_to_major table, which is shown in Figure 4-5.

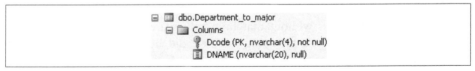

Figure 4-5. Description of Department_to_major table

The query to join the Course table to the Prereq table to the Department_to_major table with the Course/Prereq join done first is:

```
SELECT c.course_name, c.course_number, d2m.dname
FROM department_to_major d2m JOIN
(course c JOIN prereq  p
```

```
ON c.course_number=p.course_number)
ON c.offering_dept=d2m.dcode
```

In the nested JOIN, the part within the parentheses, course c JOIN prereq p ON c.course_number=p.course_number, is performed first to produce a result set. The internal result is then used to join to the third table, Department_to_major.

The result of the join is the following 12 rows:

```
course_name           course_number dname
--------------------- ------------- -------------------
MANAGERIAL FINANCE    ACCT3333      Accounting
ORGANIC CHEMISTRY     CHEM3001      Chemistry
DATA STRUCTURES       COSC3320      Computer Science
DATABASE              COSC3380      Computer Science
DATABASE              COSC3380      Computer Science
ADA - INTRODUCTION    COSC5234      Computer Science
ENGLISH COMP II       ENGL1011      English
FUND. TECH. WRITING   ENGL3401      English
WRITING FOR NON MAJO  ENGL3520      English
Math Analysis         MATH5501      Mathematics
AMERICAN GOVERNMENT   POLY2103      Political Science
POLITICS OF CUBA      POLY5501      Political Science

(12 row(s) affected)
```

Which join is performed first has performance implications. We could choose to do the Course/Department_to_major table join first, in which case the query could be written as follows:

```
SELECT c.course_name, c.course_number, d.dname
FROM (course c JOIN department_to_major d
ON c.offering_dept = d.dcode)
JOIN prereq p
ON p.course_number = c.course_number
```

For larger tables and multi-table joins, the order will determine which version of the query would be most efficient.

The OUTER JOIN

In an *equi-inner join*, rows without matching values are eliminated from the join result. For example, with the following join, we did not see information on any course that did not have a prerequisite:

```
SELECT *
FROM Course c, Prereq p
WHERE c.course_number = p.course_number
```

In some cases, it may be desirable to include rows from one table even if it does not have matching rows in the other table. This is done by the use of an OUTER JOIN. OUTER JOINs are used when we want to keep all the rows from the one table, such as Course, or all the rows from the other, regardless of whether they have matching rows in the other table. In SQL Server, an OUTER JOIN in which we want to keep all the rows from the first (left) table is called a LEFT OUTER JOIN, and an OUTER JOIN in which we want to keep all the rows from the second table (or right relation) is called the RIGHT OUTER JOIN. The term FULL OUTER JOIN is used to designate the union of the LEFT and RIGHT OUTER JOINs. In the following subsections, we illustrate the LEFT OUTER JOIN, RIGHT OUTER JOIN, and FULL OUTER JOIN.

The LEFT OUTER JOIN

LEFT OUTER JOINs include all the rows from the first (left) of the two tables, even if there are no matching values for the rows in the second (right) table. LEFT OUTER JOINs are performed in SQL Server using a LEFT OUTER JOIN statement.

 LEFT JOIN is the same as LEFT OUTER JOIN. The inclusion of the word OUTER is optional in SQL Server SQL, but we will use LEFT OUTER JOIN instead of LEFT JOIN for clarity.

The following is the simplest form of a LEFT OUTER JOIN statement:

```
SELECT columns
FROM table1 LEFT OUTER JOIN table2
ON table1.column1=table2.column1
```

For example, if we want to list all the rows in the Course table (the left, or first table), even if these courses do not have prerequisites, we type the following LEFT OUTER JOIN statement:

```
SELECT *
FROM Course c LEFT OUTER JOIN Prereq p
ON c.course_number = p.course_number
```

Here the LEFT OUTER JOIN is processed as follows: First, all the rows from the Course table that have course_number equal to the course_number in the Prereq table are joined. Then, when a row (with a course_number) from the Course table (first table) has no match in Prereq table (second table), the rows from the Course table are anyway included in the result set with a row of null values joined to the right side. This means that the courses that do not have prerequisites will get a set of null values for prerequisites. So, the output (result set) of a LEFT OUTER JOIN includes all rows from the left (first) table, which in this case is the Course table with matching Prereq rows where applicable.

 The use of the *= operator for the LEFT OUTER JOIN is considered old syntax, and hence its use is not encouraged. It is prone to ambiguities, especially when joining three or more tables.

The previous query will produce the following 33 rows of output (of which we show the first 13 rows here):

```
COURSE_NAME           COURSE_NUMBER CREDIT_HOURS OFFERING_DEPT COURSE_NUMBER PREREQ
--------------------  ------------- ------------ ------------- ------------- -------
ACCOUNTING I          ACCT2020      3            ACCT          NULL          NULL
ACCOUNTING II         ACCT2220      3            ACCT          NULL          NULL
MANAGERIAL FINANCE    ACCT3333      3            ACCT          ACCT3333      ACCT2220
ACCOUNTING INFO SYST  ACCT3464      3            ACCT          NULL          NULL
INTRO TO CHEMISTRY    CHEM2001      3            CHEM          NULL          NULL
ORGANIC CHEMISTRY     CHEM3001      3            CHEM          CHEM3001      CHEM2001
INTRO TO COMPUTER SC  COSC1310      4            COSC          NULL          NULL
TURBO PASCAL          COSC2025      3            COSC          NULL          NULL
ADVANCED COBOL        COSC2303      3            COSC          NULL          NULL
DATA STRUCTURES       COSC3320      4            COSC          COSC3320      COSC1310
DATABASE              COSC3380      3            COSC          COSC3380      COSC3320
DATABASE              COSC3380      3            COSC          COSC3380      MATH2410
OPERATIONS RESEARCH   COSC3701      3            COSC          NULL          NULL
 .
 .
 .

(33 row(s) affected)
```

Note the nulls added to courses (due to the LEFT OUTER JOIN) like ACCOUNTING I, ACCOUNTING II, ACCOUNTING INFO SYST, and so on, which are the courses (in the Course table) that do not have prerequisites.

The RIGHT OUTER JOIN

RIGHT OUTER JOINs include all the rows from the second (right) of the two tables, even if there are no matching values for the rows in the first (left) table. RIGHT OUTER JOINs are performed in SQL Server using a RIGHT OUTER JOIN statement.

 RIGHT JOIN is the same as RIGHT OUTER JOIN. The inclusion of the word OUTER is optional in SQL Server SQL, but we will use RIGHT OUTER JOIN instead of RIGHT JOIN for clarity's sake.

The following is the simplest form of a RIGHT OUTER JOIN statement:

```
SELECT columns
FROM table1 RIGHT OUTER JOIN table2
ON table1.fieldcolumn1=table2.column1
```

As an example, we will redo the previous query from the right side. If we want to list all the rows in the Course table (the right, or second table), even if these courses do not have prerequisites, we may type the following RIGHT OUTER JOIN statement:

```
SELECT *
FROM Prereq p RIGHT OUTER JOIN Course c
ON p.course_number = c.course_number
```

Here, the RIGHT OUTER JOIN is processed as follows. First, all the rows from the Prereq table that have course_number equal to the course_number in the Course table are joined. Then, when a row (with a course_number) from the Course table (second table) has no match in the Prereq table (first table), the rows from the Course table are anyway included in the result set with a row of null values joined to the left side. This means that courses that do not have prerequisites will get a set of null values joined to the left side. The output of a RIGHT OUTER JOIN includes all rows from the right (second) table, which in this case is the Course table, producing output similar to that obtained in the previous section.

The output consists of 33 rows (of which the first 13 rows are shown here):

```
COURSE_NUMBER PREREQ    COURSE_NAME          COURSE_NUMBER CREDIT_HOURS OFFERING_DEPT
------------- --------  -------------------- ------------- ------------ -------------
NULL          NULL      ACCOUNTING I         ACCT2020      3            ACCT
NULL          NULL      ACCOUNTING II        ACCT2220      3            ACCT
ACCT3333      ACCT2220  MANAGERIAL FINANCE   ACCT3333      3            ACCT
NULL          NULL      ACCOUNTING INFO SYST ACCT3464      3            ACCT
NULL          NULL      INTRO TO CHEMISTRY   CHEM2001      3            CHEM
CHEM3001      CHEM2001  ORGANIC CHEMISTRY    CHEM3001      3            CHEM
NULL          NULL      INTRO TO COMPUTER SC COSC1310      4            COSC
NULL          NULL      TURBO PASCAL         COSC2025      3            COSC
NULL          NULL      ADVANCED COBOL       COSC2303      3            COSC
COSC3320      COSC1310  DATA STRUCTURES      COSC3320      4            COSC
COSC3380      COSC3320  DATABASE             COSC3380      3            COSC
COSC3380      MATH2410  DATABASE             COSC3380      3            COSC
NULL          NULL      OPERATIONS RESEARCH  COSC3701      3            COSC
  .
  .
  .

(33 row(s) affected)
```

Once again, note the NULLs added to the unmatched rows from the second table due to the use of the RIGHT OUTER JOIN.

The FULL OUTER JOIN

The FULL OUTER JOIN includes the rows that are equi-joined from both tables, plus the remaining rows from the first table and the remaining rows from the second table. NULLs are added to the unmatched rows from both the first and second tables.

The following is the simplest form of a FULL OUTER JOIN statement:

```
SELECT columns
FROM table1 FULL OUTER JOIN table2
ON table1.column1=table2.column1
```

If we want to list all the rows for which a connection exists between the Prereq table and the Course table (result of a regular JOIN), and in addition, we want all rows from the Prereq table for which there is no corresponding row in the Course table (LEFT

OUTER JOIN), and in addition, we want all rows in the Course table for which there is no corresponding row in the Prereq table (RIGHT OUTER JOIN), we would use the following FULL OUTER JOIN statement:

```
SELECT *
FROM Prereq p FULL OUTER JOIN Course c
ON p.course_number = c.course_number
```

We will get 33 rows:

COURSE_NUMBER	PREREQ	COURSE_NAME	COURSE_NUMBER	CREDIT_HOURS	OFFERING_DEPT
NULL	NULL	ACCOUNTING I	ACCT2020	3	ACCT
NULL	NULL	ACCOUNTING II	ACCT2220	3	ACCT
ACCT3333	ACCT2220	MANAGERIAL FINANCE	ACCT3333	3	ACCT
NULL	NULL	ACCOUNTING INFO SYST	ACCT3464	3	ACCT
NULL	NULL	INTRO TO CHEMISTRY	CHEM2001	3	CHEM
CHEM3001	CHEM2001	ORGANIC CHEMISTRY	CHEM3001	3	CHEM
NULL	NULL	INTRO TO COMPUTER SC	COSC1310	4	COSC
NULL	NULL	TURBO PASCAL	COSC2025	3	COSC
NULL	NULL	ADVANCED COBOL	COSC2303	3	COSC
COSC3320	COSC1310	DATA STRUCTURES	COSC3320	4	COSC
COSC3380	COSC3320	DATABASE	COSC3380	3	COSC
COSC3380	MATH2410	DATABASE	COSC3380	3	COSC
NULL	NULL	OPERATIONS RESEARCH	COSC3701	3	COSC
NULL	NULL	ADVANCED ASSEMBLER	COSC4301	3	COSC
NULL	NULL	SYSTEM PROJECT	COSC4309	3	COSC
COSC5234	COSC3320	ADA - INTRODUCTION	COSC5234	4	COSC
NULL	NULL	NETWORKS	COSC5920	3	COSC
NULL	NULL	ENGLISH COMP I	ENGL1010	3	ENGL
ENGL1011	ENGL1010	ENGLISH COMP II	ENGL1011	3	ENGL
ENGL3401	ENGL1011	FUND. TECH. WRITING	ENGL3401	3	ENGL
NULL	NULL	TECHNICAL WRITING	ENGL3402	2	ENGL
ENGL3520	ENGL1011	WRITING FOR NON MAJO	ENGL3520	2	ENGL
NULL	NULL	CALCULUS 1	MATH1501	4	MATH
NULL	NULL	CALCULUS 2	MATH1502	3	MATH
NULL	NULL	CALCULUS 3	MATH1503	3	MATH
NULL	NULL	ALGEBRA	MATH2333	3	MATH
NULL	NULL	DISCRETE MATHEMATICS	MATH2410	3	MATH
MATH5501	MATH2333	Math Analysis	MATH5501	3	MATH
NULL	NULL	AMERICAN CONSTITUTIO	POLY1201	1	POLY
NULL	NULL	INTRO TO POLITICAL S	POLY2001	3	POLY
POLY2103	POLY1201	AMERICAN GOVERNMENT	POLY2103	2	POLY
NULL	NULL	SOCIALISM AND COMMUN	POLY4103	4	POLY
POLY5501	POLY4103	POLITICS OF CUBA	POLY5501	4	POLY

```
(33 row(s) affected)
```

Summary

After reading this chapter, you should have an appreciation of the concept of the join, a concept very fundamental to understanding relational databases. We have illustrated, with examples, the regular JOIN, CROSS JOIN and the Cartesian product, equi-joins and non-equi-joins, the self join, LEFT OUTER JOIN, RIGHT OUTER JOIN, and FULL OUTER JOIN. We have also discussed how multiple tables can be joined using a nested join.

Review Questions

1. What is a join? Why do you need a join?
2. What is an INNER JOIN?
3. Which clause[s] can be used in place of the JOIN in Server SQL?
4. What is the Cartesian product?
5. What would be the Cartesian product of a table with 15 rows and another table with 23 rows?
6. List some uses of the Cartesian product.
7. What is an equi-join?
8. What is a non-equi-join? Give an example of an non-equi-join.
9. What is a self join? Give an example of a self join.
10. What is a LEFT OUTER JOIN?
11. What is a RIGHT OUTER JOIN?
12. What is a CROSS JOIN?
13. What is a FULL OUTER JOIN?
14. Does Server SQL allow the use of *= to perform outer joins?
15. What is the maximum number of rows that a self join can produce?
16. For what kinds of joins will the associative property hold?
17. What would be the Cartesian product of the two sets {a,b,c} and {c,d,e}?

Exercises

Unless specified otherwise, use the Student_course database to answer the following questions. Also, use appropriate column headings when displaying your output.

1. Create two tables, Stu(name, majorCode) and Major(majorCode, majorDesc), with the following data. Use VARCHAR for the codes and appropriate data types for the other columns.

Stu	
name	**majorCode**
Jones	CS
Smith	AC
Evans	MA
Adams	CS
Sumon	

Major	
majorCode	**majorDesc**
AC	Accounting
CS	Computer Science
MA	Math
HI	History

a. Display the Cartesian product (no WHERE clause) of the two tables. Use SELECT *.... How many rows did you get? How many rows will you always get when combining two tables with *n* and *m* rows in them (Cartesian product)?

b. Display an equi-join of the Stu and Major tables on majorCode. First do this using the INNER JOIN, and then display the results using the equi-join with an appropriate WHERE clause. Use appropriate table aliases. How many rows did you get?

c. Display whatever you get if you leave off the column qualifiers (the aliases) on the equi-join in question 1b. (Note: This will give an error because of ambiguous column names.)

d. Use the COUNT(*) function instead of SELECT * in the query. Use COUNT to show the number of rows in the result set of the equi-join.

e. Display the name, majorCode, and majorDesc of all students regardless of whether or not they have a declared major (even if the major column is null). (Hint: You need to use a LEFT OUTER JOIN here if Stu is the first table in your equi-join query.)

f. Display a list of majorDescs available (even if the majorDesc does not have students yet) and the students in each of the majors. (Hint: You need to use a RIGHT OUTER JOIN here.)

g. Display the Cartesian product of the two tables using a CROSS JOIN.

2. Create two tables, T1(name, jobno) and T2(jobno, jobdesc). Let jobno be data type INT, and use appropriate data types for the other columns. Put three rows in T1 and two rows in T2. Give T1.jobno values 1, 2, 3 for the three rows: <..., 1>,<..., 2,>,<..., 3>, where ... represents any value you choose. Give T2.jobno the values 1, 2: <1,...>,<2,...>.

a. How many rows are in the equi-join (on jobno) of T1 and T2?

b. If the values of T2.jobno were <2,...>, <2,...> (with different jobdesc values), how many rows would you expect to get, and why? Why would the rows have to have different descriptions?

c. If the values of T2.jobno were 4, 5 as in <4,...>,<5,...>, how many rows would you expect to get?

d. If the values of T1.jobno were <..., 1>,<..., 1>,<..., 1> (with different names) and the values of T2.jobno were <1,...>,<1...> with different descriptions, how many rows would you expect to get?

e. If you have two tables, what is the number of rows you may expect from an equi-join operation (and with what conditions)? A Cartesian product?

f. The number of rows in an equi-join of two tables, whose sizes are m and n rows, is from ____ to ____ depending on these conditions: _____ .

3. Use tables T1 and T2 in this exercise. Create another table called T3(jobdesc, minpay). Let minpay be of data type SMALLMONEY. Populate the table with at least one occurrence of each jobdesc from table T2 plus one more jobdesc that is not in T2. Write and display the result of a triple equi-join of T1, T2, and T3. Use an appropriate comment on each of the lines of the WHERE clause on which there are equi-join conditions. (Note: You will need two equi-join conditions.)

    a. How many rows did you get in the equi-join?

    b. Use the COUNT(*) function and display the number of rows in the equi-join.

    c. How many rows would you get in this meaningless, triple Cartesian product (use COUNT(*))?

    d. In an equi-join of n tables, you always have _____ equi-join conditions in the WHERE clause.

In the preceding three exercises, you created tables T1, T2, T3, Stu, and Major. When you have completed the three exercises, delete these tables.

Answer questions 4 through 8 by using the Student_course database.

4. Display a list of course names for all of the prerequisite courses.

5. Use a JOIN or INNER JOIN to join the Section and Course tables.

    a. List the course names, instructors, the semesters and years they were teaching in.

    b. List the instructor, course names, and offering departments of each of the courses the instructors were teaching.

6. Use a LEFT OUTER JOIN to join the Section and Course tables.

    a. List the course names, instructors, and the semesters and years they were teaching in. Sort in descending order by instructors.

    b. List the instructor, course names, and offering departments of each of the courses the instructors were teaching.

7. Use a RIGHT OUTER JOIN to join the Section and Course tables.

   a. For each instructor, list the name of each course they teach and the semester and year in which they teach that course.

   b. For each course, list the name of the instructor and the name of the department in which it is offered.

8.

   a. Are there any differences in the answers for questions 5, 6, and 7? Why? Explain.

   b. Use a FULL OUTER JOIN to join the Section and Course tables. How do the results vary from the results of questions 5, 6, and 7?

9. Discuss the output that the following query would produce:

```
SELECT *
FROM Course AS c, Prereq AS p
WHERE c.course_number<>p.course_number
```

10. Find all the sophomores who are more senior than other students. (Hint: Use a self-join.)

11. Find all the courses that have more credit hours than other courses. (Hint: Use a self-join.)

12. Display a list of the names of all students who have dependents, the dependents name, relationship and age, ordered by the age of the dependent.

CHAPTER 5

Functions

Functions are preprogrammed mini-programs that perform a certain task. As with mathematics, functions transform values into another result. SQL Server 2005 has a wide range of built-in functions to carry out various tasks. In this chapter, we introduce several of SQL Server 2005's useful built-in functions, which can be divided into row-level functions, aggregate functions, and other special functions. Row-level functions operate on a row at a time, whereas aggregate functions operate on many rows at once.

In SQL Server, we can group the row-level functions into four types: numeric functions, string functions, conversion functions, and date functions. Numeric functions are used for calculations. An example of a numeric function is the SQUARE function, which would return the square (a row at a time) of every number (row) of a particular column. String functions are used to manipulate strings in a particular column (again, one row at a time). An example of a string function is SUBSTRING, which extracts characters from a string. Conversion functions are used to convert a particular column (a row at a time) from one data type to another. And, date functions (created using the DATETIME data type) operate on a particular data column or attribute, a row at a time. Date functions are also considered fundamental to the operations of a database.

The second category of functions that we will discuss is aggregate functions. Aggregate functions provide a one-number result after calculations based on multiple rows. Examples of aggregate functions are MIN or AVG, which stand for the minimum or average, respectively, and return the minimum or average value respectively, of multiple rows of a particular column.

The third category of functions that we will discuss is a special class of "other" functions. These other functions produce a smaller subset of rows from multiple rows. Example of these other kind of functions would be the DISTINCT function or the TOP function, both of which produce a smaller subset of rows from the complete set.

Note that most of the functions discussed in this chapter are placed in a SELECT statement, and so they are "read-only" or "display-only" functions. Any SELECT statement function will not change the underlying data in the database. To change the underlying data in a database, UPDATE (instead of SELECT) would have to be used (as shown in Chapter 3).

We begin the chapter by discussing aggregate functions. We discuss row-level functions later in the chapter.

Aggregate Functions

An *aggregate function* (or *group function*) is a function that returns a result (one number) after calculations based on multiple rows. We use the term "aggregate" (instead of "group"), because it avoids confusion later in the book (we discuss other GROUP functions in Chapter 9). An aggregate function basically combines multiple rows into a single number. Aggregate functions can be used to count the number of rows, find the sum or average of all the values in a given numeric column, and find the largest or smallest of the entries in a given column. In SQL, these aggregate functions are: COUNT, SUM, AVG, MAX, and MIN, respectively. In this section, we examine several of these aggregate functions.

The COUNT Function

The COUNT function is used to count how many (rows) of something there are, or the number of rows in a result set. Following is the general syntax for the COUNT function.

```
SELECT COUNT(*)
FROM    Table-name(s)
```

COUNT(*) returns a count of the number of rows in the table(s).

The following query counts the number of rows in the table, Grade_report:

```
SELECT COUNT(*) AS [Count]
FROM    Grade_report
```

The following is its output:

```
Count
-----------
209

(1 row(s) affected)
```

COUNT(*) counts all rows, including rows that have some (or even all) null values in some columns.

In Figure 5-1, we present the table definition of the Grade_report table to remind you of the columns available in the Grade_report table.

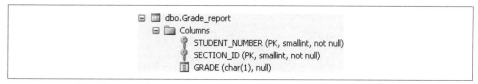

Figure 5-1. Table definition of the Grade_report table

Sometimes we want to count how many items we have in a specific column. The general syntax for counting the number of items in a specific column is:

```
SELECT COUNT(attribute_name)
FROM   Table-name(s)
```

For example, to count the number of grades in the grade column of the Grade_report table, we could type the following:

```
SELECT COUNT(grade) AS [Count of Grade]
FROM   Grade_report
```

This produces the following output:

```
Count of Grade
--------------
114

(1 row(s) affected)
```

COUNT(column) counts only non null columns. Although the Grade_report table has 209 rows, you get a count of 114 grades rather than 209 grades, because there are some null grades in the grade column.

The COUNT feature can be quite useful because it can save you from unexpectedly long results. Also, you can use it to answer "how many" queries without looking at the row-values themselves. In Chapter 4, which showed how Cartesian products are generated, you learned that SQL does not prevent programmers from asking questions that have very long or even meaningless answers. Thus, when dealing with larger tables, it is good to first ask the question, "How many rows can I expect in my answer?" This question may be vital if a printout is involved. For example, consider the question, "How many rows are there in the Cartesian product of the Student, Section, and Grade_report tables in our database?" This is answered by the query:

```
SELECT COUNT(*) AS Count
FROM   Student, Section, Grade_report
```

The following output shows the count from this query, which will be equal to the product of the table sizes of the three tables (the Cartesian product of the three tables). Obviously, in this example, it would be a good idea to first find out the number of rows in this result set before printing it.

```
Count
-----------
321024

(1 row(s) affected)
```

Contrast the previous COUNTing-query and its Cartesian product result to this query:

```
SELECT  COUNT(*) AS [Count]
FROM    Student, Grade_report, Section
WHERE   Student.stno = Grade_report.student_number
AND     Grade_report.section_id  = Section.section_id
```

The following is the result of this query:

```
Count
-----------
209

(1 row(s) affected)
```

What is requested here is a count of a three-way equi-join rather than a three-way Cartesian product, the result of which is something you probably would be much more willing to work with. Note also that you expect a count of about 209 from the sizes of the tables involved: Student (48 rows), Grade_report (209 rows), and Section (32 rows). The expected count of a join operation is of the order of magnitude of the larger number of rows in the tables.

SQL syntax will *not* allow you to count two or more columns at the same time. The following query will not work:

```
SELECT COUNT (grade, section_id)
FROM    Grade_report
```

You will get the following error message:

```
Msg 174, Level 15, State 1, Line 2
The COUNT function requires 1 argument(s).
```

The SUM Function

The SUM function totals the values in a numeric column. For example, suppose you have another table called Employee that looks like this:

```
names            wage          hours
---------------  ------------  -----------
Sumon Bagui      10.0000       40
Sudip Bagui      15.0000       30
Priyashi Saha    18.0000       NULL
Ed Evans         NULL          10
Genny George     20.0000       40

(5 row(s) affected)
```

In this Employee table, names is defined as a NVARCHAR column, wage is defined as a SMALLMONEY column, and hours is defined as SMALLINT.

 This Employee table has not been created for you in the Student_course database. You have to create and insert rows into it in order to run the following queries.

To find the sum of hours worked, use the SUM function like this:

```
SELECT SUM(Hours) AS [Total hours]
FROM    Employee
```

This query produces the following output:

```
Total hours
--------------------
120

Warning: Null value is eliminated by an aggregate or other SET operation.
(1 row(s) affected)
```

Columns that contain null values are not included in the SUM function (and not in any aggregate numeric functions except COUNT(*)).

 AS [Total hours] is an illustration of an alternative way of giving a title to a column.

The AVG Function

The AVG function calculates the arithmetic mean (the sum of non null values divided by the number of non null values) of a set of values contained in a numeric column (or attribute) in the result set of a query. For example, if you want to find the average hours worked from the Employee table, type:

```
SELECT AVG(hours) AS [Average hours]
FROM    Employee
```

This produces the following output:

```
Average hours
--------------------
30

Warning: Null value is eliminated by an aggregate or other SET operation.
(1 row(s) affected)
```

Again, note that the null value is ignored (not used) in the calculation of the average, so the total hours (120) is divided by 4 rather than 5.

The MIN and MAX Functions

The MIN function finds the minimum value from a column, and the MAX function finds the maximum value (once again, nulls are ignored). For example, to find the minimum and maximum wage from the Employee table, you could type the following:

```
SELECT MIN(wage) AS [Minimum Wage], MAX(wage) AS [Maximum Wage]
FROM    Employee
```

This query produces the following output:

```
Minimum Wage Maximum Wage
------------ ------------
20.0000

Warning: Null value is eliminated by an aggregate or other SET operation.
(1 row(s) affected)
```

The MIN and MAX functions also work with character and datetime columns. For example, if we type:

```
SELECT "First name in alphabetical order" = MIN(names)
FROM   Employee
```

We will get:

```
First name in alphabetical order
--------------------------------
Ed Evans

(1 row(s) affected)
```

And, if we type:

```
SELECT "Last name in alphabetical order" = MAX(names)
FROM   Employee
```

We will get:

```
Last name in alphabetical order
--------------------------------
Sumon Bagui

(1 row(s) affected)
```

In the case of strings, the MIN and MAX are related to the collating sequence of the letters in the string. Internally, the column that we are trying to determine the MIN or MAX of is sorted alphabetically. Then, MIN returns the first (top) of the alphabetical list, and MAX returns the last (bottom) of the alphabetical list.

Row-Level Functions

Whereas aggregate functions operate on multiple rows for a result, row-level functions operate on values in single rows, one row at a time. In this section, we look at row-level functions that are used in calculations—for example, row-level functions that are used to add a number to a column, the ROUND function, the ISNULL function, and others.

Arithmetic Operations on a Column

A row-level "function" can be used to perform an arithmetic operation on a column.

Strictly speaking a row-level "function" is not a function, but an operation performed in a result set. But the use of arithmetic operations in
result sets behaves like functions.

For example, in the Employee table, if we wanted to display every person's wage plus
5, we could type the following:

```
SELECT wage, (wage + 5) AS [wage + 5]
FROM   Employee
```

In this query, from the Employee table, first the wage is displayed, then the wage is
incremented by five with (wage + 5), and displayed.

This query produces the following output:

```
wage          wage + 5
------------  ------------
10.0000       15.0000
15.0000       20.0000
18.0000       23.0000
NULL          NULL
20.0000       25.0000

(5 row(s) affected)
```

 Similarly, values can be subtracted (with the - operator), multiplied
(with the * operator), and divided (with the / operator) to and from
columns.

Once again, note that (wage + 5) is only a "read-only" or "display-only" function,
because we are using it in a SELECT statement. The wage in the Employee table is not
actually changing. We are only displaying what the wage + 5 is. To actually increase
the wage in the Employee table by 5, we would have to use the UPDATE command. Any
other arithmetic operation may be performed on numeric data.

The ROUND Function

The ROUND function rounds numbers to a specified number of decimal places. For
example, in the Employee table, if you wanted to divide every person's wage by 3 (a
third of the wage), you would type (wage/3). Then, to round this, you could use
ROUND(wage/3), and include the precision (number of decimal places) after the
comma. In query form, this would be:

```
SELECT names, wage, ROUND((wage/3), 2) AS [wage/3]
FROM   Employee
```

This query produces the following output:

```
names                 wage                  wage/3
--------------------  --------------------  --------------------
Sumon Bagui           10.00                 3.33
Sudip Bagui           15.00                 5.00
Priyashi Saha         18.00                 6.00
Ed Evans              NULL                  NULL
Genny George          20.00                 6.67

(5 row(s) affected)
```

In this example, the values of (wage/3) are rounded up to two decimal places because of the "2" after the comma after ROUND(wage/3).

Other Common Numeric Functions

Other very common numeric functions include:

- CEILING(attribute), which returns the next larger integer value when a number contains decimal places.
- FLOOR(attribute), which returns the next lower integer value when a number contains decimal places.
- SQRT(attribute), which returns the square root of positive numeric values.
- ABS(attribute), which returns the absolute value of any numeric value.
- SQUARE(attribute), which returns a number squared.

The ISNULL Function

The results of the queries in the preceding sections show not only that nulls are ignored, but that if a null is contained in a calculation on a row, the result is always null. We will illustrate, with a couple of examples, how to handle this NULL issue.

Example 1

In the first example, we will illustrate how to handle the NULL problem and also illustrate how to create variables on the fly. SQL Server 2005 allows you to create variables on the fly using a DECLARE statement followed by a @, the variable name (a or b, in our example) and then data type of the variable (both declared as FLOAT in our example). Variables are assigned values using the SET statement. And variables can be added in the SELECT statement.

 A variable is a special place in memory used to hold data temporarily.

So, type the following sequence to declare the variables (a and b), assign values to them, and then add them together:

```
DECLARE @a FLOAT, @b FLOAT
SET @a = 3
SET @b = 2
SELECT @a + @b AS 'A + B = '
```

This query gives the result:

```
A + B =
----------------
5

(1 row(s) affected)
```

SQL Server allows the use of SELECT with no FROM clause for such calculations as we have illustrated.

Now, if you set the variable a to null, as follows:

```
DECLARE @a FLOAT, @b FLOAT
SET @a = NULL
SET @b = 2
SELECT @a + @b AS 'A + B = '
```

You get this:

```
A + B =
----------------
NULL

(1 row(s) affected)
```

To handle the null issue, SQL Server 2005 provides a row-level function, ISNULL, which returns a value if a table value is null. The ISNULL function has the following form:

```
ISNULL(expression1, ValueIfNull)
```

The ISNULL function says that if the expression (or column value) *is not* null, return the value, but if the value *is* null, return ValueIfNull. Note that the ValueIfNull must be compatible with the data type. For example, if you wanted to use a default value of zero for a null in the previous example, you could type this:

```
DECLARE @a FLOAT, @b FLOAT
SET @a = NULL
SET @b = 2
SELECT ISNULL(@a, 0) + ISNULL(@b, 0) AS 'A + B = '
```

Which would give:

```
A + B =
-----------------
2

(1 row(s) affected)
```

Here, @b is unaffected, but @a is set to zero for the result set as a result of the ISNULL function. @a is not actually changed, it is replaced for the purposes of the query.

Example 2

For the second example we will use the Employee table. To multiply the wage by hours and avoid the null-result problem by making the nulls act like zeros, a query could read:

```
SELECT names, wage, hours, ISNULL(wage, 0)*ISNULL(hours,0) AS [wage*hours]
FROM    Employee
```

This query would produce the following output:

```
names            wage         hours        wage*hours
---------------  -----------  -----------  ------------
Sumon Bagui      10.00        40           400.00
Sudip Bagui      15.00        30           450.00
Priyashi Saha    18.00        NULL         0.00
Ed Evans         NULL         10           0.00
Genny George     20.00        40           800.00

(5 row(s) affected)
```

ISNULL does not have to have a ValueIfNull equal to zero. For example, if you want to assume that the number of hours is 40 if the value for hours is null, then you could use the following expression:

```
SELECT names, wage, new_wage = ISNULL(wage, 40)
FROM    Employee
```

This query would give:

```
names            wage         new_wage
---------------  -----------  ------------
Sumon Bagui      10.00        10.00
Sudip Bagui      15.00        15.00
Priyashi Saha    18.00        18.00
Ed Evans         NULL         40.00
Genny George     20.00        20.00

(5 row(s) affected)
```

The NULLIF Function

SQL Server 2005 also has a NULLIF function, which returns a NULL if *expression1 = expression2*. If the expressions are not equal, then *expression1* is returned. The NULLIF function has the following form:

```
NULLIF(expression1, expression2)
```

For example, if we want to see whether the wage is 0, we would type:

```
SELECT names, wage, new_wage = NULLIF(wage, 0)
FROM    Employee
```

This query would give:

```
names            wage          new_wage
---------------  ------------  ------------
Sumon Bagui      10.00         10.00
Sudip Bagui      15.00         15.00
Priyashi Saha    18.00         18.00
Ed Evans         NULL          NULL
Genny George     20.00         20.00

(5 row(s) affected)
```

From these results we can see that because none of the wages are equal to 0, the wage (*expression1*) is returned in every case. Even the NULL wage (Ed Evans's wage) is not equal to 0, but NULL is returned anyway, as the value in question is NULL.

If, for example, a wage 15 was unacceptable for some reason, you could null out the value of 15 using the NULLIF function like this:

```
SELECT names, wage,
       new_wage = NULLIF(wage, 15)
FROM   Employee
```

This query would give:

```
names            wage          new_wage
---------------  ------------  ------------
Sumon Bagui      10.00         10.00
Sudip Bagui      15.00         NULL
Priyashi Saha    18.00         18.00
Ed Evans         NULL          NULL
Genny George     20.00         20.00

(5 row(s) affected)
```

Again, as can be noted from the previous set of results, you have to be very careful about the interpretation of the output obtained from a NULLIF function if there were already nulls present in the columns being tested. Ed Evans's wage was not equal to15, but had a NULL originally (and this may be wrongly interpreted when the NULLIF function is being used).

Other Row-Level Functions

Other row-level functions in SQL Server 2005 include ABS, which returns the absolute value of a numeric expression. For example, if we wanted to find the absolute value of −999.99, we could type the following:

```
SELECT ABS(-999.99) AS [Absolute Value]
```

This query would produce the following output:

```
Absolute Value
--------------
999.99

(1 row(s) affected)
```

There are also several other row-level trigonometric functions available in Server SQL 2005, including SIN, COS, TAN, LOG, and so forth. But, as these functions are less commonly used, we will not discuss them.

Other Functions

This section discusses some other useful functions, such as TOP, TOP with PERCENT, and DISTINCT. These functions help us in selecting rows from a larger set of rows.

The TOP Function

This function returns a certain number of rows. Often, the TOP function is used to display or return from a result set the rows that fall at the top of a range specified by an ORDER BY clause. Suppose you want the names of the "top 2" (first two) employees with the lowest wages from the Employee table (top 2 refers to the results in the first two rows). You would type:

```
SELECT TOP 2 names, wage
FROM    Employee
ORDER   BY wage ASC
```

This query would produce the following output:

```
names           wage
--------------- ------------
Ed Evans        NULL
Sumon Bagui     10.00

(2 row(s) affected)
```

To get this output, first the wage column was ordered in ascending order, and then the "top" two wages were selected from that ordered result set. The columns with the null wages are placed first with the ascending (ASC) command.

With the TOP command, if you do not include the ORDER BY clause (and the table has no primary key), the query will return rows based on the order in which the rows appear in the table (probably, but not guaranteed to be, the order in which the rows were entered in the table). For example, the following query does not include the ORDER BY clause:

```
SELECT TOP 2 names, wage
FROM    Employee
```

And this query returns the following output:

```
names           wage
--------------- ------------
Sumon Bagui     10.00
Sudip Bagui     15.00

(2 row(s) affected)
```

Remember that in relational database, you can never depend on where rows in a table are. Tables are sets of rows and at times the database engines may insert rows in unoccupied physical spaces. You should never count on retrieving rows in some order and always use ORDER BY if you desire an ordering.

Handling the "BOTTOM"

Since there is only a TOP command, and no similar BOTTOM command, if you want to get the "bottom" two employees meaning, the employees with the highest wages (the values in the last two ordered rows) instead of the top two employees from the Employee table, the top two employees (the highest wages) would have to be selected from the table ordered in descending order, as follows:

```
SELECT TOP 2 names, wage
FROM    Employee
ORDER   BY wage DESC
```

This query would produce the following output:

```
names            wage
---------------- ------------
Genny George     20.00
Priyashi Saha    18.00

(2 row(s) affected)
```

Handling a tie

This section answers an interesting question—what if there is a tie? For example, what if you are looking for the top two wages, and two employees have the same amount in the wage column? To handle ties, SQL Server has a WITH TIES option that can be used with the TOP function.

To demonstrate WITH TIES, make one change in the data in your Employee table, so that the value in the wage column of Sudip Bagui is also 10, as shown here:

```
names            wage          hours
---------------- ------------  ------------
Sumon Bagui      10.0000       40
Sudip Bagui      10.0000       30
Priyashi Saha    18.0000       NULL
Ed Evans         NULL          10
Genny George     20.0000       40

(5 row(s) affected)
```

You can use the following UPDATE statement to make the change in the Employee table:

```
UPDATE Employee
SET WAGE = 10
WHERE names LIKE '%Sudip%'
```

The LIKE operator is explained later in the chapter.

 You can also make this change in the Employee table by right-clicking on the table from your Object Explorer and selecting Open Table and changing the data.

Now type the following query:

```
SELECT TOP 2 WITH TIES names, wage
FROM    Employee
ORDER   BY wage ASC
```

Although you requested only the TOP 2 employees, this query produced three rows, because there was a tie in the column that you were looking for (and you used with the WITH TIES option), as shown by the following output:

```
names             wage
---------------   -----------
Ed Evans          NULL
Sumon Bagui       10.00
Sudip Bagui       10.00

(3 row(s) affected)
```

The WITH TIES option is not allowed without a corresponding ORDER BY clause.

 Remember to change the data in your Employee table back to its original state if you are doing the exercises as you read the material.

The TOP Function with PERCENT

PERCENT returns a certain percentage of rows that fall at the top of a specified range. For example, the following query returns the top 10 percent (by count) of the student names from the Student table based on the order of names:

```
SELECT TOP 10 PERCENT sname
FROM    Student
ORDER   BY sname ASC
```

This query produces the following output:

```
sname
--------------------
Alan
Benny
Bill
```

```
Brad
Brenda
```

```
(5 row(s) affected)
```

Again, there is no BOTTOM PERCENT function, so in order to get the bottom 10 percent, you would have to order the sname column in descending order and then select the top 10 percent, as follows:

```
SELECT TOP 10 PERCENT sname
FROM    Student
ORDER   BY sname DESC
```

This query would produce the following output:

```
sname
--------------------
Zelda
Thornton
Susan
Steve
Stephanie
```

```
(5 row(s) affected)
```

Note that the query can be used without the ORDER BY, but because the rows are unordered, the result is simply a sample of the first 10 percent of the data drawn from the table. Here is the same query without the use of the ORDER BY:

```
SELECT TOP 10 PERCENT sname
FROM    Student
```

As output, this query returns the first 10 percent of the names based on the number of rows. But, as the rows are unordered (and there is no primary key in this table), your output would depend on where in the database these rows reside:

```
sname
--------------------
Lineas
Mary
Zelda
Ken
Mario
```

```
(5 row(s) affected)
```

Once again, ties in this section could be handled in the same way as they were handled in the preceding section, with the WITH TIES option as shown:

```
SELECT TOP 10 PERCENT WITH TIES sname
FROM    Student
ORDER   BY sname DESC
```

 The WITH TIES option cannot be used without a corresponding ORDER BY clause.

The DISTINCT Function

The DISTINCT function omits rows in the result set that contain duplicate data in the selected columns. For example, to SELECT all grades from the Grade_report table, you could type:

```
SELECT grade
FROM   Grade_report
```

This query results in 209 rows, all the grades in the Grade_report table.

To SELECT all *distinct* grades from the Grade_report table, you would type:

```
SELECT DISTINCT grade
FROM   Grade_report
```

The result set would look like this:

```
grade
-----
NULL
A
B
C
D
F

(6 row(s) affected)
```

Observe that the syntax requires you to put the word DISTINCT first in the string of attributes, because DISTINCT implies distinct rows in the result set. The preceding statement also produces a row for null grades (regarded here as a DISTINCT grade). Note also that the result set is sorted (ordered). The fact that the result set is sorted could cause some response inefficiency in larger table queries.

Using DISTINCT with other aggregate functions

In SQL Server 2005, DISTINCT can also be used as an option with aggregate functions like COUNT, SUM and AVG. For example, to count the distinct grades from the Grade_report table, we can type:

```
SELECT "Count of distinct grades" = COUNT(DISTINCT(grade))
FROM    Grade_report
```

This query will give:

```
Count of distinct grades
------------------------
5

Warning: Null value is eliminated by an aggregate or other SET operation.

(1 row(s) affected)
```

Because an aggregate function, COUNT, is being used here with an argument, NULL values are not included in this result set.

As another example, to sum the distinct wages from the Employee table, we can type:

```
SELECT "Sum of distinct wages" = SUM(DISTINCT(wage))
FROM    Employee
```

This query will give:

```
Sum of distinct wages
---------------------
63.00

Warning: Null value is eliminated by an aggregate or other SET operation.

(1 row(s) affected)
```

String Functions

SQL Server 2005 has several functions that operate on strings; for example, functions for the extraction of part of a string, functions to find the length of a string, functions to find matching characters in strings, etc. In this section, we explore some of these common and useful string functions. String functions are not aggregates—they are row-level functions, as they operate on one value in one row at a time. String functions are read-only functions and will not change the underlying data in the database unless UPDATEs are performed. We start our discussion of string functions with string concatenation.

String Concatenation

String manipulations often require *concatenation*, which means to connect things together. In this section we look at the string concatenation operator available in SQL Server 2005, the +.

To see an example of concatenation, using the Employee table, we will first list the names of the employees using the following statement:

```
SELECT names
FROM    Employee
```

This query produces the following output:

```
names
---------------
Sumon Bagui
Sudip Bagui
Priyashi Saha
Ed Evans
Genny George

(5 row(s) affected)
```

Now, suppose you would like to concatenate each of the names with ", Esq." Type the following:

```
SELECT names + ', Esq.' AS [Employee Names]
FROM    Employee
```

This query produces:

```
Employee Names
--------------------
Sumon Bagui, Esq.
Sudip Bagui, Esq.
Priyashi Saha, Esq.
Ed Evans, Esq.
Genny George, Esq.

(5 row(s) affected)
```

As another example, suppose you want to add a series of dots (.....) to the left side of the names column. You would type:

```
SELECT ('.....'+ names) AS [Employee Names]
FROM    Employee
```

to produce the following result set:

```
Employee Names
--------------------
.....Sumon Bagui
.....Sudip Bagui
.....Priyashi Saha
.....Ed Evans
.....Genny George

(5 row(s) affected)
```

Similarly, to add ..... to the right side of names column, type:

```
SELECT (names + '.....') AS [Employee Names]
FROM     Employee
```

This query returns:

```
Employee Names
--------------------
Sumon Bagui.....
Sudip Bagui.....
Priyashi Saha.....
Ed Evans.....
Genny George.....

(5 row(s) affected)
```

String Extractors

SQL has several string extractor functions. This section briefly describes some of the more useful string extractors, like SUBSTRING, LEFT, RIGHT, LTRIM, RTRIM, and CHARINDEX. Now suppose (again) that the Employee table has the following data:

```
names             wage           hours
---------------   ------------   -----------
Sumon Bagui       10.0000        40
Sudip Bagui       15.0000        30
Priyashi Saha     18.0000        NULL
Ed Evans          NULL           10
Genny George      20.0000        40

(5 row(s) affected)
```

And suppose you want to display the names in the following format:

```
Employee Names
------------------------
Sumon, B.
Sudip, B.
Priyashi, S.
Ed, E.
Genny, G.

(5 row(s) affected)
```

You can achieve this output by using a combination of the string functions to break down names into parts, re-assemble (concatenate) those parts, and then concatenate a comma and period in their respective (appropriate) locations. Before we completely solve this particular problem, in the next few sections we will explain the string functions that you will need to get this output. Then we will show you how to get this result.

The SUBSTRING function

The SUBSTRING function returns part of a string. Following is the format for the SUBSTRING function:

```
SUBSTRING(stringexpression, startposition, length)
```

stringexpression is the column that we will be using, *startposition* tells SQL Server where in the *stringexpression* to start retrieving characters from, and *length* tells SQL Server how many characters to extract. All three parameters are *required* in SQL Server 2005's SUBSTRING function. For example, type the following:

```
SELECT names, SUBSTRING(names,2,4) AS [middle of names]
FROM   Employee
```

This query returns:

```
names            middle of names
---------------  ---------------
Sumon Bagui      umon
Sudip Bagui      udip
Priyashi Saha    riya
Ed Evans         d Ev
Genny George     enny

(5 row(s) affected)
```

SUBSTRING(names,2,4) started from the second position in the column, names, and extracted four characters starting from position 2.

Strings in SQL Server 2005 are indexed from 1. If you start at position 0, the following query will show you what you will get:

```
SELECT names, "first letter of names" = SUBSTRING(names,0,2)
FROM    Employee
```

You will get:

```
names            first letter of names
---------------  ---------------------
Sumon Bagui      S
Sudip Bagui      S
Priyashi Saha    P
Ed Evans         E
Genny George     G

(5 row(s) affected)
```

In the previous output, we got the first letter of the names because the SUBSTRING function started extracting characters starting from position zero (the position before the first letter) and went two character positions—which picked up the first letter of the names field.

We could have also achieved the same output with:

```
SELECT names, "first letter of names" = SUBSTRING(names,1,1)
FROM    Employee
```

Here the SUBSTRING function would start extracting characters starting from position 1 and go only one character position, hence ending up with only one character—which picks up the first letter of the names field.

SQL Server 2005's SUBSTRING function actually allows you to start at a negative position relative to the string. For example, if you typed:

```
SELECT names, "first letter of names" = SUBSTRING(names,-1,3)
FROM    Employee
```

You would get the same output as the previous query also, because you are starting two positions before the first character of names, and going three character places, so you get the first letter of the name.

The LEFT and RIGHT functions

These functions return a portion of a string, starting from either the left or right side of *stringexpression*. Following are the general formats for the LEFT and RIGHT functions respectively:

```
LEFT(stringexpression, n)
```

Or:

```
RIGHT(stringexpression, n)
```

The LEFT function starts from the LEFT of the *stringexpression* or column and returns *n* characters, and the RIGHT function starts from the right of the *stringexpression* or column and returns *n* characters.

For example, to get the first three characters from the names column, type:

```
SELECT names, LEFT(names,3) AS [left]
FROM    Employee
```

This query produces:

```
names            left
---------------  ----
Sumon Bagui      Sum
Sudip Bagui      Sud
Priyashi Saha    Pri
Ed Evans         Ed
Genny George     Gen

(5 row(s) affected)
```

To get the last three characters from the names column (here the count will start from the right of the column, names), type:

```
SELECT names, RIGHT(names,3) AS [right]
FROM    Employee
```

This query produces:

```
names            right
---------------  -------
Sumon Bagui      gui
Sudip Bagui      gui
Priyashi Saha    aha
Ed Evans         ans
Genny George     rge

(5 row(s) affected)
```

The LTRIM and RTRIM functions

LTRIM removes blanks from the beginning (left) of a string. For example, if three blank spaces appear to the left of a string such as ' Ranu', you can remove the blank spaces with the following query:

```
SELECT LTRIM('   Ranu') AS names
```

which produces:

```
names
-------
Ranu

(1 row(s) affected)
```

It does not matter how many blank spaces precede the non-blank character. All leading blanks will be excised.

Similarly, RTRIM removes blanks from the end (right) of a string. For example, if blank spaces appear to the right of Ranu in the names column, you could remove the blank spaces using the RTRIM, and then concatenate "Saha" with the + sign, as shown here:

```
SELECT RTRIM('Ranu    ') + ' Saha' AS names
```

This query produces:

```
names
------------
Ranu Saha

(1 row(s) affected)
```

The CHARINDEX function

The CHARINDEX function returns the starting position of a specified pattern. For example, if we wish to find the position of a space in the employee names in the Employee table, we could type:

```
SELECT names, "Position of Space in Employee Names" = CHARINDEX(' ',names)
FROM    Employee
```

This query would give:

```
names             Position of Space in Employee Names
--------------    -----------------------------------
Sumon Bagui       6
Sudip Bagui       6
Priyashi Saha     9
Ed Evans          3
Genny George      6

(5 row(s) affected)
```

  In Oracle, CHARINDEX is called INSTR.

Now that you know how to use quite a few string extractor functions, you can combine them to produce the following output, which will require a nesting of string functions:

```
Employee Names
-----------------------
Sumon, B.
Sudip, B.
Priyashi, S.
Ed, E.
Genny, G.

(5 row(s) affected)
```

Following is the query to achieve the preceding output:

```
SELECT "Employee Names" = SUBSTRING(names,1,CHARINDEX(' ',names)-1) + ', ' +
SUBSTRING(names, CHARINDEX(' ',names)+1,1) + '.'
FROM    Employee
```

In this query, we get the first name with the SUBSTRING(names,1,CHARINDEX(' ',names)-1) portion. SUBSTRING begins in the first position of names. CHARINDEX(' ',names) finds the first space. We need only the characters up to the first space, so we use CHARINDEX(' ',names) -1. We then concatenate the comma and a space with + (', '). Then, to extract the first character after the first space in the original names column, we use SUBSTRING(names, CHARINDEX(' ',names)+1,1), followed by concatenation of a period.

To display the names in a more useful manner—that is, the last name, comma, and then the first initial—we would have to use the following query:

```
SELECT "Employee Names" = SUBSTRING(names, (CHARINDEX(' ',names)+1 ), (CHARINDEX(' ',
names))) + ', ' + SUBSTRING(names,1,1) + '.'
FROM    Employee
```

which would produce the following output:

```
Employee Names
-----------------------
Bagui, S.
Bagui, S.
Saha, P.
Eva, E.
George, G.

(5 row(s) affected)
```

In this query, we get the last name with SUBSTRING(names, (CHARINDEX(' ',names)+1), (CHARINDEX(' ', names))). The SUBSTRING begins at the space and picks up the rest of the characters after the space. Then a comma and a space are concatenated, and then the first letter of the first name and a period are concatenated.

The UPPER and LOWER Functions

To produce all the fields in the result set (output) in uppercase or in lowercase, you can use the UPPER or LOWER functions. For example, to produce all the names in the Employee table in uppercase, type:

```
SELECT UPPER(names) AS [NAMES IN CAPS]
FROM   Employee
```

This query produces the following output:

```
NAMES IN CAPS
------------------------
SUMON BAGUI
SUDIP BAGUI
PRIYASHI SAHA
ED EVANS
GENNY GEORGE

(5 row(s) affected)
```

To produce all the names in lowercase, you would type:

```
SELECT LOWER(names) AS [NAMES IN SMALL]
FROM   Employee
```

To further illustrate the nesting of functions, and to produce, in all uppercase, the first name followed by the first letter of the last name, type:

```
SELECT "Employee Names" = UPPER(SUBSTRING(names,1,CHARINDEX(' ',names)-1)) + ', ' +
       SUBSTRING(names,CHARINDEX(' ',names)+1,1) + '.'
FROM     Employee
```

This query produces the following output:

```
Employee Names
----------------------------------
SUMON, B.
SUDIP, B.
PRIYASHI, S.
ED, E.
GENNY, G.

(5 row(s) affected)
```

The LEN Function

The LEN function returns the length (number of characters) of a desired string excluding trailing blanks. For example, to list the lengths of the full names (including any spaces) in the Employee table, type:

```
SELECT names, LEN(names) AS [Length of Names]
FROM     Employee
```

This query produces the following output:

```
names            Length of Names
---------------  ---------------
Sumon Bagui      11
Sudip Bagui      11
Priyashi Saha    13
Ed Evans         8
Genny George     12

(5 row(s) affected)
```

Matching Substrings Using LIKE

Often we want to use part of a string as a condition in a query. For example, consider the Section table (from our Student_course database), which has the following data:

```
SECTION_ID COURSE_NUM SEMESTER YEAR INSTRUCTOR BLDG   ROOM
---------- ---------- -------- ---- ---------- ------ ------
85         MATH2410   FALL     98   KING       36     123
86         MATH5501   FALL     98   EMERSON    36     123
87         ENGL3401   FALL     98   HILLARY    13     101
.
.
.
```

We might want to know something about Math courses—courses with the prefix MATH. In this situation, we need an operator that can determine whether a substring exists in an attribute. Although we have seen how to handle this type of question with both the SUBSTRING and CHARINDEX functions, another common way to handle this situation in a WHERE clause is by using the LIKE function.

Using LIKE as an "existence" match entails finding whether a character string exists in a string or value—if the string exists, the row is SELECTed for inclusion in the result set. Again of course, we could use SUBSTRING and/or CHARINDEX for this, but LIKE is a powerful, common and flexible alternative. This existence-type of the LIKE query is useful when the position of the character string sought may be in various places in the substring. SQL Server 2005 uses the wildcard character, %, at the beginning or end of a LIKE-string, when looking for the existence of substrings. For example, suppose we want to find all names that have "Smith" in our Student table, type the following:

```
SELECT *
FROM   Student
WHERE  sname = 'SMITH'
```

which produces the following output:

```
STNO  SNAME        MAJOR  CLASS  BDATE
-----  -----------  ------  -----  ------------------------------
88     Smith        NULL   NULL   10/15/1979 12:00:00 AM

(1 row(s) affected)
```

Note that the case (upper or lower) in the statement WHERE sname = 'SMITH' does not matter, because SQL Server 2005 is handled as if it is all uppercase (this is by default, and can be changed), although it is displayed in mixed case (and even if it had been entered in mixed case). In other words, we can say that data in SQL Server 2005 is *not* case-sensitive by default.

To count how many people have a name of "Smith," type:

```
SELECT COUNT(*) AS Count
FROM    Student
WHERE   sname = 'Smith'
```

which produces:

```
Count
-----------
1

(1 row(s) affected)
```

Using the wildcard character with LIKE

The percentage sign (%) is SQL Server 2005's wildcard character. For example, if we wanted to find all the names that had some form of "Smith" in their names from the Student table, we would use % on both ends of "Smith," as shown here:

```
SELECT *
FROM    Student
WHERE   sname LIKE '%Smith%'
```

This query produces the following output, showing any "Smith" pattern in sname:

```
STNO    SNAME                  MAJOR CLASS  BDATE
------  ---------------------  ----- ------ -----------------------
88      Smith                  NULL  NULL   1979-10-15 00:00:00
147     Smithly                ENGL  2      1980-05-13 00:00:00
151     Losmith                CHEM  3      1981-01-15 00:00:00

(3 row(s) affected)
```

To find any pattern starting with "Smith" from the Student table, you would type:

```
SELECT *
FROM    Student
WHERE   sname LIKE 'Smith%'
```

This query would produce:

```
STNO    SNAME                  MAJOR CLASS  BDATE
------  ---------------------  ----- ------ -----------------------
88      Smith                  NULL  NULL   1979-10-15 00:00:00
147     Smithly                ENGL  2      1980-05-13 00:00:00

(2 row(s) affected)
```

By default, it is not necessary to use UPPER or LOWER before sname in the previous query since data in SQL Server 2005 is not case sensitive. You can change this however, by changing SQL Server 2005's database configurations.

To find the Math courses (any course_num starting with MATH) from the Section table, you could pose a wildcard match with a LIKE as follows:

```
SELECT *
FROM    Section
WHERE   course_num LIKE 'MATH%'
```

This query would produce the following output:

SECTION_ID	COURSE_NUM	SEMESTER	YEAR	INSTRUCTOR	BLDG	ROOM
85	MATH2410	FALL	98	KING	36	123
86	MATH5501	FALL	98	EMERSON	36	123
107	MATH2333	SPRING	00	CHANG	36	123
109	MATH5501	FALL	99	CHANG	36	123
112	MATH2410	FALL	99	CHANG	36	123
158	MATH2410	SPRING	98	NULL	36	123

(6 row(s) affected)

Finding a range of characters

SQL Server 2005 allows some POSIX-compliant regular expression patterns in LIKE clauses. We will illustrate some of these extensions for pattern matching.

LIKE can be used to find a range of characters. For example, to find all grades between C and F in the Grade_report table, type:

```
SELECT DISTINCT student_number, grade
FROM    Grade_report
WHERE   grade LIKE '[c-f]'
AND     student_number > 100
```

This query produces 15 rows of output:

student_number	grade
125	C
126	C
127	C
128	F
130	C
131	C
145	F
147	C
148	C
151	C
153	C

```
158        C
160        C
161        C
163        C
```

(15 row(s) affected)

 By default, note that LIKE is also case-insensitive. You can change this, however, by changing SQL Server 2005's database configurations.

To find all grades from the Grade_report table that are *not* between C and F, we use a caret (^) before the range we do not want to find:

```
SELECT DISTINCT student_number, grade
FROM   Grade_report
WHERE  grade LIKE '[^c-f]'
AND    student_number > 100
```

This query produces the following 21 rows of output:

```
student_number grade
-------------- -----
121            B
122            B
123            A
123            B
125            A
125            B
126            A
126            B
127            A
127            B
129            A
129            B
132            B
142            A
143            B
144            B
146            B
147            B
148            B
155            B
157            B
```

(21 row(s) affected)

As another example, to find all the courses from the Section table that start with "C," but do not have "h" as the second character, we could type:

```
SELECT *
FROM   Section
WHERE  course_num LIKE 'C[^h]%'
```

This query would give the following 10 rows of output:

```
SECTION_ID COURSE_NUM SEMESTER YEAR INSTRUCTOR BLDG  ROOM
---------- ---------- -------- ---- ---------- ----- -----
90         COSC3380   SPRING   99   HARDESTY   79    179
91         COSC3701   FALL     98   NULL       79    179
92         COSC1310   FALL     98   ANDERSON   79    179
93         COSC1310   SPRING   99   RAFAELT    79    179
96         COSC2025   FALL     98   RAFAELT    79    179
98         COSC3380   FALL     99   HARDESTY   79    179
102        COSC3320   SPRING   99   KNUTH      79    179
119        COSC1310   FALL     99   ANDERSON   79    179
135        COSC3380   FALL     99   STONE      79    179
145        COSC1310   SPRING   99   JONES      79    179

(10 row(s) affected)
```

Finding a particular character

To find a particular character using LIKE, we would place the character in square brackets []. For example, to find all the names from the Student table that begin with a B or G and end in "ill," we could type:

```
SELECT sname
FROM    Student
WHERE sname LIKE '[BG]ill'
```

We would get:

```
sname
--------------------
Bill

(1 row(s) affected)
```

Finding a single character or single digit—the underscore wildcard character

A single character or digit can be found in a particular position in a string by using an underscore, _, for the wildcard in that position in the string. For example, to find all students with student_numbers in the 130s (130...139) range from the Student table, type:

```
SELECT DISTINCT student_number, grade
FROM    Grade_report
WHERE   student_number LIKE '13_'
```

This query would produce the following:

```
student_number grade
-------------- -----
130            C
131            C
132            B

(3 row(s) affected)
```

Using NOT LIKE

In SQL Server 2005, the LIKE operator can be negated with the NOT. For example, to get a listing of the non math courses and the courses that do not start in "C" from the Section table, we would type:

```
SELECT *
FROM    Section
WHERE   course_num NOT LIKE 'MATH%'
AND     Course_num NOT LIKE 'C%'
```

This query would give the following 14 rows of output:

SECTION_ID	COURSE_NUM	SEMESTER	YEAR	INSTRUCTOR	BLDG	ROOM
87	ENGL3401	FALL	98	HILLARY	13	101
88	ENGL3520	FALL	99	HILLARY	13	101
89	ENGL3520	SPRING	99	HILLARY	13	101
94	ACCT3464	FALL	98	RODRIGUEZ	74	NULL
95	ACCT2220	SPRING	99	RODRIQUEZ	74	NULL
97	ACCT3333	FALL	99	RODRIQUEZ	74	NULL
99	ENGL3401	FALL	99	HILLARY	13	101
100	POLY1201	FALL	99	SCHMIDT	NULL	NULL
101	POLY2103	SPRING	00	SCHMIDT	NULL	NULL
104	POLY4103	SPRING	00	SCHMIDT	NULL	NULL
126	ENGL1010	FALL	98	HERMANO	13	101
127	ENGL1011	SPRING	99	HERMANO	13	101
133	ENGL1010	FALL	99	HERMANO	13	101
134	ENGL1011	SPRING	00	HERMANO	13	101

```
(14 row(s) affected)
```

CONVERSION Functions

Sometimes data in a table is stored in a particular data type, but you need to have the data in another data type. For example, let us suppose that columnA of TableA is of character data type, but you need to use this column as a numeric column in order to do some mathematical operations. Similarly, there are times where you have a table with numeric data types and you need characters. What do you do? SQL Server 2005 provides three functions for converting data types—CAST, CONVERT, and STR. In the following subsections, we discuss each of these functions.

The CAST Function

The CAST function is a very useful SQL Server 2005 function that allows you to change a data type of a column. The CAST result can then be used for:

- Concatenating strings
- Joining columns that were not envisioned as related

- Performing unions of tables (unions are discussed in Chapter 7)
- Performing mathematical operations on columns that were defined as character but which actually contain numbers that need to be calculated.

Some conversions are automatic and implicit, so using CAST is not necessary. For example, converting between numbers with types INT, SMALLINT, TINYINT, FLOAT, NUMERIC, and so on is done automatically and implicitly as long as an overflow does not occur. But, converting numbers with decimal places to integer data types truncates values to the right of the decimal place without a warning, so you should use CAST if a loss of precision is possible.

The general form of the syntax for the CAST function is:

```
CAST (original_expression AS desired_datatype)
```

To illustrate the CAST function, we will use the Employee table that we created earlier in this chapter. In this table, names was defined as a NVARCHAR column, wage was defined as a SMALLMONEY column, and hours was defined as a SMALLINT column. We will use CAST to change the display of the hours column to a character column so that we can concatenate a string to it, as shown in the following query:

```
SELECT names, wage, hours = CAST(hours AS CHAR(2)) + ' hours worked per week'
FROM   Employee
```

This query will give us:

```
names                wage         hours
-------------------- ------------ ------------------------
Sumon Bagui          10.0000      40 hours worked per week
Sudip Bagui          15.0000      30 hours worked per week
Priyashi Saha        18.0000      NULL
Ed Evans             NULL         10 hours worked per week
Genny George         20.0000      40 hours worked per week

(5 row(s) affected)
```

CAST will truncate the value or column if the character length is smaller than the size required for full display.

CAST is a subset of the CONVERT function, and was added to SQL Server 2005 to comply with ANSI-92 specifications.

The STR Function

STR is a specialized conversion function that always converts from a number (for example, float or numeric) to a character data type. It allows you to explicitly specify the length and number of decimal places that should be formatted for the character string.

The general form of the syntax for the STR function is:

```
STR(float_expression, character_length, number_of_decimal_places)
```

character_length and number_of_decimal_places are optional arguments.

character_length must include room for a decimal place and a negative sign. STR rounds a value to the number of decimal places requested.

We will illustrate the use of the STR function using the Employee table that we created earlier in this chapter. In this table, the hours column is a SMALLINT column. To format it to two decimal places, we can use STR. Note that we have to make the character length 5 in this case in order to accommodate the .00 (the decimal point and zeros). Following is the query showing this:

```
SELECT names, wage, hours = STR(hours, 5, 2)
FROM   Employee
```

which produces:

```
names                  wage                   hours
---------------------  ---------------------  -----
Sumon Bagui            10.00                  40.00
Sudip Bagui            15.00                  30.00
Priyashi Saha          18.00                  NULL
Ed Evans               NULL                   10.00
Genny George           20.00                  40.00

(5 row(s) affected)
```

The CONVERT Function

Just like the CAST function, the CONVERT function is also used to explicitly convert to a given data type. But, the CONVERT function has additional limited formatting capabilities.

The general syntax for the CONVERT function is:

```
CONVERT(desired_datatype[(length)], original_expression [, style])
```

CONVERT has an optional third parameter, style, which is used for formatting. If style is not specified, it will use the default style. Because the CONVERT function has formatting capabilities, it is widely used when displaying dates in a particular format. Examples of the use of the CONVERT function are presented in the section, "Default Date Formats and Changing Date Formats" later in this chapter.

DATE Functions

Using the DATETIME and SMALLDATETIME data type, SQL Server 2005 gives you the opportunity to use several date functions like DAY, MONTH, YEAR, DATEADD, DATEDIFF, DATEPART, and GETDATE for extracting and manipulating dates (adding dates, taking the differences between dates, finding the day/month/year from dates, and so on).

Before we start discussing date functions, we will create a table, DateTable, using the SMALLDATETIME data type. Then we will discuss date formats and formatting dates.

Creating a Table with the DATETIME Data Type

Suppose that you define SMALLDATETIME types in a table like this:

```
CREATE TABLE DateTable    (birthdate      SMALLDATETIME,
                           school_date    SMALLDATETIME,
                           names          VARCHAR(20))
```

Data can now be entered into the birthdate and school_date columns, which are both SMALLDATETIME columns, and into the names column. Inserting dates is usually done by using an implicit conversion of character strings to dates. Following would be an example of an INSERT into DateTable:

```
INSERT INTO DateTable
VALUES ('10-oct-01', '12/01/2006', 'Mala Sinha')
```

You will get:

```
(1 row(s) affected)
```

Note that single quotes are required around date values. As SMALLDATETIME is not really a character column, the character strings representing date are implicitly converted provided that the character string is in a form recognizable by SQL Server.

Now if you type:

```
SELECT *
FROM   DateTable
```

The following appears in the DateTable table:

```
birthdate             school_date            names
--------------------  ---------------------  --------------------

2001-10-10 00:00:00   2006-12-01 00:00:00    Mala Sinha

(1 row(s) affected)
```

The DateTable table has not been created for you. Create it and insert the following data into it:

```
birthdate             school_date            names
--------------------  ---------------------  ------------------

2001-10-10 00:00:00   2006-12-01 00:00:00    Mala Sinha
2002-02-02 00:00:00   2006-03-02 00:00:00    Mary Spencer
2002-10-02 00:00:00   2005-02-04 00:00:00    Bill Cox
1998-12-29 00:00:00   2004-05-05 00:00:00    Jamie Runner
1999-06-16 00:00:00   2003-03-03 00:00:00    Seema Kapoor

(5 row(s) affected)
```

Default Date Formats and Changing Date Formats

By default, SQL Server 2005 reads and displays the dates in the *yyyy/mm/dd* format. We can change the format in which SQL Server *reads* in dates by using SET DATEFORMAT. DATEFORMAT controls only how SQL Server 2005 interprets date constants that are entered by you, but does not control how date values are displayed. For example, to have SQL Server 2005 first read the day, then month, and then year, we would type:

```
SET DATEFORMAT dmy
SELECT 'Format is yyyy/mon/dd' = CONVERT(datetime, '10/2/2003')
```

And we will get:

```
Format is yyyy/mon/dd
----------------------
2003-02-10 00:00:00.000

(1 row(s) affected)
```

In SQL Server 2005, if incorrect dates are used, we will get an out-of-range error. For example, if we tried to do the following insert with the 32nd day of a month:

```
INSERT INTO DateTable
VALUES ('10-oct-01', '32/01/2006', 'Mita Sinha')
```

We would get the following error message:

```
Msg 296, Level 16, State 3, Line 1
The conversion of char data type to smalldatetime data type resulted in an out-of-
range smalldatetime value.
The statement has been terminated.
```

In SQL Server 2005, if two-digit year dates are entered, SQL Server 2005's default behavior is to interpret the year as 19*yy* if the value is greater than or equal to 50 and as 20*yy* if the value is less than 50.

Date Functions

In this section we discuss some useful SQL Server 2005 date functions—DATEADD, DATEDIFF, DATEPART, YEAR, MONTH, DAY, and GETDATE.

The DATEADD function

The DATEADD function produces a date by adding a specified number to a specified part of a date.

 The date parts are: dd for day, mm for month, and yy for year.

The format for the DATEADD function is:

```
DATEADD(datepart, number, date_field)
```

datepart would be either dd, mm, or yy. *number* would be the number that you want to add to the *datepart*. *date_field* would be the date field that you want to add to.

For example, to add 2 days to the birthdate of every person in DateTable we would type:

```
SELECT names, 'Add 2 days to birthday' = DATEADD(dd, 2, birthdate)
FROM    Datetable
```

This query would give:

```
names                Add 2 days to birthday
-------------------- ----------------------
Mala Sinha           2001-10-12 00:00:00
Mary Spencer         2002-02-04 00:00:00
Bill Cox             2002-10-04 00:00:00
Jamie Runner         1998-12-31 00:00:00
Seema Kapoor         1999-06-18 00:00:00

(5 row(s) affected)
```

You can also subtract two days from the birthdate of every person in DateTable by adding a –2 (minus or negative 2) instead of a positive 2, as shown by the following query:

```
SELECT names, 'Add 2 days to birthday' = DATEADD(dd, -2, birthdate)
FROM    Datetable
```

This query would give:

```
names                Add 2 days to birthday
-------------------- ----------------------
Mala Sinha           2001-10-08 00:00:00
Mary Spencer         2002-01-31 00:00:00
Bill Cox             2002-09-30 00:00:00
Jamie Runner         1998-12-27 00:00:00
Seema Kapoor         1999-06-14 00:00:00

(5 row(s) affected)
```

The DATEDIFF function

The DATEDIFF function returns the difference between two parts of a date. The format for the DATEDIFF function is:

```
DATEDIFF(datepart, date_field1, date_field2)
```

Here again, *datepart* would be either dd, mm, or yy. And, *date_field1* and *date_field2* would be the two date fields that you want to find the difference between.

For example, to find the number of months between the two fields, birthdate and school_date of every person in DateTable, we would type:

```
SELECT names, 'Months between birth date and school date' = DATEDIFF(mm, birthdate,
school_date)
FROM Datetable
```

This query would give:

```
names                 Months between birth date and school date
--------------------  -----------------------------------------
Mala Sinha            62
Mary Spencer          49
Bill Cox              28
Jamie Runner          65
Seema Kapoor          45

(5 row(s) affected)
```

The DATEPART function

The DATEPART function returns the specified part of the date requested. The format for the DATEPART function is:

```
DATEPART(datepart, date_field)
```

Here too, *datepart* would be either dd, mm, or yy. And, *date_field* would be the date field that you want to request the dd, mm, or yy from.

For example, to find year from the birthdate of every person in DateTable we would type:

```
SELECT names, 'YEARS' = DATEPART(yy, birthdate)
FROM    Datetable
```

This query would give:

```
names                 YEARS
--------------------  -----------
Mala Sinha            2001
Mary Spencer          2002
Bill Cox              2002
Jamie Runner          1998
Seema Kapoor          1999

(5 row(s) affected)
```

The YEAR function

The YEAR(column) function will extract the year from a value stored as a SMALLDATETIME data type. For example, to extract the year from the school_date column of every person in DateTable, type:

```
SELECT names, YEAR(school_date) AS [Kindergarten Year]
FROM    Datetable
```

This query produces the following output:

```
names                 Kindergarten Year
--------------------  -----------------
Mala Sinha            2006
Mary Spencer          2006
Bill Cox              2005
```

```
Jamie Runner          2004
Seema Kapoor          2003

(5 row(s) affected)
```

We can also use the YEAR function in date calculations. For example, if you want to find the number of years between when a child was born (birthdate) and when the child went to kindergarten (the school_date column) from DateTable, type the following query:

```
SELECT names, YEAR(school_date)-YEAR(birthdate) AS [Age in Kindergarten]
FROM   DateTable
```

This query produces the following output:

```
names                 Age in Kindergarten
--------------------  --------------------
Mala Sinha            5
Mary Spencer          4
Bill Cox              3
Jamie Runner          6
Seema Kapoor          4

(5 row(s) affected)
```

Here, the YEAR(birthdate) was subtracted from YEAR(school_date).

The MONTH function

The MONTH function will extract the month from a date. Then, to add six months to the birth month of every person in DateTable, we can first extract the month by MONTH(birthdate), and then add six to it, as shown here:

```
SELECT names, birthdate, MONTH(birthdate) AS [Birth Month], ((MONTH(birthdate)) + 6 )
AS      [Sixth month]
FROM    DateTable
```

This query produces the following output:

```
names              birthdate               Birth Month Sixth month
-----------------  ----------------------  ----------- -----------
Mala Sinha         2001-10-10 00:00:00     10          16
Mary Spencer       2002-02-02 00:00:00     2           8
Bill Cox           2002-10-02 00:00:00     10          16
Jamie Runner       1998-12-29 00:00:00     12          18
Seema Kapoor       1999-06-16 00:00:00     6           12

(5 row(s) affected)
```

The DAY function

The DAY function extracts the day of the month from a date. For example, to find the day from the birthdate of every person in DateTable, type the following query:

```
SELECT names, birthdate, DAY([birthdate]) AS [Date]
FROM    DateTable
```

which produces the following output:

```
names                birthdate               Date
-------------------- ----------------------- -----------
Mala Sinha           2001-10-10 00:00:00     10
Mary Spencer         2002-02-02 00:00:00     2
Bill Cox             2002-10-02 00:00:00     2
Jamie Runner         1998-12-29 00:00:00     29
Seema Kapoor         1999-06-16 00:00:00     16

(5 row(s) affected)
```

The GETDATE function

The GETDATE function returns the current system date and time.

For example:

```
SELECT 'Today ' = GETDATE()
```

will give:

```
Today
-----------------------
2006-01-17 23:17:52.340

(1 row(s) affected)
```

To find the number of years since everyone's birthdate entered in our Datetable, and the current date, we could type:

```
SELECT names, 'Number of years ' = DATEDIFF(yy, birthdate, GETDATE())
FROM    Datetable
```

This query will give us:

```
names                Number of years
-------------------- ----------------
Mala Sinha           5
Mary Spencer         4
Bill Cox             4
Jamie Runner         8
Seema Kapoor         7

(5 row(s) affected)
```

Inserting the current date and time

Using the GETDATE() function, we can insert or update the current date and time into a column. To illustrate this, we will add a new record (row) to our DateTable, inserting the current date and time into the birthdate column of this row using the GETDATE() function, and then add five years to the current date for the school_date column of this new row. So type:

```
INSERT INTO DateTable
VALUES (GETDATE(), GETDATE()+YEAR(5), 'Piyali Saha')
```

Then type:

```
SELECT *
FROM   DateTable
```

This query produces the following output (note the insertion of the sixth row):

```
birthdate                school_date              names
--------------------     --------------------     ------------------
2001-10-10 00:00:00      2006-12-01 00:00:00      Mala Sinha
2002-02-02 00:00:00      2006-03-02 00:00:00      Mary Spencer
2002-10-02 00:00:00      2005-02-04 00:00:00      Bill Cox
1998-12-29 00:00:00      2004-05-05 00:00:00      Jamie Runner
1999-06-16 00:00:00      2003-03-03 00:00:00      Seema Kapoor
2006-01-17 23:19:00      2011-04-01 23:19:00      Piyali Saha

(6 row(s) affected)
```

Summary

This chapter provided an overview of the functions available in SQL Server 2005. In this chapter, we looked at several of SQL Server 2005's aggregate, row-level and other functions. We also presented conversion as well as date functions.

Table of Functions

Aggregate Functions	
AVG	Averages a group of row values.
COUNT	Counts the total number of rows in a result set.
MAX	Returns the highest of all values from a column.
MIN	Returns the lowest of all values from a column.
SUM	Adds all the values in a column.
Row-level Functions	
ABS	Returns an absolute value.
CEILING	Returns the next larger integer value.
FLOOR	Returns the next lower integer value.
ISNULL	Returns a true value if a data item contains a NULL.
NULLIF	Returns a NULL if a certain condition is met in an expression.
ROUND	Rounds numbers to a specified number of decimal places.
STR	Converts from a number to a character data type.
SQRT	Returns the square root of positive numeric values.
SQUARE	Returns the square of a number.

String Functions	
CHARINDEX	Returns the starting position of a specified pattern.
LEFT	Returns the left portion of a string up to a given number of characters.
LEN	Returns the length of a string.
LIKE	Option that matches a particular pattern.
LOWER	Converts a string to lower case.
RIGHT	Returns the right portion of a string.
RTRIM	Removes blanks from the right end of a string.
SUBSTRING	Returns part of a string.
UPPER	Displays all output in upper case.
Date Functions	
DATEADD	Adds to a specified part of a date.
DATEDIFF	Returns the difference between two dates.
DATEPART	Returns the specified part of the date requested.
DAY	Extracts a day from a date.
GETDATE	Returns the current system date and time.
MONTH	Extracts the month from a date.
SET DATEFORMAT	Changes the format in which SQL Server reads in dates.
YEAR	Extracts the year from a date.
Conversion Functions	
CAST	Changes a data type of a column in a result set.
CONVERT	Explicitly converts to a given data type in a result set.
Other Functions	
DISTINCT	Omits rows that contain duplicate data.
PERCENT	Return a certain percentage of records that fall at the top of a range specified.
TOP	Returns a specified number of records from the top of a result set.

Review Questions

1. What are functions?
2. What are aggregate functions? Give examples of aggregate functions. What is another term for an aggregate function?
3. What are row-level functions? Give examples of row-level functions.

4. Is COUNT an aggregate function or a row-level function? Explain why. Give at least one example of when the COUNT function may come in handy. Does the COUNT function take nulls into account?

5. Is AVG an aggregate function or a row-level function?

6. What is the NULLIF function? Explain.

7. How are ties handled in SQL Server?

8. How does the DISTINCT function work?

9. Are string functions (for example, SUBSTRING, RIGHT, LTRIM) aggregate functions or row-level functions?

10. What is the SUBSTRING function used for?

11. What is the CHARINDEX function used for?

12. What function would you use to find the leftmost characters in a string?

13. What are the LTRIM/RTRIM functions used for?

14. What function would produce the output in all lowercase?

15. What function would you use to find the length of a string?

16. What characters or symbols are most commonly used as wildcard characters in SQL Server 2005?

17. What is the concatenation operator in Server SQL 2005?

18. What does the YEAR function do?

19. What does the MONTH function do?

20. What does the GETDATE function do?

21. What will the following query produce in SQL Server 2005?
```
SELECT ('.....'+ names) AS [names]
FROM Employee
```

22. Does Server SQL allow an expression like COUNT(DISTINCT column_name)?

23. How is the ISNULL function different from the NULLIF function?

24. What function would you use to round a value to three decimal places?

25. Which functions can the WITH TIES option be used with?

26. What clause does the WITH TIES option require?

27. What is the default date format in SQL Server 2005?

28. How do dates have to be entered in Server SQL 2005?

29. What function is used to convert between data types?

30. What function is useful for formatting numbers?

31. What function is useful for formatting dates?

Exercises

Unless specified otherwise, use the Student_course database to answer the following questions. Also, use appropriate column headings when displaying your output.

1. Display the COUNT of tuples (rows) in each of the tables Grade_report, Student, and Section. How many rows would you expect in the Cartesian product of all three tables? Display the COUNT (*not* the resulting rows) of the Cartesian product of all three and verify your result (use SELECT COUNT(*) ...).

2. Display the COUNT of section-ids from the Section table. Display the COUNT of DISTINCT section-ids from the Grade_report table. What does this information tell you? (Hint: section_id is the primary key of the Section table.)

3. Write, execute, and print a query to list student names and grades (just two attributes) using the table alias feature. Restrict the list to students that have either As or Bs in courses with ACCT prefixes only.

   Here's how to complete this problem:

   a. Get the statement to work as a COUNT of a join of the three tables, Student, Grade_report, Section. Use table aliases in the join condition. Note that a join of *n* tables requires (*n* − 1) join conditions, so here you have to have two join conditions: one to join the Student and Grade_report tables, and one to join the Grade_report and Section tables. Note the number of rows that you get (expect no more rows than is in the Grade_report table). Why do you get this result?

   b. Modify the query and put the Accounting condition in the WHERE clause. Note the number of rows in the result—it should be a good bit less than in question 3a.

   c. Again, modify the query and add the grade constraints. The number of rows should decrease again. Note that if you have WHERE x *and* y *or* z, parentheses are optional, but then the criteria will be interpreted according to precedence rules.

   The reason that we want you to "start small" and add conditions is that it gives you a check on what you ought to get and it allows you to output less nonsense. Your minimal starting point should be a count of the join with appropriate join conditions.

4. Using the Student table, answer the following questions:

   a. How many students have names like Smith?

   b. How many have names that contain the letter sequence Smith?

   c. How many student names end in LD?

   d. How many student names start with S?

   e. How many student names do not have "i" as the second letter?

f. Would `SELECT * FROM Student WHERE sname LIKE 'Smith%'` find someone whose name is:

    i. LA SMITH

    ii. SMITH-JONES

    iii. SMITH JR.

    iv. SMITH, JR

5. Using the `Course` table, answer the following questions:

    a. List the junior-level COSC courses (LIKE COSC3xxx) and the name of the courses.

    b. List all the courses except the junior-level COSC courses (use `NOT LIKE`).

6. Using the `COUNT` feature, determine whether there are duplicate names or student numbers in the `Student` table.

7. Assume that all math courses start with `MATH`. How many math courses are there in the `Section` table? From the count of courses, does it appear that there any math courses in the `Section` table that are not in the Course table? Again, using `COUNT`s, are there any math courses in the `Course` table that are not in the `Section` table? Does it appear that there are any courses at all that are in the `Grade_report`, `Section`, or `Course` tables that are not in the others? (We will study how to ask these questions in SQL in a later chapter.) Note that a query like the following would not work:

```
SELECT g.section_id
FROM Grade_report g, Section t
WHERE g.section_id <> t.section_id
```

Explain why `WHERE .. <> ..` will not work to produce the desired output.

8. For every table in the `Student_course` database, we would like to compile the following information: attributes, number of rows, number of distinct rows, and rows without nulls. Find this information using different queries and compile the information in a table as shown here:

Table	Attribute	Rows	Distinct Rows	Rows without Nulls
Student	Stno	48	48	48
	Sname	48	47	48
	Major	48	8	
	Class	etc.	etc.	etc.
Section	Section_id	etc.	etc.	etc.

The other tables in the `Student_course` database are `Grade_report`, `Dependent`, `Section`, `Room`, `Course`, `Prereq`, and `Department_to_major`.

Hint: You can use the following query:

```
SELECT COUNT(*)
FROM Student
WHERE sname IS NULL
```

9. Find the count, sum, average, minimum, and maximum capacity of rooms in the database. Format the output using the STR function.

   a. Where there is a null value for the capacity, assume the capacity to be 40, and find the average room size again.

10. Using the Student table, display the first 10 rows with an appended initial. For the appended initial, choose the halfway letter of the name, so that if a name is Evans, the initial is A (half of the length +1). If the name is Conway, the initial is W (again, (half of the length +1)). You do not need to round up or down, just use (LEN(Name)/2)+1 as the starting place to create the initial. Use appropriate column aliases. Your result should look like this (actual names may vary depending on the current database):

```
PERSON#    NAMES
--------   ------------------------
1          Lineas, E.
2          Mary, R.
3          Brenda, N.
4          Richard, H.
5          Kelly, L.
6          Lujack, A.
7          Reva, V.
8          Elainie, I.
9          Harley, L.
10         Donald, A.
```

   a. Display the preceding output in all capital letters.

11. Find the names of the bottom 50 percent of the students, ordered by grade.

   a. Find the names of the top 25 percent of the seniors, ordered by grade.

   b. Now use the WITH TIES option with part (b). Is there any difference in the output?

12. Count the number of courses taught by each instructor.

   a. Count the number of distinct courses taught by each instructor.

13. Count the number of classes each student is taking.

14. Display all the names that are less than five characters long from the Student table.

15. List all the students with student numbers in the 140s range.

16. Find all the students (the student names should be listed only once) who received As and Bs.

17. Would you call TOP an aggregate function? Why or why not?

18. Add an asterisk (*) to the names of all juniors and seniors who received at least one A. (This question will take a few steps, and you will have to approach this problem in a step-by-step manner.)

19. In this chapter, we used a table called `Employee`. Add a `birthdate` column and an `employment_date` column to the `Employee` table. Insert values into both the columns.

   a. Display the current ages of all the employees.

   b. Find the youngest employee.

   c. Find the oldest employee.

   d. Find the youngest employee at the time of employment.

   e. Find the oldest employee at the time of employment.

   f. Add five years to the current ages of all employees. Will any of the employees be over 65 in five years?

   g. List the birth months and names of all employees.

CHAPTER 6

Query Development and Derived Structures

A problem in SQL—and in all programming, for that matter—is the development of long queries or statements. One way to create long queries is to begin modestly and to incrementally build or develop the query of interest. This is the approach described in this chapter, which we will illustrate by developing a few queries. And, as you'll find out, often the appropriate placement of parentheses within the query is required to get the right answer to a question.

Another way to develop queries is to use derived structures—a pseudo-table, of sorts. In Server SQL 2005, derived structures include such things as views (both real and inline views) and temporary tables (both temporary and global), both of which enable us to easily manipulate partial displays of tables. The partial displays can then be connected to answer a complicated database query. This chapter discusses derived structures, focusing specifically on views and temporary tables, and how query development can be aided with the use of derived structures.

Query Development

Queries are sometimes developed after some initial experimentation, yet other times they are the result of modifying previously stored queries. The best way to understand how the query building process works is to look at an example. Suppose we want to find the names of all students in the Student_course database who major in computer science (COSC) and have earned a grade of B in some course. To do so, we can follow these steps:

1. Type the following query to find students who major in computer science:

   ```
   SELECT *
   FROM    Student
   WHERE   major = 'COSC'
   ```

   This query produces the following 10 rows of output:

   ```
   STNO   SNAME                 MAJOR CLASS  BDATE
   ------ --------------------  ----- ------ ----------------------
   ```

3	Mary	COSC	4	1978-07-16 00:00:00
5	Zelda	COSC	NULL	1978-02-12 00:00:00
8	Brenda	COSC	2	1977-08-13 00:00:00
14	Lujack	COSC	1	1977-02-12 00:00:00
17	Elainie	COSC	1	1976-08-12 00:00:00
31	Jake	COSC	4	1978-02-12 00:00:00
121	Hillary	COSC	1	1977-07-16 00:00:00
128	Brad	COSC	1	1977-09-10 00:00:00
130	Alan	COSC	2	1977-07-16 00:00:00
142	Jerry	COSC	4	1978-03-12 00:00:00

```
(10 row(s) affected)
```

2. To find the student rows in the preceding output who have earned a B in a course, we first need to add the Grade_report table, shown in Figure 6-1, with a join (to get the grades of those students who are computer science majors).

Figure 6-1. Table definition of the Grade_report table

The join query now looks like (note the choice of columns in the SELECT statement, so that we can see the student names, majors, sections and grades):

```
SELECT    stu.sname, stu.major, g.section_id, g.grade
FROM      Student stu, Grade_report g
WHERE     stu.major = 'COSC'
  AND         stu.stno = g.student_number
```

This query produces 48 rows of output (of which we show the first 20 rows):

```
sname                 major section_id grade
--------------------  ----- ---------- -----
Mary                  COSC  85         A
Mary                  COSC  87         B
Mary                  COSC  90         B
Mary                  COSC  91         B
Mary                  COSC  92         B
Mary                  COSC  96         B
Mary                  COSC  101        NULL
Mary                  COSC  133        NULL
Mary                  COSC  134        NULL
Mary                  COSC  135        NULL
Zelda                 COSC  90         C
Zelda                 COSC  94         C
Zelda                 COSC  95         B
Brenda                COSC  85         A
Brenda                COSC  92         A
Brenda                COSC  94         C
Brenda                COSC  95         B
Brenda                COSC  96         C
```

```
Brenda              COSC  102      B
Brenda              COSC  133      NULL
.
.
.
(48 row(s) affected)
```

3. To add the condition for Bs, we need to add another AND clause in the WHERE condition, by adding a fifth line to the query:

```
SELECT  stu.sname, major, section_id, grade
FROM    Student stu, Grade_report g
WHERE   stu.major = 'COSC'
  AND       stu.stno = g.student_number
  AND       g.grade = 'B'
```

This query produces the following 14 rows of output:

```
sname                major section_id grade
-------------------- ----- ---------- -----
Mary                 COSC  87         B
Mary                 COSC  90         B
Mary                 COSC  91         B
Mary                 COSC  92         B
Mary                 COSC  96         B
Zelda                COSC  95         B
Brenda               COSC  95         B
Brenda               COSC  102        B
Lujack               COSC  102        B
Lujack               COSC  145        B
Lujack               COSC  158        B
Hillary              COSC  90         B
Hillary              COSC  94         B
Hillary              COSC  95         B

(14 row(s) affected)
```

4. To get only the student names from the preceding output, we reduce the result set by typing:

```
SELECT  stu.sname
FROM    Student stu, Grade_report g
WHERE   stu.major = 'COSC'
  AND       stu.stno = g.student_number
  AND       g.grade = 'B'
```

This query produces the following output, a list of all the students who are majoring in COSC and received a grade of B:

```
sname
--------------------
Mary
Mary
Mary
Mary
Mary
Zelda
Brenda
```

```
Brenda
Lujack
Lujack
Lujack
Hillary
Hillary
Hillary
```

```
(14 row(s) affected)
```

The point of this process is that it allows us to test as we go, verify that the query works up to that point, and ensure that we have a reasonable result before we move to the next enhancement.

5. To get the answer in a more reasonable "easy-to-read" orderly manner, a final presentation using DISTINCT (to find the distinct names) and ORDER BY (to order by names) could be added to the query, as follows:

```
SELECT   DISTINCT(stu.sname)
FROM     Student stu, Grade_report g
WHERE    stu.major = 'COSC'
   AND       stu.stno = g.student_number
   AND       g.grade = 'B'
   ORDER BY stu.sname
```

which would give:

```
sname
--------------------
Brenda
Hillary
Lujack
Mary
Zelda
```

```
(5 row(s) affected)
```

But note that the DISTINCT and ORDER BY do not have to be used together. When the DISTINCT is used, the ORDER BY is not necessary. DISTINCT automatically orders the result set. So writing the previous query without the ORDER BY clause would give you the same output. Try it.

Parentheses in SQL Expressions

As queries get longer, they can become very ambiguous to humans without the appropriate use of parentheses. In programming languages like C, you can write a statement like this:

```
x = y + z * w
```

How is this statement computed? The answer depends on precedence rules. Usually in programming languages (and in SQL), clauses in parentheses have the highest precedence. The authors of this book advocate *fully* parenthesized expressions for three reasons:

- It makes the expression easier to debug.
- It tells anyone else who looks at your expression that it is written as you intended, because you explicitly and unambiguously wrote the expression in a fully parenthesized way.
- There is no guarantee that another SQL language will behave like the one you learned.

In SQL, the precedence problem occurs when AND and OR are used in the same query. For example, what does the following query request? Does AND or OR have precedence or is the rule "left to right"?

```
SELECT  *
FROM    Student
WHERE   class = 3 OR class = 4 AND stno < 100
```

This query produces the following 12 rows of output:

STNO	SNAME	MAJOR	CLASS	BDATE
3	Mary	COSC	4	1978-07-16 00:00:00
13	Kelly	MATH	4	1980-08-12 00:00:00
20	Donald	ACCT	4	1977-10-15 00:00:00
24	Chris	ACCT	4	1978-02-12 00:00:00
31	Jake	COSC	4	1978-02-12 00:00:00
49	Susan	ENGL	3	1980-03-11 00:00:00
62	Monica	MATH	3	1980-10-14 00:00:00
122	Phoebe	ENGL	3	1980-04-15 00:00:00
131	Rachel	ENGL	3	1980-04-15 00:00:00
143	Cramer	ENGL	3	1980-04-15 00:00:00
151	Losmith	CHEM	3	1981-01-15 00:00:00
160	Gus	ART	3	1978-10-15 00:00:00

```
(12 row(s) affected)
```

The point is that you do not have to know the precedence rules to write an unambiguous expression. If you use parentheses appropriately, you make the expression clear and unambiguous. Consider the following examples. If we type the following:

```
SELECT  *
FROM    Student
WHERE   class = 3 OR (class = 4 AND stno < 100)
```

we get the following 12 rows of output:

STNO	SNAME	MAJOR	CLASS	BDATE
3	Mary	COSC	4	1978-07-16 00:00:00
13	Kelly	MATH	4	1980-08-12 00:00:00
20	Donald	ACCT	4	1977-10-15 00:00:00
24	Chris	ACCT	4	1978-02-12 00:00:00
31	Jake	COSC	4	1978-02-12 00:00:00
49	Susan	ENGL	3	1980-03-11 00:00:00

```
62     Monica           MATH  3     1980-10-14 00:00:00
122    Phoebe           ENGL  3     1980-04-15 00:00:00
131    Rachel           ENGL  3     1980-04-15 00:00:00
143    Cramer           ENGL  3     1980-04-15 00:00:00
151    Losmith          CHEM  3     1981-01-15 00:00:00
160    Gus              ART   3     1978-10-15 00:00:00

(12 row(s) affected)
```

The preceding query has the parentheses around the AND clause, the result of which is that the AND is performed first. The following query has the parentheses around the OR clause, meaning that the OR is performed first:

```
SELECT  *
FROM    Student
WHERE   (class = 3 OR class = 4) AND stno < 100
```

This query results in the following seven rows of output:

```
STNO   SNAME                MAJOR CLASS  BDATE
------ -------------------- ----- ------ -----------------------
3      Mary                 COSC  4      1978-07-16 00:00:00
13     Kelly                MATH  4      1980-08-12 00:00:00
20     Donald               ACCT  4      1977-10-15 00:00:00
24     Chris                ACCT  4      1978-02-12 00:00:00
31     Jake                 COSC  4      1978-02-12 00:00:00
49     Susan                ENGL  3      1980-03-11 00:00:00
62     Monica               MATH  3      1980-10-14 00:00:00

(7 row(s) affected)
```

As the preceding two query statements demonstrate, appropriate placement of parentheses eliminates any ambiguity in queries that contain both AND and OR.

Operator Precedence

In SQL Server 2005, when complex expressions use multiple operators, precedence rules determine the sequence in which the operations are performed. The order of execution can significantly affect the resulting value (as you saw in the example in the preceding section). Although we can usually control precedence with parentheses, it is important to learn, or have at least a reference, to the order of precedence.

Operators have the following precedence (the following list is shown from the highest level of precedence to the lowest level of precedence):

```
* (multiply), / (divide), % (modulo)
+ (add), + (concatenate), - (subtract)
=, >, <, >=, <=, != (not equal to), !>, !<
NOT
AND
BETWEEN, IN, LIKE, OR
= (assignment)
```

Data Type Precedence

When an operator combines two expressions of different data types, the data type precedence rules specify which data type is converted to the other. The data type with the lower precedence is converted to the data type with the higher precedence. Here we list the precedence order for SQL Server 2005 data types (again shown from the highest level of precedence to the lowest level of precedence):

- SQL_VARIANT
- DATETIME
- SMALLDATETIME
- FLOAT
- REAL
- DECIMAL
- MONEY
- SMALLMONEY
- BIGINT
- INT
- SMALLINT
- TINYINT
- BIT
- NTEXT
- TEXT
- IMAGE
- UNIQUEIDENTIFIER
- NVARCHAR
- NCHAR
- VARCHAR
- CHAR
- BINARY

This order means that if a number of an INT data type is multiplied to a number that is of a FLOAT data type, the result would be a FLOAT data type. To illustrate something like this, we will use the Employee table that we created in the last chapter. The design of the Employee table is shown in Figure 6-2.

Note that the data type of the hours column is SMALLINT. If we multiply this column (hours) by 0.75 (a FLOAT), we get a FLOAT data type in the result set, as shown here:

```
SELECT  names, hours, 'Hours * .75' = hours *  .75
FROM    Employee
```

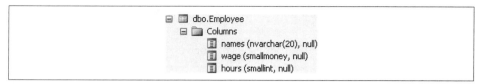

Figure 6-2. Table definition of the Employee table

This query gives us:

```
names                hours  Hours * .75
-------------------- ------ ---------------------------------------
Sumon Bagui          40     30.00
Sudip Bagui          30     22.50
Priyashi Saha        NULL   NULL
Ed Evans             10     7.50
Genny George         40     30.00

(5 row(s) affected)
```

Derived Structures

Derived structures may become necessary as the queries we build get larger and we have to use a more step-by-step approach to find a result. Derived structures help us to build queries on top of other queries. In this section, we discuss two of the most commonly used derived structures—views and temporary tables.

Views

In SQL, a *view* (also called a *virtual table*) is a mechanism to procure a restricted subset of data that is accessible in ways akin to ordinary tables. We use the word "akin" because some operations on views (such as some updates and deletes) may be restricted which otherwise would be allowed if performed on the underlying structure itself.

A view serves several purposes:

- It helps to develop a query step by step.
- It can be used to restrict a set of users from seeing part of the database in a multiuser system—this can be considered a security feature.
- Views provide a layer of abstraction to data, facilitating backward compatibility and horizontal and vertical partitioning of data.
- Views provide a seamless way to combine data from multiple sources.
- Views do not occupy much disk space, as they have no data of their own.

- When you use a view for queries, you use it just as you would use the underlying table(s).
- Views can be used to create other views or queries.

 Views are typically a way of building queries on top of other queries.

Creating views

A view can be regarded as a named SELECT statement that produces a result set (a view) that you can further work on. The SELECT statement that is used to create a view can be from one or more underlying tables or from other views in the current or other databases.

The general SQL syntax used to create a view is:

```
CREATE VIEW view_name AS
SELECT ...
```

The following example creates a view called namemaj, which is a view of students' names and majors from the Student table. To create the view namemaj, type the following in the SQL query editor screen:

```
CREATE VIEW namemaj AS
SELECT      sname, major
FROM        Student
```

And then execute this query in the regular way. A view will be created.

You will get the following message:

```
Command(s) completed successfully.
```

To view namemaj, click on Views in the Object Explorer, and then click dbo.namemaj and then Columns, as shown in Figure 6-3.

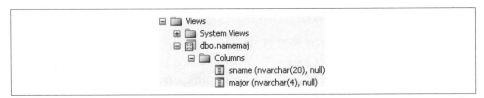

Figure 6-3. Viewing the view namemaj

A view is a stored SELECT statement. Each time a view is accessed, the SELECT statement in the view is run.

Using views

The new view can be used just like a table in the FROM clause of any SELECT statement, as shown here:

```
SELECT   *
FROM     namemaj
```

This query will give 48 rows of output, of which we show the first 10 rows:

sname major

```
-------------------- -----
Lineas               ENGL
Mary                 COSC
Zelda                COSC
Ken                  POLY
Mario                MATH
Brenda               COSC
Romona               ENGL
Richard              ENGL
Kelly                MATH
Lujack               COSC
.
.
.

(48 row(s) affected
```

Just like an ordinary table, a view can be filtered and used in a SELECT. For example, type the following query:

```
SELECT   n.major AS [Major], n.sname AS [Student Name]
FROM     namemaj AS n, Department_to_major AS d
WHERE    n.major = d.dcode
AND      d.dname LIKE 'COMP%'
```

which produces the following output:

```
Major Student Name
----- --------------------
COSC  Mary
COSC  Zelda
COSC  Brenda
COSC  Lujack
COSC  Elainie
COSC  Jake
COSC  Hillary
COSC  Brad
COSC  Alan
COSC  Jerry

(10 row(s) affected)
```

ORDER BY in views

SQL Server 2005 does not allow you to use an `ORDER BY` when creating views. For example, if we try to create an ordered view called `namemaj1`, as follows:

```
CREATE VIEW namemaj1 AS
SELECT      sname, major
FROM        Student
ORDER BY    sname
```

we will get the following error message:

```
Msg 1033, Level 15, State 1, Procedure namemaj1, Line 4
The ORDER BY clause is invalid in views, inline functions, derived tables,
subqueries, and common table expressions, unless TOP or FOR XML is also specified.
```

 Some SQL languages, such as Oracle, allow the use of `ORDER BY` when creating views.

But an `ORDER BY` can be used in the `FROM` clause after the view has been created, as shown:

```
SELECT    *
FROM      namemaj
ORDER BY major
```

This query produces 48 rows, of which we show the first 10 rows here:

```
sname                   major
--------------------- -----
Smith                   NULL
Thornton                NULL
Lionel                  NULL
Sebastian               ACCT
Harrison                ACCT
Francis                 ACCT
Donald                  ACCT
Chris                   ACCT
Gus                     ART
Benny                   CHEM
.
.
.
(48 row(s) affected)
```

SELECT INTO in views

You cannot use a `SELECT INTO` statement when creating a view, because it is a combined data definition language (DDL) and data manipulation language (DML) statement, as shown here:

```
CREATE VIEW new_view AS
SELECT      * INTO new_view
FROM        Employee
```

You will get the following error message:

```
Msg 156, Level 15, State 1, Procedure new_view, Line 2
Incorrect syntax near the keyword 'INTO'.
```

You can, however, issue a SELECT INTO statement when the view is used in the FROM clause, as shown:

```
CREATE VIEW new_view AS
SELECT      *
FROM        namemaj
WHERE       major = 'MATH'
```

You will get:

```
Command(s) completed successfully.
```

And now if you type:

```
SELECT * INTO copy_of_new_view
FROM    new_view
```

You will get:

```
(7 row(s) affected)
```

Now if you type:

```
SELECT *
FROM    copy_of_new_view
```

You will get the following 7 rows:

```
sname                 major
--------------------- -----
Mario                 MATH
Kelly                 MATH
Reva                  MATH
Monica                MATH
Sadie                 MATH
Stephanie             MATH
Jake                  MATH

(7 row(s) affected)
```

Column aliases in views

Column aliases can be used instead of column names in views. For example, type the following to create a view called namemaj2 with column aliases:

```
CREATE VIEW namemaj2 AS
SELECT      sname AS [name], major AS [maj]
FROM        Student
WHERE       major = 'COSC'
```

You will get:

```
Command(s) completed successfully.
```

Then type:

```
SELECT *
FROM   namemaj2
```

This query produces the following 10 rows of output, with the column aliases in the column headings:

```
name                 maj
-------------------- ----
Mary                 COSC
Zelda                COSC
Brenda               COSC
Lujack               COSC
Elainie              COSC
Jake                 COSC
Hillary              COSC
Brad                 COSC
Alan                 COSC
Jerry                COSC

(10 row(s) affected)
```

To use the column aliases in a query, the name of the view or table alias (in this case, a view alias) has to precede the column alias, as shown in this query:

```
SELECT  namemaj2.[name], namemaj2.[maj]
FROM    namemaj2
WHERE   namemaj2.[name] LIKE 'J%'
```

This query produces the following output:

```
name                 maj
-------------------- ----
Jake                 COSC
Jerry                COSC

(2 row(s) affected)
```

The same query could also be written as follows, where n is the table (view) alias:

```
SELECT  n.[name], n.[maj]
FROM    namemaj2 AS n
WHERE   n.[name] LIKE 'J%'
```

Data in views

A view consists of a set of named columns and rows of data, just like a real table; however, a view has no data of its own. Data is stored only in the underlying table used to create the view, and not in the view. The view stores only the SELECT statement (rather than the actual data), and data is dynamically produced from the underlying table when the view is used. Therefore, views depend on the underlying tables and act like a filter on the underlying tables.

When data in the original table is changed, the view is automatically updated. Therefore, the view is always up to date. And, when data is changed through a view, the original (underlying) table is also automatically updated.

Changing data in views. To demonstrate how changing data through a view automatically updates the original table, begin with the following Employee table, which we created and used in Chapter 5:

```
names            wage          hours
---------------  ------------  ----------
Sumon Bagui      10.0000       40
Sudip Bagui      15.0000       30
Priyashi Saha    18.0000       NULL
Ed Evans         NULL          10
Genny George     20.0000       40

(5 row(s) affected)
```

1. Create a view called Employee_view from the Employee table, as follows:

```
CREATE VIEW Employee_view AS
SELECT      names
FROM        Employee
```

2. To output the entire contents of the view, type the following query:

```
SELECT *
FROM   Employee_view
```

which produces the following output:

```
names
--------------------
Sumon Bagui
Sudip Bagui
Priyashi Saha
Ed Evans
Genny George

(5 row(s) affected)
```

3. To update the data in the view, Employee_view, type the following UPDATE query:

```
UPDATE Employee_view
SET    names = 'Mala Saha'
WHERE  names LIKE 'Priya%'
```

You will get:

```
(1 row(s) affected)
```

1. Now, to view the contents of the view, Employee_view, type:

```
SELECT *
FROM   Employee_view
```

This query now produces the following output (the third name has changed):

```
names
--------------------
Sumon Bagui
Sudip Bagui
Mala Saha
Ed Evans
Genny George

(5 row(s) affected)
```

2. Then, view the contents of the underlying table by typing the following (and note that the third name of this table has changed too):

```
SELECT *
FROM    Employee
```

This now gives:

```
names             wage          hours
---------------   ------------   -----------
Sumon Bagui       10.0000        40
Sudip Bagui       15.0000        30
Mala   Saha       18.0000        NULL
Ed Evans          NULL           10
Genny George      20.0000        40

(5 row(s) affected)
```

If a row were added or deleted from the view, Employee_view, the same change would also appear in the underlying table.

Therefore, when adding, changing, or deleting data in views, you should always be very careful, because you do not want to unintentionally change the original underlying table. Remember that a view may sometimes be only a partial section of a table.

Changing data in tables. If data is changed in the original table, such as our Employee table, the same data in all the views related to this underlying table also gets changed.

Deleting views

A view can be deleted with a DROP VIEW. For example, to delete the view called Employee_view, you would type:

```
DROP VIEW Employee_view
```

You will get:

```
Command(s) completed successfully.
```

Temporary Tables

In SQL Server 2005, temporary tables reside in SQL Server 2005's default temporary database, tempdb. Every time that SQL Server 2005 is stopped and restarted, a brand new copy of tempdb is built. So temporary tables are automatically destroyed when the user who created them disconnects from SQL Server 2005.

Though temporary tables involve extra storage as well as extra programming effort, temporary tables are useful for doing work that requires multiple passes to avoid doing repetitive work. Temporary tables are useful for doing work on a "picture of the data" in the database. As the name implies, no permanent storage of the temporary structure is anticipated; when the use of the temporary data is over, the table is deleted. Data in temporary tables is static and not reflective of updates to the original table(s). As with views, temporary tables may also allow you to develop SQL queries in a step-by-step manner and may be used to simplify complex queries.

Creating temporary tables

In SQL Server 2005, temporary tables are created in the same way that permanent tables are created; that is, with a CREATE TABLE or a SELECT INTO statement; however, temporary table names must begin with either # or ##.

Creating local temporary tables. Local temporary tables are created with # in front of the table name and are visible only to the user who is currently connected to the database. They are deleted when the user disconnects from this instance of SQL Server. They are local to the session in which they are created. Thus they are not visible in any other session, not even to one from the same host or login.

You cannot have foreign key constraints on a temporary table.

 We discuss foreign key constraints in Chapter 11.

The general SQL Server 2005 syntax for creating a local temporary table is:

```
SELECT column_name, ..., column_name INTO #local_temporary_tablename
FROM permanent_tablename
WHERE...
```

As an example of how to create a local temporary table, #Temp1, type the following SELECT query:

```
SELECT s.sname, s.stno, d.dname, s.class INTO #Temp1
FROM   Student s, Department_to_major d
WHERE  s.major = d.dcode
AND    (s.class = 1 or s.class = 2)
AND    s.major = 'COSC';
```

You will get:

```
(6 row(s) affected)
```

This query creates a local temporary table called #Temp1. You can use #Temp1 as a regular table for this session. To view the data in #Temp1, type the following:

```
SELECT *
FROM    #Temp1
```

This query produces the following six rows of output:

```
sname                stno  dname             class
-------------------- ----- ----------------- -----
Brenda               8     Computer Science  2
Lujack               14    Computer Science  1
Elainie              17    Computer Science  1
Hillary              121   Computer Science  1
Brad                 128   Computer Science  1
Alan                 130   Computer Science  2

(6 row(s) affected)
```

You can view the local temporary table from the tempdb under Object Explorer. From the Object Explorer, click Databases, System Databases, tempdb, and then Temporary Tables. You will see the temporary table, #Temp1, as shown in Figure 6-4.

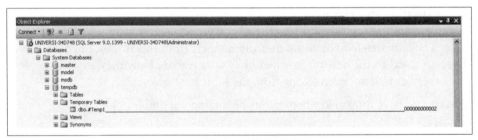

Figure 6-4. Viewing the local temporary table from the Object Explorer

As in Figure 6-4, in SQL Server 2005, the local temporary table that you create is appended by a system generated suffix—a 12-digit number with leading zeros. The local temporary table name that you provide cannot be more than 116 characters, allowing 128 characters for the name of the local temporary table. This is done by SQL Server because SQL Server allows a number of sessions to create a local temporary table with the same name without the names colliding with each other.

Creating global temporary tables. Global temporary tables are created with a prefix of ##. Global temporary tables can be accessed by anyone who logs onto the database, as long as the creator of the global temporary table is still logged on. The global temporary table will be dropped automatically when the session that created it ends and when all other processes that reference it have stopped referencing it. Therefore, even

---

though the process that created the table may have ended, if another process is still using it, then it will still be alive.

The general SQL Server syntax for creating a global temporary table is:

```
SELECT column_name, ..., column_name INTO ##global_temporary_tablename
FROM permanent_tablename
WHERE...
```

As an example of how to create a global temporary table, type the following SELECT query:

```
SELECT s.sname, s.stno, d.dname, s.class INTO ##Temp1
FROM    Student s, Department_to_major d
WHERE   s.major = d.dcode
AND     (s.class = 1 or s.class = 2)
AND     s.major = 'COSC';
```

You will get:

```
(6 row(s) affected)
```

This query creates a global temporary table called ##Temp1. You can use ##Temp1 as a regular table for this session. To view the data in ##Temp1, type the following:

```
SELECT *
FROM    ##Temp1
```

You will get the same output given previously (for the local temporary table).

A global temporary table can also be viewed from the tempdb option of the Object Explorer. From the Object Explorer, click Databases, System Databases, tempdb, and then Temporary Tables, and you will see the global temporary table, ##Temp1, as shown in Figure 6-5.

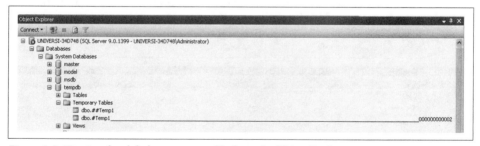

Figure 6-5. Viewing the global temporary table from the Object Explorer

 Unlike with views, updating data in local or global temporary tables does not change the data in the underlying original table.

You will note that, unlike the local temporary table, the global temporary table does not have a system generated suffix attached to the name of the global temporary table. In fact, when creating global temporary tables, you have to be careful that one with the same name does not already exist, so as to prevent collisions between tables in any one session. There can be only one instance of a global temporary table with any particular name.

For example, if you type the following query and try to create another global temporary called ##Temp1:

```
SELECT  s.sname, s.stno, d.dname, s.class INTO ##Temp1
FROM    Student s, Department_to_major d
WHERE   s.major = d.dcode
AND     (s.class = 1 or s.class = 2)
AND     s.major = 'MATH';
```

You will get the following error message:

```
Msg 2714, Level 16, State 6, Line 1
There is already an object named '##Temp1' in the database.
```

Deleting temporary tables. If you want to delete a temporary table (local or global) before ending the session, you can use the DROP TABLE statement, just as you would to delete a permanent table.

For example, with the following query

```
DROP TABLE ##Temp1
```

you will get this message:

```
Command(s) completed successfully.
```

To view this change (drop), click on select Temporary Tables and then select Refresh, and you will see that the temporary table ##Temp1 no longer exists, as shown in Figure 6-6.

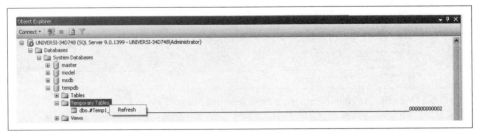

Figure 6-6. Viewing the global temporary table from the Object Explorer

Query Development with Derived Structures

In this section, we discuss how derived structures such as views and temporary tables can be used in query development.

To illustrate this process, we will list from our standard database, Student_course, the name, student number, and department name of students who are freshman or sophomores and computer science majors.

In Step 1, we will develop a query, and in Step 2, we will show how to use this query with derived structures. In Step 2, Option 1 shows how the query can be turned into a view, Option 2 shows how the query can be turned into an inline view, and Option 3 shows how the query can be used to create a temporary table.

Step 1: Develop a Query Step by Step

1. The first step is to see which columns we need and in which tables these columns are found. We need student names (sname) and numbers (stno), which are found in the Student table. Department names (dname) are found in the Department_to_major table. To find the department names that correspond to the student majors, we have to combine the Student and Department_to_major tables. To combine these two tables, we will join the tables where major from the Student table joins with the dcode from the Department_to_major table as follows (because the statements eventually will be filtered by class, we include class in the result set):

```
SELECT s.sname, s.stno, d.dname, s.class
FROM   Student s, Department_to_major d
WHERE  s.major = d.dcode
```

After you type the query and run it, you will get the following 45 rows of output:

```
sname                  stno   dname                  class
---------------------- ------ ---------------------- ------
Lineas                 2      English                1
Mary                   3      Computer Science       4
Zelda                  5      Computer Science       NULL
Ken                    6      Political Science      NULL
Mario                  7      Mathematics            NULL
Brenda                 8      Computer Science       2
Romona                 9      English                NULL
Richard                10     English                1
Kelly                  13     Mathematics            4
Lujack                 14     Computer Science       1
Reva                   15     Mathematics            2
Elainie                17     Computer Science       1
Harley                 19     Political Science      2
Donald                 20     Accounting             4
Chris                  24     Accounting             4
Jake                   31     Computer Science       4
Lynette                34     Political Science      1
```

Susan	49	English	3
Monica	62	Mathematics	3
Bill	70	Political Science	NULL
Hillary	121	Computer Science	1
Phoebe	122	English	3
Holly	123	Political Science	4
Sadie	125	Mathematics	2
Jessica	126	Political Science	2
Steve	127	English	1
Brad	128	Computer Science	1
Cedric	129	English	2
Alan	130	Computer Science	2
Rachel	131	English	3
George	132	Political Science	1
Jerry	142	Computer Science	4
Cramer	143	English	3
Fraiser	144	Political Science	1
Harrison	145	Accounting	4
Francis	146	Accounting	4
Smithly	147	English	2
Sebastian	148	Accounting	2
Losmith	151	Chemistry	3
Genevieve	153	NULL	NULL
Lindsay	155	NULL	1
Stephanie	157	Mathematics	NULL
Gus	160	Art	3
Benny	161	Chemistry	4
Jake	191	Mathematics	2

```
(45 row(s) affected)
```

2. To find all the freshmen and sophomores (class 1 and 2) from the Student table,
   add AND (s.class = 1 or s.class = 2) to the end of the previous query, as follows:

```
SELECT s.sname, s.stno, d.dname, s.class
FROM   Student s, Department_to_major d
WHERE  s.major = d.dcode
AND (s.class = 1 or s.class = 2)
```

Running this query produces the following 21 rows of output:

sname	stno	dname	class
Lineas	2	English	1
Brenda	8	Computer Science	2
Richard	10	English	1
Lujack	14	Computer Science	1
Reva	15	Mathematics	2
Elainie	17	Computer Science	1
Harley	19	Political Science	2
Lynette	34	Political Science	1
Hillary	121	Computer Science	1
Sadie	125	Mathematics	2
Jessica	126	Political Science	2
Steve	127	English	1

```
Brad            128    Computer Science    1
Cedric          129    English             2
Alan            130    Computer Science    2
George          132    Political Science   1
Fraiser         144    Political Science   1
Smithly         147    English             2
Sebastian       148    Accounting          2
Lindsay         155    NULL                1
Jake            191    Mathematics         2
```

(21 row(s) affected)

3. Now that we have the department names of all the freshmen and sophomores, we need to find the computer science majors from this group, so we add AND s. major = 'COSC' to the previous query as follows:

```
SELECT s.sname, s.stno, d.dname, s.class
FROM    Student s, Department_to_major d
WHERE   s.major = d.dcode
AND (s.class = 1 or s.class = 2)
AND s.major = 'COSC'
```

This query produces the following output (six rows), which finally gives us the student name, student number, and department name of students who are freshman or sophomores and computer science majors:

```
sname                stno   dname                 class
-------------------- ------ --------------------- ------
Brenda               8      Computer Science      2
Lujack               14     Computer Science      1
Elainie              17     Computer Science      1
Hillary              121    Computer Science      1
Brad                 128    Computer Science      1
Alan                 130    Computer Science      2
```

(6 row(s) affected)

Note that in each case where we add more filtering in the WHERE clause, the number of rows declines. If the number of rows does not decline, that could represent a problem.

Step 2: Using a Derived Structure

This step shows how the previous query (developed in Step 1) can be turned into a view (Option 1), inline view (Option 2), or temporary table (Option 3). Each one of these derived structures will produce the same end results, so as you develop your own queries, you may use whichever derived structure you become most comfortable with and/or is most appropriate.

 Derived structures are also very useful when you wish to use nested functions.

Option 1: Turning your query into a view

To create a view (called stu_view) using the previous example query, type:

```
CREATE VIEW stu_view AS
SELECT   s.sname, s.stno, d.dname, s.class
FROM     Student s, Department_to_major d
WHERE    s.major = d.dcode
AND        (s.class = 1 or s.class = 2)
AND        s.major = 'COSC'
```

You can now SELECT from the view by typing:

```
SELECT *
FROM    stu_view
WHERE   sname LIKE 'BR%'
```

This query produces the following output, which includes all the names in the view stu_view that start with "Br":

```
sname                   stno  dname                 class
-------------------     ----- -------------------   ------
Brenda                  8     Computer Science      2
Brad                    128   Computer Science      1

(2 row(s) affected)
```

Remember that the view always reflects the database as it is, and a view takes up no extra storage in the database, because no data is stored in a view.

Option 2: Using an inline view

You can also place a query in the FROM clause of a SELECT statement and thereby create what is called an *inline view*. An inline view exists only during the execution of a query. The main purpose of an inline view is to simplify the development of a one-time query. In a typical development scenario, a person would probably devise a SELECT statement, test it, examine the result, wrap it in parentheses, and continue with the development by using the inline view.

Follow these general steps to develop an inline view:

1. Develop a query:

```
SELECT column1, column2, ...
FROM    TableName
WHERE  ...
```

2. Wrap the results into parentheses and make it into an inline view:

```
SELECT *
FROM    (SELECT column1, column2, ... FROM TableName WHERE ...)
```

3. Display the columns in the inline view:

```
SELECT v.column1, v.column2, ...
FROM    (SELECT column1, column2, ... FROM TableName WHERE ...) v
```

You could then proceed to make the previous query an inline view and add more complexity as needed. The beauty of creating a query in steps is that you can examine each step using counts and TOP qualifiers to see whether you're heading in the right direction.

Let's look at an example of an inline view for our sample problem. In this example, we create the same view as previously inline — that is, we create the view on the fly, give it an alias of v, and use it just as we would use a stored table or view, as follows:

```
SELECT   v.sname, v.dname, v.class
FROM     (SELECT s.sname, s.stno, d.dname, s.class
FROM     Student AS s, Department_to_major AS d
WHERE    s.major = d.dcode
  AND      (s.class = 1 or s.class = 2)
  AND      s.major = 'COSC') AS v
```

This query produces the following six rows of output:

```
sname                 dname                class
--------------------  -------------------- ------
Brenda                Computer Science     2
Lujack                Computer Science     1
Elainie               Computer Science     1
Hillary               Computer Science     1
Brad                  Computer Science     1
Alan                  Computer Science     2
(6 row(s) affected)
```

In the final result set of the outer query, the column names reference the names used in the inline view result set.

Option 3: Using a global temporary table

To create a global temporary table (called ##Temp2) using the query developed in Step 1, type:

```
SELECT  s.sname, s.stno, d.dname, s.class INTO ##Temp2
FROM    Student s, Department_to_major d
WHERE   s.major = d.dcode
AND       (s.class = 1 or s.class = 2)
AND       s.major = 'COSC'
```

Once you run or execute your query, you have created a temporary table called ##Temp2.

Now if you type:

```
SELECT *
FROM ##Temp2
```

You should get the following six rows of output, which should be exactly the same as you received in the other options:

```
sname                 stno   dname                   class
--------------------  ------ ----------------------  ------
Brenda                8      Computer Science        2
Lujack                14     Computer Science        1
Elainie               17     Computer Science        1
Hillary               121    Computer Science        1
Brad                  128    Computer Science        1
Alan                  130    Computer Science        2

(6 row(s) affected)
```

In all the examples of views and temporary tables, the SQL programmer weighs programming effort (individual and team), storage costs, and query efficiency to choose which structure is appropriate.

Summary

In this chapter, we provided you with an overview of different derived structures available in SQL Server. Each of these derived structures has its own advantages and disadvantages, and once you have knowledge of the different derived structures, it is up to you to select the derived structure that you wish to use to make your work easier or more efficient. Oftentimes it is not easy to formulate a query all at once. The derived structures will help you formulate your queries in a more systematic step-by-step manner.

Review Questions

1. Which has precedence, AND or OR?
2. Why do we need derived structures?
3. What is a view?
4. List some advantages of using views.
5. List some advantages of using temporary tables.
6. Can temporary tables replace views in all cases?
7. What is the difference between a view and temporary table?
8. What is the difference between a local temporary table and global temporary table?
9. If data is changed in a view, is it changed in the original table?
10. If data is changed in a temporary table, does it automatically change data in the original table?
11. What happens to local temporary tables after the session has been ended?

---

12. What happens to global temporary table after the session has been ended?

13. Which type of temporary table has a system-generated suffix attached to it? What does this suffix mean?

14. Why are inline views helpful?

15. In SQL Server, is the ORDER BY clause allowed during the creation of a view?

16. Is SELECT INTO allowed in a view? Why or why not?

17. Where is the data stored in a view?

18. How do you delete views?

19. How do you delete a temporary table?

20. Do you need to delete a local temporary table? Why or why not?

21. Which operators have the highest/lowest precedence?

22. In SQL Server, if a column of FLOAT data type were divided by a column of REAL data type, what data type would the resulting column have? (Hint: refer to the section on Data Type Preference.)

23. Is an ORDER BY clause necessary when you use a DISTINCT? Why or why not?

Exercises

Unless specified otherwise, use the Student_course database to answer the following questions. Also, use appropriate column headings when displaying your output.

1. Develop and execute a query to find the names of students who had HERMANO as an instructor and earned a grade of B or better in the class. Develop the query by first finding sections where HERMANO was the instructor. Save this query. Edit the query and modify it to join the Section table with the Grade_report table. Add the grade constraint.

2. Using the Student table, create a duplicate table called Stutab that contains all rows from the Student table. Hint: Look at the design of the Student table to see the columns and their definitions. Create the Stutab table with a CREATE TABLE command. Insert data into Stutab using the INSERT INTO .. SELECT option.

   Using the newly created Stutab table:

   a. List student names and majors of the juniors and seniors.

   b. List student names of the COSC majors.

   c. Create a view (call it vstu) that contains student names and majors for the COSC majors.

   d. List the student names and majors from vstu in descending order by name.

   e. Modify a row in your view of your table so that a student changes his or her major.

f. Display of the view. Did modifying the view, vstu, also change the parent table, Stutab?

g. Try to modify the view again, but this time, change the major to COMPSC—an obviously invalid column in the Stutab table, because the column was defined as four characters. Can you do it? What happens?

h. Using Stutab, create a local temporary table (call it #stutemp) that contains student names and majors for the COSC majors.

i. List the student names and majors from #stutemp in ascending order by name.

j. Modify a row in #stutemp so that a student changes his or her major.

k. Display the local temporary table. Did modifying your temporary table, #stutemp, also change the parent table, Stutab.

l. Try to modify the local temporary table again, but this time change the major to COMPSC—again, an obviously invalid field in Stutab, because the field was defined as four characters. Can you do it? What happens?

m. Using Stutab, create a global temporary table (call it ##gstutemp) that contains student names and majors for the COSC majors.

n. List the student names and majors from ##gstutemp in ascending order by name.

o. Modify a row in ##gstutemp so that a student changes his or her major.

p. Display the global temporary table. Did modifying your temporary table, ##gstutemp, also change the parent table, Stutab.

q. Try to modify the global temporary table again, but this time change the major to COMPSC—again, an obviously invalid field in Stutab, because the field was defined as four characters. Can you do it? What happens?

r. Create an inline view (call it invstu) that contains student names and majors for COSC majors.

3. Perform an experiment to determine the precedence in a query with three conditions linked by AND and OR. Which precedence is followed: AND, OR, or left-to-right?

   Run this query:
   ```
   SELECT *
   FROM    Student
   WHERE   stno < 100 AND major = 'COSC' OR major = 'ACCT'
   ```

   Then run the following two queries and determine which one gives you the same output as the preceding non parenthesized statement:
   ```
   SELECT *
   FROM    Student
   WHERE   (stno < 100 AND major = 'COSC') OR major = 'ACCT'
   ```

or:

```
SELECT *
FROM    Student
WHERE   stno < 100 AND (major = 'COSC' OR major = 'ACCT')
```

What happens if you put the OR first instead of the AND and run the query without parentheses?

4. Develop a query to find the instructor name and course name for computer science courses (use the Section table).

   a. Convert your query into a view.

   b. Convert the query into an inline view with column aliases and test it.

   c. Include an ORDER BY clause outside of the inline view in the main query and run your query again.

CHAPTER 7

Set Operations

In Chapter 4, we looked at how data can be retrieved from multiple tables using joins. In this chapter, we discuss how data can also be retrieved from multiple tables by using set operations. We look at the set operations available in SQL Server 2005. Because not all the SQL set operations are explicitly available in SQL Server 2005, we will also look at the IN predicate and its negation, NOT..IN, which are ways around the explicit set operations. In the final section of this chapter, we look at the UNION operation in relation to the join operation, and how the UNION operation can be used to get the results of some joins.

Introducing Set Operations

A *set* is a collection of objects. In relational databases, a table can be regarded as a set of rows. Elements in a set do not have to be ordered. In relational databases, rows do not have to be ordered as they are entered or stored. *Set operations* are used in SQL to retrieve data from multiple sets, and include a binary union, binary intersection and binary set difference. A result set is obtained in SQL from the result of a SELECT.

A *binary union* is a set operation on two sets, the result of which contains all the elements of both sets. A *binary intersection* generates values in common between two sets. And, a *binary set difference* generates values in one set less those contained in another set.

Three explicit set operations are used in SQL: UNION, INTERSECT, and MINUS (for set difference). SQL Server 2005 allows the explicit use of the UNION and INTERSECT operations. Because the MINUS set operation cannot be explicitly used in SQL Server 2005, we will illustrate the MINUS operation by using the very common IN predicate and its negation, NOT..IN, which enable us to accomplish the same result as using INTERSECT and MINUS.

The format of a set statement is as follows:

```
set OPERATOR set
```

where OPERATOR is a UNION, INTERSECT or MINUS, and where "set" is defined by a SELECT.

First we will discuss the UNION operator; the INTERSECT operator will be discussed later in the chapter.

The following is the syntax for a general form of an UNION:

```
SELECT *
FROM    TableA
UNION
SELECT *
FROM TableB
```

Set statements allow us to combine two distinct sets of data (two result sets) only if we insure union compatibility, as explained in the next section.

Union Compatibility

Union compatibility, the commonly used SQL terminology for *set compatibility*, means that when using set operations, the two sets (in this case, the results of two SELECTs) being unioned have to have the same number of similar columns and the columns have to have compatible data types. Next we will explain what compatible data types means, and we will return to the issue of "similar" columns in a later section.

So what does "compatible" data types mean? The data types of the columns of the two sets being unioned do not necessarily have to be exactly the same, meaning that they may differ in length and even type, but they have to be "well-matched." For union compatibility, the three basic data types are numeric, string, and dates. All numeric columns are compatible with one another, all string columns are compatible with one another, and all date columns are compatible with one another. For numbers, SQL will convert integers, floating-point numbers, and decimals into a numeric data type, to make them compatible with one another. So any numeric column (for example, integers) can be unioned with any other numeric column (for example, decimals). Likewise, any fixed-length character column and any variable-length character column will be converted to a character data type, and take on the larger size of the character columns being unioned. Similarly, date columns will be combined to a date data type.

> For union compatibility, the three basic data types are numeric, string, and dates.

Union compatibility can happen in several ways:

- By unioning two tables or views that have identical columns (which implies the same domains as well).
- By taking two subsets from a table and combining them.
- By using two views from two tables respectively with the columns chosen so that they are compatible.

For the data type precedence rules, refer to the "Data Type Precedence" section in Chapter 6.

The UNION Operation

In SQL Server 2005, a binary union is performed with the UNION set operation. A UNION takes the result sets from two (or more) queries and returns all rows from the results sets as a single result set (removing the duplicates). In this section, we illustrate how a UNION works; although there are other ways to retrieve this information, we are showing the UNION alternative.

Suppose that we want to find the names of all students who are computer science (COSC) majors, along with all students who are MATH majors from the Student table, we may write the following query that uses the UNION set operator:

```
SELECT sname
FROM Student
WHERE major = 'COSC'
   UNION
SELECT sname
FROM Student
WHERE major = 'MATH'
```

 The two sets being unioned must have the same number of columns in the result sets of the SELECT clauses.

While executing the UNION, SQL first executes the first part of the query:

```
SELECT sname
FROM Student
WHERE major = 'COSC'
```

This part virtually produces the following 10 rows of output:

```
sname
--------------------
Mary
Zelda
Brenda
Lujack
Elainie
Jake
Hillary
Brad
Alan
Jerry

(10 row(s) affected)
```

Then SQL executes the second part of the query:

```
SELECT sname
FROM Student
WHERE major = 'MATH'
```

This part virtually produces the following 7 rows of output:

```
sname
--------------------
Mario
Kelly
Reva
Monica
Sadie
Stephanie
Jake

(7 row(s) affected)
```

SQL then combines the two virtual sets of results (the UNION operation), which includes throwing out any duplicates (an extra "Jake," in this case), leaving us with the following 16 rows of output:

```
sname
--------------------
Alan
Brad
Brenda
Elainie
Hillary
Jake
Jerry
Kelly
Lujack
Mario
Mary
Monica
Reva
Sadie
Stephanie
Zelda

(16 row(s) affected)
```

Prior to SQL Server 7, SQL Server always returned the result of a UNION in sorted order. This was so because the UNION eliminated duplicate rows using a sorting strategy. The ordering was simply a by-product of the sorting to eliminate duplicates. Newer versions of SQL Server, however, have several alternative strategies available for removing duplicates, so there is no guarantee of any particular order when you use UNION. If you would like to order the output, you should explicitly use ORDER BY at the end of your last SELECT statement.

The maximum number of rows possible when a UNION is used is the sum of the number of rows in the two result sets (or tables) in the two SELECT clauses.

Similar Columns in Unions

Earlier, we mentioned that for a union to be successful, there has to be union compatibility, and the two sets being unioned have to have similar columns. So what does similar columns mean?

If we wrote the earlier UNION example like this:

```
SELECT major
FROM Student
WHERE major = 'COSC'
    UNION
SELECT sname
FROM Student
WHERE major = 'MATH'
```

We would get a result set, but would the result set (output) be valid? The answer is *no*. You are trying to union majors and student names. These are not similar columns (though the data types of the two columns are compatible), and it does not make sense to union two different types of columns. So, before performing a union operation, you have to be very careful that you union like columns, and not "apples and oranges."

Unioning Constants or Variables

In SQL Server 2005, a group of SELECT statements can also be used to union constants or variables:

```
SELECT col1=100, col2=200
UNION
SELECT col1=400, col2=500
UNION
SELECT col1=100*3, col2=200*3
UNION
SELECT 900, 400
```

This query will produce:

```
col1        col2
----------- -----------
100         200
300         600
400         500
900         400

(4 row(s) affected)
```

Note that the output here happens to be sorted by the first column.

The UNION ALL Operation

UNION ALL works exactly like UNION, but does not expunge duplicates or sort the results. UNION ALL is more efficient in execution (because UNION ALL does not have to expunge the duplicates), and occasionally you may need to keep duplicates (just to keep all occurrences or records), in which case you can use UNION ALL.

The following is the same query previously shown for UNION, but using UNION ALL instead of UNION:

```
SELECT sname
FROM Student
WHERE major = 'COSC'
    UNION ALL
SELECT sname
FROM Student
WHERE major = 'MATH'
```

This query results in 17 unsorted rows, including one duplicate, Jake; using UNION produced 16 rows with no duplicates:

```
sname
--------------------
Mary
Zelda
Brenda
Lujack
Elainie
Jake
Hillary
Brad
Alan
Jerry
Mario
Kelly
Reva
Monica
Sadie
Stephanie
Jake

(17 row(s) affected)
```

Handling UNION and UNION ALL Situations with an Unequal Number of Columns

As has been mentioned earlier, in order to successfully UNION or UNION ALL result sets, the result sets being unioned have to have the same number of columns. That is, all queries in a UNION or UNION ALL operation must return the same number of columns.

But what if all the queries being used in the UNION or UNION ALL do not return the same number of columns?

If we want to union two result sets that do not have the same number of columns, we have to use NULL (or other) values in the column-places as place holders. For example, from our Student_course database, if we want to union the Course table and the Prereq table with all the columns, under normal circumstances, this would not be possible, because the Course table has four columns and the Prereq table has only two. Therefore, to perform a UNION ALL operation, we would have to place NULL values or some other values in the columns that will be empty, as follows (this example uses NULL as a place holder):

```
SELECT c.*, NULL
FROM Course c
WHERE c.credit_hours = 4
UNION ALL
SELECT NULL, p.course_number, NULL, NULL, p.prereq
FROM Prereq p
```

This query produces the following 18 rows of output:

COURSE_NAME	COURSE_NUMBER	CREDIT_HOURS	OFFERING_DEPT	
INTRO TO COMPUTER SC	COSC1310	4	COSC	NULL
DATA STRUCTURES	COSC3320	4	COSC	NULL
ADA - INTRODUCTION	COSC5234	4	COSC	NULL
CALCULUS 1	MATH1501	4	MATH	NULL
SOCIALISM AND COMMUN	POLY4103	4	POLY	NULL
POLITICS OF CUBA	POLY5501	4	POLY	NULL
NULL	ACCT3333	NULL	NULL	ACCT2220
NULL	CHEM3001	NULL	NULL	CHEM2001
NULL	COSC3320	NULL	NULL	COSC1310
NULL	COSC3380	NULL	NULL	COSC3320
NULL	COSC3380	NULL	NULL	MATH2410
NULL	COSC5234	NULL	NULL	COSC3320
NULL	ENGL1011	NULL	NULL	ENGL1010
NULL	ENGL3401	NULL	NULL	ENGL1011
NULL	ENGL3520	NULL	NULL	ENGL1011
NULL	MATH5501	NULL	NULL	MATH2333
NULL	POLY2103	NULL	NULL	POLY1201
NULL	POLY5501	NULL	NULL	POLY4103

```
(18 row(s) affected)
```

We can also use other values (other than NULL) as placeholders, as shown here:

```
SELECT c.*, COU_NUM = 'XXXXXXXXXXXX'
FROM Course c
WHERE c.credit_hours = 4
UNION ALL
SELECT 'XXXXXXXXXXXX', p.course_number, 00000000000, 'XXXXXXXXXXXX', p.prereq
FROM Prereq p
```

This query gives the same output as the previous query, but this time we have used a series of Xs and 0s as placeholders instead of NULL (we have 18 rows of output):

```
COURSE_NAME              COURSE_NUMBER CREDIT_HOURS OFFERING_DEPT COU_NUM
----------------------   ------------- ------------ ------------- ------------
INTRO TO COMPUTER SC COSC1310         4            COSC          XXXXXXXXXXXX
DATA STRUCTURES          COSC3320      4            COSC          XXXXXXXXXXXX
ADA - INTRODUCTION       COSC5234      4            COSC          XXXXXXXXXXXX
CALCULUS 1               MATH1501      4            MATH          XXXXXXXXXXXX
SOCIALISM AND COMMUN POLY4103         4            POLY          XXXXXXXXXXXX
POLITICS OF CUBA         POLY5501      4            POLY          XXXXXXXXXXXX
XXXXXXXXXXXX             ACCT3333      0            XXXXXXXXXXXX ACCT2220
XXXXXXXXXXXX             CHEM3001      0            XXXXXXXXXXXX CHEM2001
XXXXXXXXXXXX             COSC3320      0            XXXXXXXXXXXX COSC1310
XXXXXXXXXXXX             COSC3380      0            XXXXXXXXXXXX COSC3320
XXXXXXXXXXXX             COSC3380      0            XXXXXXXXXXXX MATH2410
XXXXXXXXXXXX             COSC5234      0            XXXXXXXXXXXX COSC3320
XXXXXXXXXXXX             ENGL1011      0            XXXXXXXXXXXX ENGL1010
XXXXXXXXXXXX             ENGL3401      0            XXXXXXXXXXXX ENGL1011
XXXXXXXXXXXX             ENGL3520      0            XXXXXXXXXXXX ENGL1011
XXXXXXXXXXXX             MATH5501      0            XXXXXXXXXXXX MATH2333
XXXXXXXXXXXX             POLY2103      0            XXXXXXXXXXXX POLY1201
XXXXXXXXXXXX             POLY5501      0            XXXXXXXXXXXX POLY4103

(18 row(s) affected)
```

NULL does not have a data type, so it can be used as a placeholder for both numeric and character columns. But when using other values as placeholders, the data types have to match. Hence we used 'XX...' (in the query with the single quotes) for the character columns, and 000s (in the query without quotes) for the numeric columns.

The IN and NOT..IN Predicates

Although SQL Server 2005 does not have the MINUS (difference) operator, it does have an IN predicate and its negation, the NOT..IN, which enables us to create differences. Let us look at this predicate from a set point of view. If we find the objects from set A that are not in set B, we have found the difference of set A and B (A − B).

Using IN

The following is a simple example of an IN predicate with constants in a SELECT statement:

```
SELECT  sname, class
FROM    Student
WHERE   class IN (3,4)
```

In this example, IN (3,4) is called a *subquery-set*, where (3, 4) is the set in which we are testing membership. This query says: "Find all student names from the Student table where the class is in the set (3, 4)." It produces the following 17 rows of output:

```
sname                class
-------------------- ------
Mary                 4
Kelly                4
Donald               4
Chris                4
Jake                 4
Susan                3
Monica               3
Phoebe               3
Holly                4
Rachel               3
Jerry                4
Cramer               3
Harrison             4
Francis              4
Losmith              3
Gus                  3
Benny                4

(17 row(s) affected)
```

The preceding query produces the same output as the following query:

```
SELECT  sname, class
FROM    Student
WHERE   class = 3 OR class = 4
```

In other words, the IN(3,4) means belonging to either set (3) OR set (4), as shown by the WHERE class = 3 OR class = 4.

Using IN as a subquery

We can expand the IN predicate's subquery-set part to be an actual query. For example, consider the following query:

```
SELECT Student.sname
FROM    Student
WHERE   Student.stno IN
   (SELECT  g.student_number
    FROM    Grade_report g
    WHERE   g.grade = 'A')
```

 Subqueries will be discussed at length in the next chapter.

Note the following about this query:

- WHERE Student.stno references the name of the column in the Student table.
- g.student_number is the column name in the Grade_report table.
- stno in the Student table and student_number in the Grade_report table have the same domain.

Note also that you must retrieve the information from the same domains for purposes of union compatibility.

The preceding query produces the following 14 rows of output:

```
sname
--------------------
Lineas
Mary
Brenda
Richard
Lujack
Donald
Lynette
Susan
Holly
Sadie
Jessica
Steve
Cedric
Jerry

(14 row(s) affected)
```

You could view the preceding query as a result derived from the *intersection* of the sets A and B, where set A is the set of student numbers in the student set (from the Student table) and set B is the set of student numbers in the grade set (from the Grade_report table) that have As.

To make this command behave like a set operator (as if it were an INTERSECT operator), you can add the qualifier DISTINCT to the result set as follows:

```
SELECT DISTINCT (Student.sname)
FROM   Student
WHERE Student.stno IN
  (SELECT DISTINCT (g.student_number)
   FROM Grade_report g
   WHERE g.grade = 'A')
```

This query produces the following 14 rows of output:

```
sname
--------------------
Brenda
Cedric
Donald
Holly
```

```
Jerry
Jessica
Lineas
Lujack
Lynette
Mary
Richard
Sadie
Steve
Susan

(14 row(s) affected)
```

Here, SQL Server 2005 sorts the results for you and does not return duplicates.

The INTERSECT Operator

From a set point of view, an INTERSECT means if we find objects from set A that are also in set B (and vice versa), we have found the intersection of sets A and B. SQL Server 2005 has an INTERSECT operator.

The following query is the previous query written using an INTERSECT (but we displayed student numbers instead of student names):

```
SELECT s.stno
FROM Student s
INTERSECT
SELECT g.student_number
FROM Grade_report g
WHERE g.grade = 'A'
```

This query gives the following 14 rows of output:

```
stno
-------------
2
3
8
10
14
20
34
49
123
125
126
127
129
142

(14 row(s) affected)
```

In this query, we had to display student numbers (stno) instead of the student names (sname) because of the set compatibility issue discussed earlier. INTERSECT is a set operator, so the two sets being intersected have to have the same number of columns and the columns have to have compatible data types.

Another example of the use of the INTERSECT operator would be, for example, if we wanted to find all the students who had dependents, in which case we could type:

```
SELECT s.stno
FROM Student s
INTERSECT
SELECT d.pno
FROM Dependent d
```

This query would give the following 19 rows of output:

```
stno
------------------
2
10
14
17
20
34
62
123
126
128
132
142
143
144
145
146
147
153
158

(19 row(s) affected)
```

Though the INTERSECT operator gives us the right answer, in some ways the IN as a subquery (discussed earlier) is better to use, because when SQL Server 2005 performs the INTERSECT, it selects sets based on what is mentioned in the SELECT statements. So, for example, if we wanted the student names in addition to the student numbers, and we typed:

```
SELECT s.stno, s.sname
FROM Student s
INTERSECT
SELECT d.pno, relationship
FROM Dependent d
```

The query would not work.

Here we would have to use an IN with a subquery as discussed earlier:

```
SELECT s.stno, s.sname
FROM Student AS s
WHERE (s.stno IN
(SELECT pno
FROM Dependent AS d))
```

giving us the following 19 rows of output:

```
stno    sname
----    ------------------
2       Lineas
10      Richard
14      Lujack
17      Elainie
20      Donald
34      Lynette
62      Monica
123     Holly
126     Jessica
128     Brad
132     George
142     Jerry
143     Cramer
144     Fraiser
145     Harrison
146     Francis
147     Smithly
153     Genevieve
158     Thornton

(19 row(s) affected)
```

Using NOT..IN

The NOT..IN is really a negated IN predicate. If you use the NOT..IN in your query, your query may perform poorly. The reason is that when NOT..IN is used, no indexing can be used, because the NOT..IN part of the query has to test the set with *all* values to find out what is *not* in the set. For smaller tables, no difference in performance will likely be detected. Nonetheless, we discuss how to use NOT..IN in this section, to demonstrate the logical negative of the IN predicate, which will help to complete your overall understanding of the SQL language. Instead of using NOT..IN, it is often preferable to use NOT EXISTS or outer join techniques, both of which are discussed later on.

 Indexing is discussed in detail in Chapter 11.

Sometimes the NOT..IN may seem to more easily describe the desired outcome or may be used for a set difference. For a simple example, consider the following query:

```
SELECT sname, class
FROM   Student
WHERE  class IN (1,3,4)
```

This query produces the following 28 rows of output:

```
sname                 class
--------------------  ------
Lineas                1
Mary                  4
Richard               1
Kelly                 4
Lujack                1
Elainie               1
Donald                4
Chris                 4
Jake                  4
Lynette               1
Susan                 3
Monica                3
Hillary               1
Phoebe                3
Holly                 4
Steve                 1
Brad                  1
Rachel                3
George                1
Jerry                 4
Cramer                3
Fraiser               1
Harrison              4
Francis               4
Losmith               3
Lindsay               1
Gus                   3
Benny                 4

(28 row(s) affected)
```

Contrast the preceding query to the following query:

```
SELECT sname, class
FROM   Student
WHERE  class NOT IN (2)
```

The output in this case is the same as the preceding output because the Student table only has classes 1, 2, 3, and 4. If counts (results) did not "add up," this would show that some value of class was not 1, 2, 3, or 4.

As another example, suppose that you want the names of students who are not computer science (COSC) or math (MATH) majors. The query would be:

```
SELECT  sname, major
FROM    Student
WHERE   major NOT IN ('COSC','MATH')
```

which produces the following output (28 rows):

```
sname                 major
--------------------  -----
Lineas                ENGL
Ken                   POLY
Romona                ENGL
Richard               ENGL
Harley                POLY
Donald                ACCT
Chris                 ACCT
Lynette               POLY
Susan                 ENGL
Bill                  POLY
Phoebe                ENGL
Holly                 POLY
Jessica               POLY
Steve                 ENGL
Cedric                ENGL
Rachel                ENGL
George                POLY
Cramer                ENGL
Fraiser               POLY
Harrison              ACCT
Francis               ACCT
Smithly               ENGL
Sebastian             ACCT
Losmith               CHEM
Genevieve             UNKN
Lindsay               UNKN
Gus                   ART
Benny                 CHEM

(28 row(s) affected)
```

The example output gave all majors other than COSC and MATH. But you must be very careful with the NOT..IN predicate, because if nulls are present in the data, you may get odd answers with NOT..IN.

As an example, consider the following table called Stumajor:

```
name                  major
--------------------  --------------------
Mary                  Biology
Sam                   Chemistry
Alice                 Art
Tom                   NULL

(4 row(s) affected)
```

The table Stumajor has not been created for you in the Student_course database. You have to create it, insert the records shown, and then run the queries that follow.

If you perform the following query:

```
SELECT *
FROM Stumajor
WHERE major IN ('Chemistry','Biology')
```

It produces the following output:

```
name                 major
-------------------- --------------------
Mary                 Biology
Sam                  Chemistry

(2 row(s) affected)
```

If you perform the following query:

```
SELECT *
FROM Stumajor
WHERE major NOT IN ('Chemistry','Biology')
```

It produces the following output:

```
name                 major
-------------------- --------------------
Alice                Art

(1 row(s) affected)
```

The value, null, is not equal to anything. You might expect that NOT..IN would give you <Tom,null>, but it does not. Why? Because nulls in the selection column (here, major) are not matched with a NOT..IN.

Using NOT..IN in a subquery

A NOT..IN can also be used in a subquery. For example, assume that we have another table called Instructor, as shown here:

```
iname                teaches
-------------------- --------------------
Richard              COSC
Subhash              MATH
Tapan                BIOCHEM

(3 row(s) affected)
```

The Instructor table has not been created for you in the Student_course database. You have to create it, insert the records shown, and then run the queries that follow.

Now, if we want to find all the departments that do not have instructors, we could type the following query:

```
SELECT *
FROM department_to_major d
WHERE d.dcode NOT IN
    (SELECT dcode
    FROM department_to_major d, instructor i
    WHERE d.dcode=i.teaches)
```

This query produces the following output (6 rows):

```
Dcode DNAME
----- --------------------
ACCT  Accounting
ART   Art
CHEM  Chemistry
ENGL  English
POLY  Political Science
UNKN  NULL

(6 row(s) affected)
```

Note that in this case, the NOT..IN "behaved" correctly and reported the NULL value for DNAME!

The Difference Operation

Because SQL Server 2005 does not support the MINUS predicate, we will show the set difference operation using a NOT..IN with two examples.

Example 1

Suppose that set A is the set of students in classes 2, 3, or 4 and set B is the set of students in class 2. We could use the NOT..IN predicate to remove the students in set B from set A (a difference operation) by typing the following query:

```
SELECT sname, class
FROM    Student
WHERE class IN (2,3,4)
   AND NOT class IN (2)
```

which produces the following output (17 rows):

```
sname                class
-------------------- ------
Mary                 4
Kelly                4
Donald               4
Chris                4
Jake                 4
Susan                3
Monica               3
```

Phoebe	3
Holly	4
Rachel	3
Jerry	4
Cramer	3
Harrison	4
Francis	4
Losmith	3
Gus	3
Benny	4

(17 row(s) affected)

Example 2

To illustrate another difference operation, we will use views with the NOT..IN to give the effect of a difference operation. Suppose for example, you wanted to find the names of those students who do not major in COSC or MATH but delete from that set those students who have made an A in some course.

First, using the NOT..IN, we will create a view (view1) of the names and majors of the students who are not COSC or MATH majors using the following query:

```
CREATE VIEW view1 AS
SELECT sname, major
FROM    Student
WHERE   major NOT IN ('COSC', 'MATH')
```

View1 will have the same 28 rows of output as shown earlier in this chapter.

Then, using the IN predicate, we will create another view (view2) of names and majors of students who have received As using the following query:

```
CREATE VIEW view2 AS
SELECT Student.sname, Student.major
FROM    Student
WHERE   Student.stno IN
   (SELECT g.student_number
    FROM   Grade_report g
    WHERE  g.grade = 'A')
```

If we type:

```
SELECT *
FROM view2;
```

We get the following 14 rows of output:

sname	major
Lineas	ENGL
Mary	COSC
Brenda	COSC
Richard	ENGL
Lujack	COSC

```
Donald      ACCT
Lynette     POLY
Susan       ENGL
Holly       POLY
Sadie       MATH
Jessica     POLY
Steve       ENGL
Cedric      ENGL
Jerry       COSC
```

```
(14 row(s) affected)
```

Then, to find those students who are not majoring in COSC or MATH, and remove from that set those who made an A in some course, the difference operation could be approached using the NOT..IN as follows, using the views created earlier:

```
SELECT sname
FROM view1
WHERE sname NOT IN
  (SELECT sname
   FROM view2)
```

This query produces the following output (19 rows):

```
sname
--------------------
Ken
Romona
Harley
Chris
Bill
Phoebe
Rachel
George
Cramer
Fraiser
Harrison
Francis
Smithly
Sebastian
Losmith
Genevieve
Lindsay
Gus
Benny
```

```
(19 row(s) affected)
```

This query has the same effect as view1–view2 (all students who are not majoring in COSC or MATH, MINUS students who made an A in some course).

The Union and the Join

In Chapter 4, we discussed joins. In this section, we discuss some differences between the two operations, the UNION and the JOIN. Although the UNION operation and the JOIN operation are similar in that they both combine two tables or sets of data, the approaches used by the two operations are different. We will first present an example of when a JOIN may be used versus when a UNION may be used, and then we will present some other differences between the UNION and the JOIN.

When a JOIN May Be Used Versus When a UNION May Be Used

A JOIN is very commonly used in queries. As we discussed previously (in Chapter 4), JOINs (specifically, equi-joins) involve a result set created based on tables where the tables are linked via some common column. The UNION operator is mostly used to combine two sets of information where the genesis of the information is not as straightforward as in a join. Consider the following two examples.

Example 1: A straightforward join operation

Suppose that we wanted to find the names of students who took accounting courses. This is a straightforward join example. This type of query would involve joining the Student, Section, and Course tables and selecting the student names from the result set. In this case though, we actually have to join the Student table to the Grade_report table first, and then join that result to the Section table, because we cannot directly join the Student table to the Section table. Then, we join that combined result to the Course table—so this ends up becoming a four-table join, with the Grade_report table acting like a bridge between Student and Section. The JOIN query would be:

```
SELECT DISTINCT(sname)
FROM Course c JOIN (Section se JOIN
(Student s JOIN Grade_report g
ON s.stno = g.student_number)
ON se.section_id = g.section_id)
ON c.course_number = se.course_num
AND c.course_name LIKE 'ACC%'
```

This query would give the following 20 rows of output:

```
sname
---------------
Alan
Bill
Brad
Brenda
Cedric
Chris
Donald
Hillary
```

```
Holly
Jessica
Kelly
Ken
Mario
Monica
Phoebe
Romona
Sadie
Steve
Susan
Zelda

(20 row(s) affected)
```

Note that we had to use a DISTINCT in the previous query, as the result of a JOIN gives duplicates.

This example query could also be answered using subqueries, which are discussed later, but the point is that it is easy to see the relationship between the three (actually four) tables.

Example 2: A not-so-straightforward query

Suppose that we wanted to find something like the names of the students who take accounting courses and combine them with the names of students who also major in subjects that use overhead projectors in the courses they take. This could be done using a join with this database, but it would involve finding a join-path through most of the database. For a much larger database, it might be very impractical to consider such a large join. It would be easier to first find the set of names of students who take accounting courses (call this set A) and then find students who major in subjects that use projectors (set B), then union sets A and B. The UNION approach allows us to simplify the problem and check intermediate results, so we will present this problem using a UNION. Further, each part of the problem can be done with joins or subqueries as needed for efficiency and then the results finally unioned. Set operations allow us to create sets of results any way we can and then combine the result sets using set operations; UNION is a set operation.

Following, we present the UNION approach to doing this query. The first step is to do the parts individually. That is, first find the set of names of students who take accounting courses (this is the first half of the query before the UNION). Once this is done, then do the second part individually; that is, find the students who major in subjects that use projectors. Once you have the result for both parts, UNION the two results. We will not need the DISTINCT here, as UNION does not keep the duplicates. Here is a query that shows this approach:

```
SELECT sname
FROM Course c JOIN (Section se JOIN
(Student s JOIN Grade_report g
```

```
ON s.stno = g.student_number)
ON se.section_id = g.section_id)
ON c.course_number = se.course_num
AND c.course_name LIKE 'ACC%'
UNION
SELECT sname
FROM Student s JOIN
(Department_to_major d
JOIN (Course c JOIN
(Room r JOIN Section se
ON r.room = se.room)
ON se.course_num = c.course_number)
ON c.offering_dept = d.dcode)
ON s.major = d.dcode
AND r.ohead = 'Y'
```

This query produces 30 rows:

```
sname
--------------------
Alan
Bill
Brad
Brenda
Cedric
Chris
Cramer
Donald
Elainie
Hillary
Holly
Jake
Jerry
Jessica
Kelly
Ken
Lineas
Lujack
Mario
Mary
Monica
Phoebe
Rachel
Richard
Romona
Sadie
Smithly
Steve
Susan
Zelda

(30 row(s) affected)
```

A Summary of the Other Differences Between the UNION and the JOIN

In this section, we summarize our JOIN/UNION discussion with three abstract tables containing three rows each of symbolic data. Relations or tables are *sets of rows*.

We will first show the union. Assume that we have the following two tables.

Table A

ColumnA	ColumnB	ColumnC
X1	Y1	Z1
X2	Y2	Z2
X3	Y3	Z3

Table B

ColumnA	ColumnB	ColumnC
X4	Y4	Z4
X5	Y5	Z5
X6	Y6	Z6

A SQL UNION can be shown would be:

```
SELECT * FROM TableA
UNION
SELECT * FROM TableB
```

which produces the following table as a result:

Table C

ColumnA	ColumnB	ColumnC
X1	Y1	Z1
X2	Y2	Z2
X3	Y3	Z3
X4	Y4	Z4
X5	Y5	Z5
X6	Y6	Z6

Using a similar set of diagrams, the join operation could be shown as follows with the following two tables (joining TableA and TableD into TableE):

Table A

ColumnA	ColumnB	ColumnC
X1	Y1	Z1
X2	Y2	Z2
X3	Y3	Z3

Table D

ColumnA	ColumnD	ColumnE
X1	D1	E1
X2	D2	E2
X3	D3	E3

Now, a SQL JOIN would be:

```
SELECT *
FROM TableA a JOIN TableD d
ON a.ColumnA = d.ColumnA
```

Giving the following table:

Table E

TableA. ColumnA	TableA. ColumnB	TableA. ColumnC	TableB. ColumnA	TableB. ColumnD	TableB. ColumnE
X1	Y1	Z1	X1	D1	E1
X2	Y2	Z2	X2	D2	E2
X3	Y3	Z3	X3	D3	E3

Following are the major differences between UNIONs and JOINs:

- In a UNION, all the rows in the resulting tables (sets) being unioned have to be compatible; in a JOIN, only the joining columns of the tables being joined have to be compatible—the other columns may be different.

- In a UNION, no "new" columns can be added to the final result of the UNION; in a JOIN, new columns can be added to the result of the JOIN.

- In a UNION, the number of columns in the result set has to be the same as the number of columns in the sets being unioned; in a JOIN, the number of columns in the result set may vary.

A UNION Used to Implement a Full Outer Join

In Chapter 4, you read that the outer join adds rows to the result set that would otherwise be dropped from an inner join of both tables due to the join condition. Remember that an inner join (also known as an equi-join, ordinary join or regular join) combines two tables by finding common values on some column(s) common to the two tables. In an outer join, we are saying, "we want all the rows from one table and only the joined rows from the other." In SQL Server 2005, the outer joins are in two classes—left and right, depending on how the query is written. A full outer join means that we want all rows from both tables being joined, and "fill in those rows where a join does not produce a result with nulls." In SQL Server 2005, a UNION can also be used to achieve this full outer join.

 Some SQL languages do not directly support the full outer join, but SQL Server 2005 directly supports it.

In SQL Server 2005, you can create a full outer join by writing a union of the left outer join and the right outer join, like this:

```
SELECT with right outer join
UNION
SELECT with left outer join
```

The order of the left outer join and the right outer join does not matter and can be reversed. To illustrate the workings of the UNION version of the full outer join, let us again use the table called Instructor, created earlier in this chapter:

```
iname                teaches
-------------------- --------------------
Richard              COSC
Subhash              MATH
Tapan                BIOCHEM
```

If we want to get a listing of all instructors and the names of the departments for which they teach (which will be done by a regular equi-join) plus a listing of the rest of the instructors, regardless of whether they belong to a department, plus a listing of the rest of the departments, regardless of whether they have instructors, we would write the following query to achieve the full outer join effect with a UNION:

```
SELECT *
FROM Department_to_major AS d LEFT JOIN Instructor AS I
ON d.dcode=i.teaches
    UNION
SELECT *
FROM Department_to_major AS d RIGHT JOIN Instructor AS I
ON d.dcode=i.teaches
```

This query produces the following output (9 rows):

```
Dcode DNAME                 iname                teaches
----- -------------------- -------------------- --------------------
NULL  NULL                 Tapan                BIOCHEM
ACCT  Accounting           NULL                 NULL
ART   Art                  NULL                 NULL
CHEM  Chemistry            NULL                 NULL
COSC  Computer Science     Richard              COSC
ENGL  English              NULL                 NULL
MATH  Mathematics          Subhash              MATH
POLY  Political Science    NULL                 NULL
UNKN                       NULL                 NULL

(9 row(s) affected)
```

First, the LEFT JOIN was done, outer joining the department_to_major table and the Instructor table (so that all the rows of the department_to_major table were added to the result set). Then, a RIGHT JOIN was done, again joining the department_to_major table to the Instructor table (but this time all the rows of the Instructor table were added to the result set). Finally, a UNION of the two results sets was performed, creating the effect of a full outer join (where the rows from both the tables were added back after the join).

Summary

In this chapter, we discussed the set operators available in SQL Server 2005. After reading this chapter, you should have an appreciation of how and when to use UNIONs and INTERSECTs, and how to handle the difference problem, although SQL Server 2005 does not have an explicit MINUS operator. Oftentimes queries can be approached in more than one way. In several places, we also showed how the same queries could also be approached without the use of set operators.

Review Questions

1. What are the major differences between the UNION operation and the JOIN operation?

2. What is the major difference between the UNION and the UNION ALL?

3. What major set operator does SQL Server 2005 not have? How can these problems be resolved?

4. What does union compatibility mean?

5. What data types are union-compatible?

6. What is the maximum number of rows that can result from a UNION of two tables—one with 5 rows and the other with 6 rows?

7. What is the maximum number of rows that can result from a JOIN of two tables—one with 5 rows and the other with 6 rows?

8. How can a UNION be used to implement an outer join? Explain.

9. Does SQL Server 2005 support the MINUS operation? How can this be resolved? Give examples.

10. What is a full outer join? Does SQL Server 2005 directly support a full outer join?

11. Do you need the same number of columns to perform a union?

12. Do you need the same data types to perform a union?

13. Do you need the same number of columns to perform a join?

14. From the examples given in the chapter, what does the UNION JOIN appear to do?

15. If a VARCHAR column were unioned with a CHAR column, what would the resulting column be? (Hint: refer to the "Data Type Precedence" section in Chapter 6.)

16. What does set compatibility mean?

17. What is the maximum number of rows that can result from a INTERSECT of two tables—one with 5 rows and the other with 6 rows?

18. Do you need the same number of columns to perform an INTERSECT operation?

19. Do you need the same data types to perform an INTERSECT operation?

Exercises

Unless specified otherwise, use the Student_course database to answer the following questions. Also, use appropriate column headings when displaying your output.

1. In this exercise, you'll test the UNION statement. Having seen how the UNION statement works, demonstrate some permutations to see what will work "legally" and what won't. First, create two tables as follows:

Table 1	
A	B
x1	y1
r1	s1

Table 2			
A	B	C	D
x2	y2	z2	w2
r2	s2	t2	u2

Make the type of As and Bs CHAR(2). Let the type of C in Table2 be VARCHAR(2) and D in Table2 be VARCHAR(3).

Try the following statements and note the results:

```
SELECT * FROM Table1 UNION SELECT * FROM Table2
SELECT * FROM Table1 UNION SELECT A,B FROM Table2
SELECT * FROM Table1 UNION SELECT B,A FROM Table1
SELECT * FROM Table1 UNION SELECT A,C FROM Table2
SELECT * FROM Table1 UNION SELECT A,D FROM Table2
CREATE VIEW viewx AS
SELECT A,B
FROM Table2
SELECT *
FROM Table1
   UNION
SELECT *
FROM viewx
```

Feel free to experiment with any other combinations that you deem appropriate or that you wonder about.

2. Create and print the result of a query that generates the names, class, and course numbers of students who have earned Bs in computer science courses. Store this query as Q7_2. Then, revise Q7_2 to delete from the result set those students who are sophomores (class = 2). Use NOT..IN to select those students who are sophomores.

3. Find the names, grades, and course numbers of students who have earned As in computer science or math courses. Join the Section and Grade_report tables (be careful to not create the Cartesian product). Then, UNION the set of "course numbers COSC% and A" with the set of "course number MATH% and A."

   Hint: Start with the query to get names, grades, and course numbers for COSC% and A, and then turn this into a view. Do the same for MATH% and A, and then execute the UNION statement as follows (using your view names):

```
SELECT *
FROM view1a
   UNION
SELECT *
FROM view1b
```

4. Find the names and majors of students who have made a C in any course. Make the "who have made a C in any course" a subquery for which you use IN.

5. A less-obvious example of a difference query is to find a difference that is not based on simple, easy-to-get sets. Suppose that set A is the set of student names who have made As and Bs in computer science (COSC) courses. Suppose further that set B is the set of students who have taken math courses (regardless of what grade they earned).

   Then, set A minus set B would contain names of students who have made As or Bs in computer science courses, less those who have taken math courses. Similarly, set B minus set A would be the set of students who took math courses, less those who took COSC courses and made an A or a B in some COSC course.

Build these queries into set difference queries as views based on student numbers and execute them, as follows:

  a. Write a query that gives the student number, name, course, and grade for each set. Save each query as Q7_5a and Q7_5b.

  b. Reconstruct each query into a view of just student numbers, verify that it works, and then create views to create set A and set B. Verify that you have the same number of tuples in set A as you have in Q7_5a, and the same number of tuples in set B as you have in Q7_5b.

  c. Display the student numbers of students in each set difference—show (set A minus set B) and (set B minus set A). Look at the original queries, Q7_5a and Q7_5b, to verify your result.

6. Create two tables, T1 and T2, that contain a name and a salary column. In the first table, order the columns by name, and then by salary. In the second table, order the columns by salary, and then by name. Use the same data types for each - VARCHAR(20), NUMBER, for example. Populate the tables with two tuples each.

7. Can you UNION the two tables in the preceding question with the following query?

```
SELECT *
FROM T1
  UNION
SELECT *
FROM T2
```

Why or why not? If not, can you force the union of the two tables? Illustrate how. Be sure to DROP the tables when you are finished.

8. Using the Instructor table you created in this chapter (as well as the tables supplied in the Student_course database), find the following (use the UNION or INTERSECT operator if you feel it is appropriate):

  a. All departments that have instructors. First do this using an IN predicate, and then using a regular join.

  b. Find all students who are also instructors.

  c. Find all instructors who are not students.

  d. Find all students who are not instructors.

  e. Find all students as well as instructors.

9. Using the Student table, find all the students who major in math and are seniors. Hint: Use the INTERSECT operator for this.

Optional Exercise

1. *De Morgan's Theorem.* In the binary case, DeMorgan's Theorem tells us that [not(A and B)] = [not(A) or not(B)]. For example, suppose that A is the set of rows where students are juniors and B is the set of rows where students are females. And suppose that you were asked the question, "Find the students who are not (female and juniors)." Clearly this is the set [not(A and B)]. You can answer this question by finding the set of students who are not juniors [not(A)] and then or-ing this with the set of students who are not females [not(B)]. At times it is easier to find one or the other of the results via a query, and the point here is that the two methods of finding a result is equivalent.

   Question: Find the result set for all sections that are offered in building 13 and call this set A. Find the result set for all sections that are offered in building 36 and call this set B. Construct the SQL to find the following result sets:

   a. The result of set A OR set B (use WHERE building = 13 or building = 36).

   b. The result of the complement of (a): NOT(set A OR set B).

   c. The result of NOT(set A) AND NOT(set B).

   d. The count of all rows in the Section table.

   Is the count in d = a + b? Is the result of c the same as the result of b? Explain why or why not in each case (Hint: You may apply the De Morgan's Theorem which states that NOT(set A or set B) = NOT(set A) and NOT(set b).

CHAPTER 8

Joins Versus Subqueries

The purpose of this chapter is to demonstrate the use of subqueries. Subqueries may often be used as alternatives to joins. There are two main issues to consider when choosing between subqueries and joins (and other techniques for combining tables). First, you must consider how to get the information. By understanding the limitations of joins and subqueries (as well as sets and other table-combining techniques), you will increase your choices as to how to get information from the database. Second, you must also consider performance. You usually a have choice of how to get multi-table information—joins, sets, subqueries, views, and so forth. In larger databases, you need to be flexible and consider other choices if a query performs poorly and/or if the query is done often.

 Although set operations logically are also viable choices for retrieving data from multiple tables, set operations (discussed in Chapter 7) are less common and usually less efficient than joins and subqueries.

Subquery with an IN Predicate

Suppose that a query requests a list of names and numbers of students (which are in the Student table in our Student_course database) who have made As or Bs in any course (grades are in the Grade_report table in our Student_course database). You can complete this query as either a subquery or a join. As a subquery with an IN predicate, it will take the following form:

```
SELECT Student.sname, Student.stno
FROM   Student
WHERE  "link to Grade_report"
   IN  ("link to Student" - subquery involving Grade_report)
```

In this format, the part of the query that contains:

```
SELECT Student.sname, Student.stno
FROM   Student
WHERE  "link to Grade_report"
```

is said to be the *outer query*. The part of the query that contains:

```
("link to Student" - subquery involving Grade_report)
```

is the *inner query*.

The link between the Student table and the Grade_report table is the student number. In the Student table, the appropriate column is stno, and in the Grade_report table, it is student_number. When linking the tables in the subquery with an IN predicate, the linking columns are all that can be mentioned in the WHERE..IN and in the result set of the subquery. Thus, the statement with a subquery is as follows:

```
SELECT Student.sname, Student.stno
FROM    Student
WHERE   Student.stno
   IN (SELECT   gr.student_number
       FROM     Grade_report gr
       WHERE    gr.grade = 'B' OR gr.grade = 'A')
ORDER BY Student.stno
```

 The part of the query *before* the IN is often called the *outer query*. The part of the query *after* the IN is called the *inner query*.

This query produces the following output (31 rows):

sname	stno
Lineas	2
Mary	3
Zelda	5
Ken	6
Mario	7
Brenda	8
Richard	10
Kelly	13
Lujack	14
Reva	15
Harley	19
Donald	20
Chris	24
Lynette	34
Susan	49
Hillary	121
Phoebe	122
Holly	123
Sadie	125
Jessica	126
Steve	127
Cedric	129
George	132
Jerry	142
Cramer	143

```
Fraiser            144
Francis            146
Smithly            147
Sebastian          148
Lindsay            155
Stephanie          157

(31 row(s) affected)
```

The Subquery as a Join

An alternative way to perform the preceding query would be to use a join instead of a subquery, as follows:

```
SELECT  Student.sname, Student.stno
FROM    Student, Grade_report gr
WHERE   Student.stno = gr.student_number
AND        (gr.grade = 'B' OR gr.grade = 'A')
```

This query produces 67 rows of output (of which we show the first 15 rows here):

```
sname      stno
---------  ------
Lineas     2
Lineas     2
Lineas     2
Lineas     2
Mary       3
Mary       3
Mary       3
Mary       3
Mary       3
Mary       3
Brenda     8
Brenda     8
Brenda     8
Richard    10
Kelly      13
   .
   .
   .

(67 row(s) affected)
```

Now, the question is why the join has 67 rows of output instead of 31 rows of output (produced by the subquery).

When the join version is used to combine tables, any Student-Grade_report row (tuple) that has equal student numbers and a grade of A or B is selected. Thus, you should expect many duplicate names in the output. To get the result without duplicates, add the qualifier DISTINCT to the join query as follows:

```
SELECT DISTINCT Student.sname, Student.stno
FROM     Student, Grade_report AS gr
WHERE    Student.stno = gr.student_number
AND      (gr.grade = 'B' OR gr.grade = 'A')
```

This query produces the following output (31 rows):

```
sname                  stno
-------------------- ------
Lineas                 2
Mary                   3
Zelda                  5
Ken                    6
Mario                  7
Brenda                 8
Richard                10
Kelly                  13
Lujack                 14
Reva                   15
Harley                 19
Donald                 20
Chris                  24
Lynette                34
Susan                  49
Hillary                121
Phoebe                 122
Holly                  123
Sadie                  125
Jessica                126
Steve                  127
Cedric                 129
George                 132
Jerry                  142
Cramer                 143
Fraiser                144
Francis                146
Smithly                147
Sebastian              148
Lindsay                155
Stephanie              157

(31 row(s) affected)
```

When DISTINCT is used, internal sorting is performed before the result set is displayed. Such internal sorting may decrease response time for a query.

In the subquery version of the query, duplication of names does not occur in the output. This is so because you are setting up a set (the subquery) from which you will choose names—a given name is either in the subquery set or it is not. Remember that the student number (stno) is unique in the Student table.

Also, the question of which is more efficient, the join or the subquery, depends on which SQL language and database you are using. Without using extra tools, one way to test alternatives is to try the queries on the data or a subset of the data. Database systems such as SQL Server 2005 provide ways (tools) to find out how queries are executed.

When the Join Cannot Be Turned into a Subquery

When a column from a table needs to be in the result set, that table has to be in the outer query. If two tables are being used, and if columns from both tables have to be in the result set, a join is necessary. This type of join cannot be turned into a subquery, because information from *both* tables has to be in the result set. But if the result set does not need the columns from more than one table, then the join can be turned into a subquery. The other tables can be included such that the filtering conditions can be in the subquery (or inner query), and the table that has the needed result set columns is in the outer query.

Consider this example. Our original query (the first query discussed in this chapter), requested the list of names and student numbers of students who made As or Bs in any course. Student names and numbers are both in the Student table; the Grade_report table is needed only as a filter, so we could write this as a subquery, and also turn it into a join.

Now, if this original query had asked for output from the Grade_report table also, such as, "list the names, numbers, *and* grades of all students who have made As or Bs," the query would be asking for information from both the Student and Grade_report tables. In this case, you would have to join the two tables to get the information; you could not just query the Grade_report table, because that table has no names in it. Similarly, the Student table contains no grades. So you would not be able to write this as a subquery. Refer again to the original query example:

```
SELECT Student.sname, Student.stno
FROM    Student
WHERE   Student.stno
   IN (SELECT   gr.student_number
        FROM     Grade_report gr
        WHERE    gr.grade = 'B' OR  gr.grade = 'A')
ORDER BY Student.stno
```

This query asks for information only from the Student table (student names and numbers). Although the query used the Grade_report table, nothing from the Grade_report table was in the outer result set. Again, the Grade_report table is needed only as a filter (to get the student numbers of those who have As and Bs); hence we were able to write this as a subquery.

The following join query asks for information from both the Student and Grade_report tables (a result set that lists both names and grades of all students who have made As or Bs in any course):

```
SELECT DISTINCT Student.sname, gr.grade
FROM    Student, Grade_report gr
WHERE   Student.stno = gr.student_number
AND     (gr.grade = 'B' OR gr.grade = 'A')
```

This query produces 41 rows of output (of which we show the first 25 rows here):

```
sname                grade
-------------------- -----
Brenda               A
Brenda               B
Cedric               A
Cedric               B
Chris                B
Cramer               B
Donald               A
Fraiser              B
Francis              B
George               B
Harley               B
Hillary              B
Holly                A
Holly                B
Jerry                A
Jessica              A
Jessica              B
Kelly                B
Ken                  B
Lindsay              B
Lineas               A
Lineas               B
Lujack               A
Lujack               B
Lynette              A
   .
   .
   .

(41 row(s) affected)
```

As this example demonstrates, if information from a table is needed in a result set, then that table cannot be buried in a subquery—it must be in the outer query.

More Examples Involving Joins and IN

The purpose of this section is to further demonstrate several queries that will and will not allow the use of the subquery. As we have discussed, some joins can be expressed as subqueries whereas others cannot. Further, all subqueries with the IN predicate can be re-formed as a join. Whether you can use a subquery depends on the final, outer result set. Some more examples will help clarify this point.

Example 1

Find the names of all the departments that offer a course with INTRO in the title. To formulate our query, we need to use the Course table (to find the course names) and the Department_to_major table (to find the names of the departments).

Begin by viewing the column names in the tables.

 If you have forgotten how to view the column names of a table, refer to Figure 1-21.

Figure 8-1 gives the column names in the Course table:

```
☐ ▦ dbo.Course
   ☐ ▣ Columns
        ▤ COURSE_NAME (nvarchar(20), null)
        🔑 COURSE_NUMBER (PK, nvarchar(8), not null)
        ▤ CREDIT_HOURS (smallint, null)
        ▤ OFFERING_DEPT (nvarchar(4), null)
```

Figure 8-1. Column names of the Course table

Figure 8-2 gives the column names of the Department_to_major table:

```
☐ ▦ dbo.Department_to_major
   ☐ ▣ Columns
        🔑 Dcode (PK, nvarchar(4), not null)
        ▤ DNAME (nvarchar(20), null)
```

Figure 8-2. Column names of the Department_to_major table

Our query needs a department name (dname) from the Department_to_major table. We also need course information from the Course table, because our query depends on a course name; however, no course information appears in the result set. We did not ask for the names of the courses, just that they have INTRO in the title. The result set asks only for department names. We can find this result by using a subquery, with the Department_to_major table as the outer query, because all the information in the result set is contained in the outer query. The query would be as follows:

```
SELECT  d2m.dname
FROM    Department_to_major d2m
WHERE   d2m.dcode
    IN (SELECT      Course.offering_dept
        FROM        Course
        WHERE       Course.course_name LIKE '%INTRO%')
```

which produces the following output:

```
dname
--------------------
Computer Science
Political Science
Chemistry

(3 row(s) affected)
```

Example 2

List the student name, student major code, and section identifier of students who earned Cs in courses taught by Professor Hermano (HERMANO).

First, we determine which tables are needed. We want to find the student name and major code, and a section identifier for courses taken, so we need the Student and Grade_report tables for the result set. We will need to use the Section table for a filter. The instructor does not appear in the result set. Again, it is a good idea to look at the column names in each of the tables first.

Figure 8-3 gives the column names of the Student table.

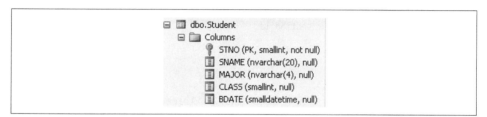

Figure 8-3. Columns names of the Student table

Figure 8-4 gives the column names of the Grade_report table.

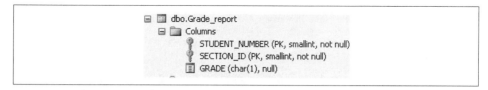

Figure 8-4. Column names of the Grade_report table

Figure 8-5 gives the column names of the Section table.

After we have determined which tables we need, we have to determine where the columns that are needed in the result set are located. We need to get the names and major codes from the Student table, and the section identifiers from the Grade_report table. So the result set part of the query (the outer query) must contain the Student and Grade_report tables. The rest of the query can contain any other tables that we

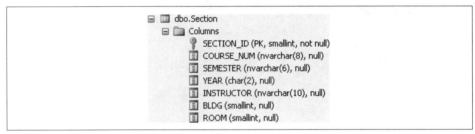

Figure 8-5. Column names of the Section table

need to locate the columns. The resulting query may look like this (a combination of a join and a subquery):

```
SELECT    s.sname, s.major, g.section_id
FROM      Student s, Grade_report g
WHERE     g.student_number = s.stno
AND           g.grade = 'C'
AND           g.section_id IN
   (SELECT t.section_id
    FROM    Section t
    WHERE   t.instructor LIKE 'HERMANO')
```

which produces the following output:

```
sname                   major section_id
--------------------    ----- ----------
Richard                 ENGL  126

(1 row(s) affected)
```

The previous query could also have been done as a three-table join, as follows:

```
SELECT  s.sname, s.major, t.section_id
FROM    Student s, Grade_report g, Section t
WHERE   s.stno = g.student_number
AND         g.section_id =t.section_id
AND         g.grade='C'
AND         t.instructor LIKE 'HERMANO'
```

Example 3

List the name and major code of students who earned Cs in courses taught by Professor King (KING).

Again, we first need to determine which tables are needed. We need to collect student names and major codes in the result set and we need the Grade_report and Section tables for filtering conditions. (You viewed the columns available in each of these tables in the preceding example.) Next, we need to determine where the columns that are needed in the result set are located. In this example, they are all in the Student table.

Because the only table needed in the outer query is the Student table, we can structure the query in any of the following ways:

1. Student join Grade_report join Section *[three-table join]*
2. Student subquery (Grade_report join Section) *[Student outer, join in subquery]*
3. Student join Grade_report subquery (Section) *[similar to Example 2 but with a different result set]*
4. Student (subquery Grade_report (subquery Section)) *[a three-level subquery]*

Each of these queries produces the same result set with different efficiencies. We'll study them further in the exercises at the end of the chapter.

Using Subqueries with Operators

In this section, we look at examples that demonstrate the use of subqueries with comparison operators. These examples are based on the Room table, which has the following data:

```
BLDG   ROOM   CAPACITY  OHEAD
-----  -----  --------  -----
13     101    85        Y
36     123    35        N
58     114    60        NULL
79     179    35        Y
79     174    22        Y
58     112    40        NULL
36     122    25        N
36     121    25        N
36     120    25        N
58     110    NULL      Y

(10 row(s) affected)
```

In previous chapters, you have seen SELECTs with conditions like the following:

```
SELECT *
FROM   Room
WHERE  capacity = 25
```

In this example, 25 is a constant and = is a comparison operator. The constant can be replaced by a subquery, and the operator can be any of the comparison operators (=, <>, <, >, <=, or >=). For example, we could devise a query to tell us which classrooms have a below-average capacity by computing the average in a subquery and using a comparison operator, like this:

```
SELECT *
FROM   Room
WHERE  capacity <
  (SELECT AVG(capacity)
   FROM   Room)
```

This query produces the following six rows of output, showing six rooms with below-average capacity:

```
BLDG    ROOM    CAPACITY OHEAD
------  ------  -------- -----
36      120     25       N
36      121     25       N
36      122     25       N
36      123     35       N
79      174     22       Y
79      179     35       Y
```

```
Warning: Null value is eliminated by an aggregate or other SET operation.
```

```
(6 row(s) affected)
```

The only problem with using subqueries in this fashion is that *the subquery must return only one row*. If an aggregate function is applied to a table in the subquery in this fashion, you will always get only one row—even if there is a WHERE clause that excludes all rows, the subquery returns one row with a null value. For example, if we were to change the preceding query to the following and force multiple rows in the subquery,

```
SELECT *
FROM    Room
WHERE   capacity <
   (SELECT AVG(capacity)
    FROM    Room
    WHERE   bldg = 99)
```

we would get:

```
BLDG    ROOM    CAPACITY OHEAD
------  ------  -------- -----
```

```
(0 row(s) affected)
```

We get no rows selected because there is no bldg = 99. If we were to change the query to the following:

```
SELECT *
FROM    Room
WHERE   bldg =
    (SELECT  bldg
     FROM     Room
     WHERE    capacity > 10)
```

we would get the following error message:

```
BLDG    ROOM    CAPACITY OHEAD
------  ------  -------- -----
Msg 512, Level 16, State 1, Line 1
Subquery returned more than 1 value. This is not permitted when the subquery follows
=, !=, <, <= , >, >= or when the subquery is used as an expression.
```

When using comparison operators, only single values are acceptable from the sub-query. Again, to ensure that we get only one row in the subquery and hence a workable query, we can use an aggregate with no GROUP BY or HAVING (to be discussed in Chapter 9).

 As with all queries, the caveat to audit the result is always applicable.

Summary

In this chapter, we have introduced the subquery. We have given examples of situations in which it would be good to use subqueries, cases where subqueries could be turned into joins, and cases where they cannot be turned into joins. After reading this chapter, you should have a better appreciation for subqueries and joins.

Review Questions

1. What is a subquery?

2. Which part of the query/subquery is considered the inner query, and which part is considered the outer query?

3. Can a subquery always be done as a join? Why or why not?

4. When writing a query that will have a subquery, how do you determine which table/tables will go in the outer query?

5. Which predicate can usually be reformulated into a join?

6. When using operators, are many values acceptable from a result of a subquery?

7. What can you do to insure a working subquery?

Exercises

Unless specified otherwise, use the Student_course database to answer the following questions. Also, use appropriate column headings when displaying your output.

Use the techniques from this chapter to construct and execute the following queries:

1. Find the student numbers of students who have earned As or Bs in courses taught in the fall semester. Do this in two ways: first using a subquery, and then using a join.

2. Find all students who took a course offered by the Accounting department. List the student name and student number, the course name, and the grade in that course. (Hint: Begin with Department_to_major and use an appropriate WHERE.) Note that this task cannot be done with a multilevel subquery. Why?

3. For every students who is a sophomore (class = 2), find the name and the name of the department that includes the student's major.

4. Find the names of the departments that offer courses at the junior or senior levels (either one) but not at the freshman level. The course level is the first digit after the prefix; for example, AAAA3yyy is a junior course, and so on.

   Hint: Begin by creating the outer query—the names of departments that offer courses at the junior or senior levels. Save this query as q8_4. Then, construct the subquery—a list of departments that offer courses at the freshman level. Save the subquery as a view. Examine both lists of departments. When you have the outer query and the subquery results, recall the original query that you saved (q8_4) and add the subquery. Check your result with the department lists you just generated. Redo the last part of the experiment with your view. You should get the same result.

5. Find the names of courses that are prerequisites for other courses. List the course number and name, and the number and name of the prerequisite.

6. List the names of instructors who teach courses that have other than three-hour credits. Do the problem in two ways: once with IN and once with NOT..IN.

7. Create a table called Secretary with the columns dcode (of data type CHAR(4)) for department code and name (of data type VARCHAR(20)) for the secretary name. Populate the table as follows:

Secretary	
dCode	name
ACCT	Beryl
COSC	Kaitlyn
ENGL	David
HIST	Christina
BENG	Fred
HINDI	Chloe

   a. Create a query that lists the names of departments that have secretaries (use IN and the Secretary table in a subquery with the Department_to_major table in the outer query). Save this query as q8_7a.

   b. Create a query that lists the names of departments (using the Department_to_major table) that do not have secretaries (use NOT IN). Save this query as q8_7b.

   c. Add one more row to the Secretary table that contains <null,'Brenda'> (which you could see, for example, in a situation in which you have hired Brenda but have not yet assigned her to a department).

d. Recall q8_7a and rerun it. Recall q87_b and rerun it.

The behavior of NOT..IN when nulls exist may surprise you. If nulls may exist in the subquery, then NOT..IN either should not be used (Chapter 10 shows how to use another predicate, NOT EXISTS, which is a workaround to this problem), or should include AND whatever IS NOT NULL. If you use NOT.. IN in a subquery, you must either ensure that nulls will not occur in the subquery or use some other predicate (such as NOT EXISTS). Perhaps the best advice is to avoid NOT..IN unless you cannot figure out another way to solve a problem.

e. To see a correct answer, add the phrase WHERE dcode IS NOT NULL to the subquery in the IN and NOT..IN cases and run them again.

Do *not* delete the Secretary table, because we will revisit this problem in Chapter 10.

8. Devise a list of course names that are offered in the fall semester in rooms where the capacity is equal to or above the average room size.

CHAPTER 9

Aggregation and GROUP BY

The SQL construction GROUP BY is a SELECT statement clause that is designed to be used in conjunction with aggregation (discussed in Chapter 5) to group data of similar types. An aggregate function is one that extracts information—such as a COUNT of rows or an average, minimum, or maximum—by operating on multiple rows. We first discuss using GROUP BY on one column, and then on two columns. Then, we look at how to use GROUP BY in conjunction with the ORDER BY, HAVING, and WHERE clauses. Finally, we discuss aggregation with subqueries and complexities that nulls present in aggregate functions and other queries. As we introduce the GROUP BY and HAVING, and expand on the ORDER BY (which has been introduced earlier) in this chapter, we first present a SELECT in modified BNF showing the GROUP BY, HAVING and ORDER BY, before we start the rest of the discussion.

A SELECT in Modified BNF

BNF, short for *Backus Naur Form*, is used to describe syntax rules. A general form (in modified BNF) of the SELECT statement for SQL Server, with the FROM, WHERE, GROUP BY, HAVING and ORDER BY would be:

```
SELECT result-set
[FROM Tables]
[WHERE row-filter]
[GROUP BY column names]
[HAVING after-filter on groups]
[ORDER BY column names]
```

The [..] notation means that the contained code is optional.

The GROUP BY Clause

GROUP BY is used in conjunction with aggregate functions to group data on the basis of the same values in a column. GROUP BY returns one row for each *value* of the column(s) that is grouped. You can use GROUP BY to group by one column or multiple columns.

As an example of how to group by one column, the following statement shows how you can use the aggregate COUNT to extract the number of class groups (number of students in each class) from the Student table:

```
SELECT       class, COUNT(*) AS [count]
FROM         Student
GROUP BY  class
```

This query produces the following five rows of output, which is grouped by one column, class:

```
class count
----- -----------
NULL  10
1     11
2     10
3     7
4     10

(5 row(s) affected)
```

This type of statement gives you a new way to retrieve and organize aggregate data. Other aggregate functions would have a similar syntax.

 You have to group by at least the attributes/expressions you are aggregating.

If a GROUP BY clause contains a two-column specification, the result is aggregated and grouped by two columns. For example, the following is COUNT of class and major from the Student table:

```
SELECT       class, major, COUNT(*)  AS [count]
FROM         Student
GROUP BY  class, major
```

This query produces the following output (24 rows), which is grouped by class within major:

```
class major    count
----- -----    -----------
NULL  NULL     3
2     ACCT     1
4     ACCT     4
3     ART      1
3     CHEM     1
4     CHEM     1
NULL  COSC     1
1     COSC     4
2     COSC     2
4     COSC     3
NULL  ENGL     1
1     ENGL     3
```

```
2      ENGL    2
3      ENGL    4
NULL   MATH    2
2      MATH    3
3      MATH    1
4      MATH    1
NULL   POLY    2
1      POLY    3
2      POLY    2
4      POLY    1
NULL   UNKN    1
1      UNKN    1

(24 row(s) affected)
```

The sequence of the columns in a GROUP BY clause has the effect of ordering the output. If we change the order of the GROUP BY like this:

```
SELECT      class, major, COUNT(*)  AS [count]
FROM        Student
GROUP BY major, class
```

our result will look like this:

```
class major count
----- ----- -----------
NULL  NULL  3
NULL  COSC  1
NULL  ENGL  1
NULL  MATH  2
NULL  POLY  2
NULL  UNKN  1
1     COSC  4
1     ENGL  3
1     POLY  3
1     UNKN  1
2     ACCT  1
2     COSC  2
2     ENGL  2
2     MATH  3
2     POLY  2
3     ART   1
3     CHEM  1
3     ENGL  4
3     MATH  1
4     ACCT  4
4     CHEM  1
4     COSC  3
4     MATH  1
4     POLY  1

(24 row(s) affected)
```

Here the output is grouped by major within class.

A statement like the following will cause a syntax error, because it says that you are to count both class and major, but GROUP BY class only:

```
SELECT      class, major, COUNT(*)
FROM        Student
GROUP BY  class
```

This query results in the following error message:

```
Msg 8120, Level 16, State 1, Line 1
Column 'Student.MAJOR' is invalid in the select list because it is not contained in
either an aggregate function or the GROUP BY clause.
```

To be syntactically and logically correct, you must have all the non aggregate columns of the result set in the GROUP BY clause. For example, let's take a look at the data of Table 9-1.

Table 9-1. Room table

BLDG	ROOM	CAPACITY	OHEAD
13	101	85	Y
36	123	35	N
58	114	60	NULL
79	179	35	Y
79	174	22	Y
58	112	40	NULL
36	122	25	N
36	121	25	N
36	120	25	N
58	110	NULL	Y

```
(10 row(s) affected)
```

The following query would be improper, because you must GROUP BY "ohead" to SUM capacities for each ohead value:

```
SELECT   ohead, SUM(capacity)
FROM     Room
```

 ohead, an attribute in the Room table (in our Student_Course database), is short for rooms with overhead projectors.

This query would produce an error message similar to what we saw previously:

```
Msg 8120, Level 16, State 1, Line 1
Column 'Room.OHEAD' is invalid in the select list because it is not contained in
either an aggregate function or the GROUP BY clause.
```

If you SELECT columns *and* use an aggregate function, you must GROUP BY the non aggregate attributes. The correct version of the last statement is as follows:

```
SELECT      ohead, SUM(capacity) AS [sum]
FROM        Room
GROUP BY  ohead
```

which produces the following three rows of output:

```
ohead sum
----- -----------
NULL  100
N     110
Y     142

Warning: Null value is eliminated by an aggregate or other SET operation.

(3 row(s) affected)
```

This is the sum of room capacities for rooms that have no overhead projectors (N), rooms that have overhead projectors (Y), and rooms in which the overhead projector capacity is unknown (null).

Observe that in the Room table, some rooms have null values for ohead, and the null rows are summed and grouped along with the non-null rows.

GROUP BY and ORDER BY

To enhance the display of a GROUP BY clause, you can combine it with an ORDER BY clause. Consider the following example:

```
SELECT      class, major, COUNT(*) AS [count]
FROM        Student
GROUP BY class, major
```

The output for this query was presented earlier in the chapter.

This result set can also be ordered by any other column from the result set using the ORDER BY. For instance, the following example orders the output in descending order by COUNT(*):

```
SELECT class, major, COUNT(*)  AS [count]
FROM    Student
GROUP BY class, major
ORDER BY COUNT(*) DESC
```

This query produces the following output (24 rows):

```
class  major count
------ ----- -----------
4      ACCT  4
1      COSC  4
3      ENGL  4
2      MATH  3
4      COSC  3
1      ENGL  3
NULL   NULL  3
1      POLY  3
2      POLY  2
```

```
NULL   POLY   2
2      COSC   2
2      ENGL   2
NULL   MATH   2
3      MATH   1
4      MATH   1
NULL   ENGL   1
2      ACCT   1
3      ART    1
3      CHEM   1
4      CHEM   1
NULL   COSC   1
4      POLY   1
NULL   UNKN   1
1      UNKN   1
```

(24 row(s) affected)

GROUP BY and DISTINCT

When a SELECT clause includes all the columns specified in a GROUP BY clause, the use of the DISTINCT function is unnecessary and inefficient, because the GROUP BY clause groups rows in such a way that the column(s) that are grouped will not have duplicate values.

The HAVING Clause

The GROUP BY and HAVING clauses are used together. The HAVING clause is used as a final filter (rather than as a conditional filter) on the aggregate column values in the result set of a SELECT statement. In other words, the query has to be grouped before the HAVING clause can be applied. For example, consider the following statement, which displays the count of students in various classes (classes of students = 1, 2, 3, 4, corresponding to freshman, sophomore, and so on):

```
SELECT      class, COUNT(*) AS [count]
FROM        Student
GROUP BY    class
```

This query produces the following output:

```
class count
----- -----------
NULL  10
1     11
2     10
3     7
4     10
```

(5 row(s) affected)

If you are interested only in classes that have more than a certain number of students in them, you could use the following statement:

```
SELECT      class, COUNT(*) AS [count]
FROM        Student
GROUP BY class
HAVING COUNT(*) > 9
```

which produces the following four rows of output:

```
class count
----- -----------
NULL  10
1     11
2     10
4     10

(4 row(s) affected)
```

HAVING and WHERE

Whereas HAVING is a final filter in a SELECT statement, the WHERE clause, which excludes rows from a result set, is a conditional filter. HAVING is used to filter based on aggregate values, WHERE cannot do that. Consider the following two queries:

```
SELECT      class, COUNT(*) AS [count]
FROM        Student
GROUP BY    class
HAVING      class = 3
```

```
SELECT      class, COUNT(*) AS [count]
FROM        Student
WHERE       class = 3
GROUP BY    class
```

Both queries produce the following output:

```
class count
----- -----------
3     7

(1 row(s) affected)
```

In a typical implementation, the first of these two queries is less efficient because the query engine has to complete the query before removing rows WHERE class = 3 from the result. In the second version, the rows WHERE class = 3 are removed before the grouping takes place. WHERE is not always a substitute for HAVING, but when it can be used instead of HAVING, it should be. Notice that in the example:

```
SELECT      class, COUNT(*) AS [count]
FROM        Student
GROUP BY class
HAVING COUNT(*) > 9
```

HAVING and WHERE are not interchangeable because the grouping has to take place before the HAVING could have an effect. You cannot know in advance what the counts for each class are until they are counted.

Consider the following query, its meaning, and the processing that is required to finalize the result set:

```
SELECT      class, major, COUNT(*) AS [count]
FROM        Student
WHERE       major = 'COSC'
GROUP BY    class, major
HAVING COUNT(*) > 2
```

This query produces the following output:

```
class major count
----- ----- -----------
1     COSC  4
4     COSC  3

(2 row(s) affected)
```

In this example, all computer science (COSC) majors (per the WHERE clause) will be grouped and COUNTed and then displayed only if COUNT(*) > 2. The query might erroneously be interpreted as "Group and count all COSC majors by class, but only if there are more than two in a class." This interpretation is wrong, because SQL applies the WHERE, then applies the GROUP BY, and, finally, filters with the HAVING criterion.

GROUP BY and HAVING: Aggregates of Aggregates

A "usual" GROUP BY has an aggregate and a column that are grouped like this:

```
SELECT      COUNT(stno) AS [count of student no], class
FROM        Student
GROUP BY class
```

This produces a result set of 5 rows of counts by class:

```
count of student no      class
-------------------      -----
10                       NULL
11                       1
10                       2
7                        3
10                       4

(5 row(s) affected)
```

Although you must have class or some other attribute in the GROUP BY, you do not have to have the class in the result set. Consider the following query, which generates the same numeric information as the previous query, but does not report the class in the result:

```
SELECT      COUNT(stno) AS [count of student no]
FROM        Student
GROUP BY class
```

This query produces the following five rows of output:

```
count of student no
-------------------
10
11
10
7
10

(5 row(s) affected)
```

This previous example may seem contradictory to the preceding discussion, but it is not. You must have all the non aggregate columns from the result set in the GROUP BY, but you do not have to have the columns in the result set that you are grouping. That example may prove useful when a grouped result is needed in a filter. For example, how would you find the class with the most students?

Aggregation and Grouping in SQL Server 2005

SQL Server 2005 will not allow you to handle aggregation and grouping by nesting aggregates. For example, suppose you want to find the class with the minimum number of students. You might try the following query:

```
SELECT MIN(COUNT(stno))
FROM Student
GROUP BY class
```

Though it may seem logical, this query will not work in SQL Server 2005. It will produce the following error message:

```
Msg 130, Level 15, State 1, Line 1
Cannot perform an aggregate function on an expression containing an aggregate or a
subquery.
```

The MIN function is an aggregate function, and aggregate functions operate on rows within tables. In this case, the query is asking MIN to operate on a table of counted classes that have not yet been calculated. The point is that SQL Server 2005 does not handle this mismatch of aggregation and grouping.

 This mismatch of aggregation and grouping can be handled by other SQL languages, such as Oracle.

To handle this mismatch of aggregation and grouping in SQL Server 2005, you can use derived structures such as temporary tables, inline views, or regular views (derived structures are covered in Chapter 6). Using either a temporary table or an inline view is the most logical way to solve this problem, so only these two choices are described here.

Aggregation and grouping handled with a global temporary table

This section shows how we can handle the mismatch of aggregation and grouping (described earlier) using a global temporary table.

The following steps describe how to use a global temporary table to find the class with the minimum number of students:

1. Display the counts of classes, grouped by class:

```
SELECT      COUNT(stno) AS [count of students]
FROM        Student
GROUP BY class
```

This query produces the following five rows of output:

```
count       class
----------- ------
10          NULL
11          1
10          2
7           3
10          4

(5 row(s) affected)
```

2. To find the minimum number of students in a class, count the students (you could use stno for student number) grouped by class, and put this result in ##Temp1 (a global temporary table)—shown by the first query following, and then find the minimum number of students in a class from the global temporary table, ##Temp1, with SELECT MIN(count) AS [MINIMUM COUNT] FROM ##Temp1, and then use this information in a subquery with a HAVING clause as follows: First type the query:

```
SELECT (COUNT([stno])) AS [count], class INTO ##Temp1
FROM Student
GROUP BY [class]
```

After executing the previous query, type:

```
SELECT COUNT(stno) AS [count of stno], class
FROM Student
GROUP BY class
HAVING COUNT(stno) =
(SELECT MIN(count) AS [Minimum count]
FROM ##Temp1)
```

This query produces the desired output (the class with the minimum number of students):

```
count of stno    class
------------     -----
7                3

(1 row(s) affected)
```

Aggregation and grouping handled with an inline view

As described in Chapter 6, you can put a query in the FROM clause of a SELECT statement to create an inline view. An inline view exists only during the execution of a query.

The following steps describe how to use an inline view to find the class with the minimum number of students:

1. Count the stno in the FROM clause of the SELECT statement as follows:

   ```
   SELECT "Min of Count" = MIN(c)
   FROM (SELECT c = COUNT(stno)
   FROM Student
   GROUP BY class) AS in_view
   ```

   Because SQL Server 2005 cannot directly find aggregates of aggregates, in the previous query, we give a name to the COUNT in the inline view, c, to temporarily store the aggregate result in the inline view, in_view. We then operate on the inline view as though it were a table and find the minimum value for c.

   The previous query produces the following output:

   ```
   Min of Count
   ------------
   7

   (1 row(s) affected)
   ```

2. To find out which class has the minimum count, you can write the final query using the previous query as a subquery with a HAVING clause in the outer part of the final query, as follows:

   ```
   SELECT class, "Count of Class" = COUNT(*)
   FROM Student
   GROUP BY class
   HAVING COUNT(*) =
   (SELECT MIN(c)
   FROM (SELECT COUNT(stno) AS [c]
   FROM Student
   GROUP BY class) AS in_view)
   ```

This query produces the desired output:

```
class    Count of Class
-----    --------------
3        7
```

(1 row(s) affected)

So, although SQL Server 2005 does not handle a mismatch of aggregation and HAVING, you can use your knowledge of temporary tables and inline views to work around the problem. This problem may also be solved using regular views. It is also noteworthy to see the process of query development in that some problems require using small queries and building from them to a final result.

 Once again, Chapter 6 covers the advantages and disadvantages of using each one of the derived structures.

Auditing in Subqueries

In this section, we consider a potential problem of using aggregation with subqueries. As with Cartesian products and joins, aggregation hides details and should always be audited. The two tables that follow will be used to illustrate this problem.

Table 9-2 is similar to the Grade_report table and contains a student section identifier (ssec), grades (gd), and student names (sname).

Table 9-2. GG table

```
ssec         gd    sname
-----------  ----  ------------
100          A     Brenda
110          B     Brenda
120          A     Brenda
200          A     Brenda
210          A     Brenda
220          B     Brenda
100          A     Richard
100          B     Doug
200          A     Richard
110          B     Morris
```

(10 row(s) affected)

 Tables 9-2 and 9-3 (GG and SS) have not been created for you. You have to create them (and insert the records shown) and then run the queries that follow.

Table 9-3 is similar to the Section table and contains a section identifier (sec) and an instructor name (iname).

Table 9-3. SS table

```
sec          iname
-----------  ------------
100          Jones
110          Smith
120          Jones
200          Adams
210          Jones

(5 row(s) affected)
```

Now suppose that you want to find out how many As each instructor awarded. You might start with a join of the GG and SS tables. A normal equi-join would be as follows:

```
SELECT *
FROM    GG, SS
WHERE   GG.ssec = SS.sec
```

This query would produce the following output (nine rows):

```
ssec         gd    sname         sec          iname
-----------  ----  ------------  -----------  ------------
100          A     Brenda        100          Jones
110          B     Brenda        110          Smith
120          A     Brenda        120          Jones
200          A     Brenda        200          Adams
210          A     Brenda        210          Jones
100          A     Richard       100          Jones
100          B     Doug          100          Jones
200          A     Richard       200          Adams
110          B     Morris        110          Smith

(9 row(s) affected)
```

In addition, the following query tells you that there are six As in the GG table:

```
SELECT COUNT(*) AS [Count of As]
FROM    GG
WHERE   gd = 'A'
```

giving:

```
Count of As
------------
6

(1 row(s) affected)
```

Now, if you want to find out which instructor gave the As, you would type this query:

```
SELECT  SS.iname
FROM    SS, GG
WHERE   SS.sec = GG.ssec
  AND   GG.gd = 'A'
```

You get the following six rows of output:

```
iname
------------
Jones
Jones
Adams
Jones
Jones
Adams

(6 row(s) affected)
```

Now, to find "how many" As each instructor gave, include a COUNT and GROUP BY as follows:

```
SELECT  SS.iname AS [iname], COUNT(*) AS [count]
FROM    SS, GG
WHERE   SS.sec = GG.ssec
  AND   GG.gd = 'A'
GROUP BY SS.iname
```

This query produces the following output:

```
iname        count
------------ -----------
Adams        2
Jones        4

(2 row(s) affected)
```

This shows that instructor Adams gave two As and instructor Jones gave four As. So far, so good. You should note that the final count/grouping has the same number of As as the original tables—the sum of the counts equals 6. Now, if you had devised a COUNT query with a sub-SELECT, you could get an answer that looked correct but in fact was not. For example, consider the following subquery version of the preceding join query:

```
SELECT  SS.iname AS [iname], COUNT(*) AS [count]
FROM    SS
WHERE   SS.sec IN
    (SELECT  GG.ssec
     FROM    GG
     WHERE   GG.gd = 'A')
GROUP BY SS.iname
```

This query produces the following output:

```
iname         count
-----------   -----------
Adams         1
Jones         3
```

(2 row(s) affected)

The reason that you get this output is that the second query is counting names of instructors and whether an A is present in the set of courses that this instructor teaches—not how many As are in the set, just whether any exist. The previous join query gives you all the As in the joined table and hence gives the correct answer to the question "How many As did each instructor award?" The sub-SELECTed query answers a different question: "In how many sections did the instructor award an A?"

The point in this example is that if you are SELECTing and COUNTing, it is a very good idea to *audit* your results often. If you want to COUNT the number of As by instructor, begin by first counting how many As there are. Then, you can construct a query to join and count. You should be able to total and reconcile the number of As to the number of As by instructor. The fact that the result makes sense is very useful in determining (albeit not proving) correctness.

Nulls Revisited

Nulls present a complication with regard to aggregate functions and other queries, because nulls are never equal to, less than, greater than, or not equal to any value. Using aggregates by themselves on columns that contain nulls will ignore the null values. For example, suppose you have the following Table 9-4 called Sal.

Table 9-4. Sal table

```
Name          salary
-----------   -----------
Joe           1000.00
Sam           2000.00
Bill          3000.00
Dave          NULL
```

(4 row(s) affected)

 Table 9-4 (Sal) has not been created for you. You have to create it to run the queries that follow.

Now consider the following query:

```
SELECT COUNT(*) AS [count], AVG(salary) AS [average], SUM(salary) AS [sum],
MAX(salary) AS [max], MIN(salary) AS [min]
FROM Sal
```

which produces the following output:

```
count       average     sum         max         min
----------- ----------- ----------- ----------- -----------
4           2000.00     6000.00     3000.00     1000.00
```

Warning: Null value is eliminated by an aggregate or other SET operation.

(1 row(s) affected)

COUNT (*) counts all the rows. But, the AVERAGE, SUM, MAX, and MIN functions ignore the nulled salary row in computing the aggregates. Counting columns also indicates the presence of nulls. If you count by using the following query:

```
SELECT COUNT(name) AS [Count of Names]
FROM   Sal
```

you get:

```
Count of Names
--------------
4
```

(1 row(s) affected)

If you use the "salary" column, you get:

```
SELECT COUNT(salary) AS [Count of salary]
FROM   Sal
```

which produces:

```
Count of salary
--------------
3
```

Warning: Null value is eliminated by an aggregate or other SET operation.

(1 row(s) affected)

This result indicates that you have a null salary. If you want to include nulls in the aggregate and have a rational value to substitute for a value that is not known (a big assumption), you can use the ISNULL function.

 The ISNULL function was introduced and discussed in Chapter 5.

ISNULL returns a value if the value is null. ISNULL has the form ISNULL(*column name, value if null*), which is used in place of the column name. For example, if you type the following:

```
SELECT name, ISNULL(salary, 0) AS [salary]
FROM   Sal
```

you get the following output:

```
name          salary
------------  -----------
Joe           1000.00
Sam           2000.00
Bill          3000.00
Dave          0.00

(4 row(s) affected)
```

If you type the following:

```
SELECT COUNT(ISNULL(salary,0)) AS [Count of salary]
FROM    Sal
```

you get:

```
Count of salary
---------------
4

(1 row(s) affected)
```

The "Count of salary" is now 4 instead of the 3 that you received earlier when the ISNULL function was not used.

If you type the following:

```
SELECT AVG(ISNULL(salary, 0)) AS [Average of salary]
FROM    Sal
```

you get:

```
Average of salary
-----------------
1500.00

(1 row(s) affected)
```

The "Average of salary" is now 1500.00, instead of the 2000.00 that you had received earlier because the zero value for the null was used in the calculation. What seems almost contradictory to these examples is that when grouping is added to the query, nulls in the grouped column are included in the result set. So, if the Sal table had another column like this:

```
Name          salary       job
------------  -----------  --------------------
Joe           1000.00      Programmer
Sam           2000.00      NULL
Bill          3000.00      Plumber
Dave          NULL         Programmer
```

And if you ran a query like this:

```
SELECT SUM(salary) AS [Sum of salary], job
FROM    Sal
GROUP BY job
```

You would get the following output:

```
Sum of salary Job
------------- --------------------
2000.00       NULL
3000.00       Plumber
1000.00       Programmer

Warning: Null value is eliminated by an aggregate or other SET operation.

(3 row(s) affected)
```

The aggregate will ignore values that are null, but grouping will compute a value for the nulled column value.

Summary

In this chapter we not only introduced the GROUP BY and HAVING clauses, but we also discussed what would and would not work and some efficiency issues. We discussed how aggregates and grouping can be handled in SQL Server 2005 and how it is always important to audit your queries and the results for correctness.

Review Questions

1. What do aggregate functions do?
2. How does the GROUP BY clause work?
3. What is the difference between a GROUP BY and ORDER BY?
4. What is the HAVING clause used for?
5. Can the WHERE clause always be considered a substitute for the HAVING clause? Why or why not?
6. Do functions of functions have to be handled in a special way in Server SQL 2005?
7. Will nulls in grouped columns be included in a result set?
8. How do aggregate functions treat nulls?
9. Does the sequence of the columns in a GROUP BY clause have an effect on the end result?
10. When would it not make sense to use the GROUP BY and DISTINCT functions together?
11. Is GROUP BY affected by nulls?
12. Which comes first in a SELECT statement, an ORDER BY or GROUP BY? Why?
13. The GROUP BY and _____ clauses are used together.

Exercises

Unless specified otherwise, use the Student_course database to answer the following questions. Also, use appropriate column headings when displaying your output.

1. Display a list of courses (course names) that have prerequisites and the number of prerequisites for each course. Order the list by the number of prerequisites.

2. How many juniors (class = 3) are there in the Student table?

3. Group and count all MATH majors by class and display the count if there are two or more in a class. (Remember that class here refers to freshman, sophomore, and so on and is recorded as 1, 2, and so on.)

4. Print the counts of As, Bs, and so on from the Grade_report table.

    a. Using temporary tables (local or global), print the minimum counts of the grades (that is, if there were 20 As, 25 Bs, and 18 Cs, you should print the minimum count of grades as C) from the Grade_report table.

    b. Using inline views, print the maximum counts of the grades (that is, if there were 20 As, 25 Bs, and 18 Cs, you should print the maximum count of grades as B) from the Grade_report table.

    c. Why would you not want to use views for this problem?

5. Print the counts of course numbers offered in descending order by count. Use the Section table only.

6. Create a table with names and number-of-children (NOC). Populate the table with five or six rows. Use COUNT, SUM, AVG, MIN, and MAX on the NOC attribute in one query and confirm that the numbers you get are what you expect.

7. Create a table of names, salaries and job locations. Populate the table with at least 10 rows and no fewer than three job locations. (There will be several employees at each location.) Find the average salary for each job location with one SELECT.

8. Print an ordered list of instructors and the number of As they assigned to students. Order the output by number of As (lowest to greatest). You can (and probably will) ignore instructors that assign no As.

9. Create a table called Employees with a name, a salary and job title. Include exactly six rows. Make the salary null in one row, the job title null in another, and both the salary and the job title in another. Use this data:

Name	Salary	Title
Mary	1000	Programmer
Brenda	3000	
Stephanie		Artist

Name	Salary	Title
Alice		
Lindsay	2000	Artist
Christina	500	Programmer

    a. Display the table.

    b. Display count, sum, maximum, minimum, and average salary.

    c. Display count, sum, maximum, minimum, and average salary, counting salary as 0 if no salary is listed.

    d. Display the average salary grouped by job title on the table as is.

    e. Display the average salary grouped by job title when null salary is counted as 0.

    f. Display the average salary grouped by job title when salary is counted as 0 if it is null and include a value for "no job title."

10. Find the instructor and the section where the maximum number of As were awarded.

11. Find the COUNT of the number of students by class who are taking classes offered by the computer science (COSC) department. Perform the query in two ways: once using a condition in the WHERE clause and once filtering with a HAVING clause. (Hint: These queries need a five-table join.)

Delete (DROP) all of your "scratch" tables (the ones you created just for this exercise: Employees, NOC, and any others you may have created).

CHAPTER 10

Correlated Subqueries

A *correlated subquery* is an inner subquery whose information is referenced by the main, outer query such that the inner query may be thought of as being executed repeatedly. In this chapter, we discuss correlated subqueries in detail. We discuss existence queries (EXISTS) and correlation as well as NOT EXISTS. We also take a look at SQL's universal and existential qualifiers. Before discussing correlated subqueries in detail however, let's make sure that you understand what constitutes a noncorrelated subquery.

Noncorrelated Subqueries

A *noncorrelated subquery* is a subquery that is independent of the outer query. In other words, the subquery could be executed on its own. The following is an example of a query that is *not* correlated:

```
SELECT   s.sname
FROM     Student s
WHERE    s.stno IN
              (SELECT gr.student_number
               FROM    Grade_report gr
               WHERE   gr.grade = 'A')
```

The first part of the preceding query (the first three lines) is the main, outer query, and the second part (the part in parentheses) is the subquery (also referred to as an *inner, nested,* or *embedded query*). To demonstrate that this subquery is an independent entity, you could run it by itself:

```
SELECT   gr.student_number
FROM     Grade_report gr
WHERE    gr.grade = 'A'
```

which would produce the following output (17 rows):

```
student_number
--------------
2
3
```

```
8
8
10
14
20
129
142
129
34
49
123
125
126
127
142
```

(17 row(s) affected)

The preceding subquery is thought of as being evaluated first, creating the set of student numbers who have As. Then, the subquery's result set is used to determine which rows (tuples) in the main query will be SELECTed. So, the full query results in the following output (14 rows):

```
sname
--------------------
Lineas
Mary
Brenda
Richard
Lujack
Donald
Lynette
Susan
Holly
Sadie
Jessica
Steve
Cedric
Jerry
```

(14 row(s) affected)

Correlated Subqueries

As stated at the beginning of the chapter, a *correlated subquery* is an inner subquery whose information is referenced by the main, outer query such that the inner query may be thought of as being executed repeatedly.

Correlated subqueries present a different execution scenario to the database manipulation language (DML) than do ordinary, noncorrelated subqueries. The correlated subquery cannot stand alone, as it depends on the outer query; therefore, completing the subquery prior to execution of the outer query is not an option. The efficiency of the correlated subquery varies; it may be worthwhile to test the efficiency of correlated subqueries versus joins or sets.

 One situation in which you cannot avoid correlation is the "for all" query, which is discussed later in this chapter.

To illustrate how a correlated subquery works, the following is an example of the non-correlated subquery from the previous section revised as a correlated subquery:

```
SELECT  s.sname
FROM    Student s
WHERE   s.stno IN
  (SELECT   gr.student_number
   FROM     Grade_report gr
   WHERE    gr.student_number = s.stno
   AND      gr.grade = 'A')
```

This query produces the following output (14 rows), which is the same as the output of the noncorrelated subquery (shown earlier):

```
sname
--------------------
Lineas
Mary
Brenda
Richard
Lujack
Donald
Lynette
Susan
Holly
Sadie
Jessica
Steve
Cedric
Jerry

(14 row(s) affected)
```

In this example, the inner query (the part in parentheses) references the outer one—observe the use of s.stno in the WHERE clause of the inner query. Rather than thinking of this query as creating a set of student numbers that have As, each row from the outer query can be considered to be SELECTed individually and tested against all rows of the inner query one at a time until it is determined whether a given student number is in the inner set and whether that student earned an A.

This query was illustrated with and without correlation. You might think that a correlated subquery is less efficient than doing a simple subquery, because the simple subquery is done once, whereas the correlated subquery is done once for each outer row. However, the internal handling of how the query executes depends on the SQL and the optimizer for that database engine.

The correlated subquery acts like a nested DO loop in a programming language, where the first row from the Student table is SELECTed and tested against all the rows in the Grade_report table, and then the second Student row is SELECTed and tested against all rows in the Grade_report table. The following is the DO loop in pseudocode:

```
LOOP1: For each row in Student  s  DO
     LOOP2: For each row in Grade_report  gr  DO
          IF (gr.student_number = s.stno) THEN
               IF (gr.grade = 'B') THEN TRUE
     END LOOP2;
     IF TRUE, THEN Student row is SELECTed
END LOOP1
```

Existence Queries and Correlation

Correlated queries are often written so that the question in the inner query is one of existence. For example, suppose you want to find the names of students who have taken a computer science (COSC) class and have earned a grade of B in that course. This query can be written in several ways. For example, you can write it as a noncorrelated subquery as follows:

```
SELECT   s.sname
FROM     Student s
WHERE    s.stno IN
  (SELECT   gr.student_number FROM Grade_report gr, Section
   WHERE    Section.section_id = gr.section_id
   AND         Section.course_num LIKE 'COSC%'
   AND         gr.grade = 'B')
```

This query produces the following output (17 rows):

```
sname
--------------------
Lineas
Mary
Brenda
Lujack
Reva
Harley
Chris
Lynette
Hillary
Phoebe
Holly
George
Cramer
Fraiser
Francis
Lindsay
Stephanie

(17 row(s) affected)
```

You can think of this query as first forming the set of student numbers of students who have made Bs in COSC courses—the inner query result set. In the inner query, you must have both the Grade_report table (for the grades) and the Section table (for the course numbers). Once you form this set of student numbers (by completing the inner query), the outer query looks through the Student table and SELECTs only those students who are in the inner query set.

 This query could also be done by creating a double-nested subquery containing two INs, or it could be written using a three-table join.

Had we chosen to write the query with an unnecessary correlation, it might look like this:

```
SELECT   s.sname
FROM     Student s
WHERE    s.stno IN
  (SELECT      gr.student_number
   FROM        Grade_report gr, Section
   WHERE       Section.section_id = gr.section_id
   AND           Section.course_num LIKE 'COSC%'
   AND           gr.student_number = s.stno
   AND           gr.grade = 'B')
```

The output of this query would be the same as the previous query. In this case, the use of the Student table in the subquery is unnecessary. Although correlation is unnecessary, this example is included to show the following:

- When correlation is necessary
- How to untangle unnecessarily correlated queries
- How you might migrate your thought process toward correlation, should it be necessary

First, let's look at situations in which the correlation of a subquery *is* necessary, and introduce a new predicate: EXISTS.

Using EXISTS

In situations in which the correlation of a subquery *is* necessary, you can write the correlated subquery with the EXISTS predicate, which looks like this:

```
SELECT s.sname
FROM    Student s
WHERE EXISTS
  (SELECT 1 FROM Grade_report gr, Section
   WHERE Section.section_id = gr.section_id
   AND     Section.course_num LIKE 'COSC%'
   AND     gr.student_number = s.stno
   AND     gr.grade = 'B')
```

The output of this query would be the same as the output (17 rows) of both of the previous queries.

Let's dissect this query. The EXISTS predicate says, "Choose the row from the Student table in the outer query if the subquery is true (that is, if a row in the subquery exists that satisfies the condition in the subquery WHERE clause)." Because no actual result set is formed, "SELECT 1" is used as a "dummy" result set to indicate that the subquery is true (1 is returned) or false (no rows are returned). In the noncorrelated case, we tied the student number in the Student table to the inner query by the IN predicate as follows:

```
SELECT    s.stno
FROM      Student s
WHERE     s.stno IN
   (SELECT "student number ...)
```

When using the EXISTS predicate, we do not use any column of the Student table, but rather are seeking only to find whether the subquery WHERE can be satisfied.

We have indicated that we are using EXISTS with (SELECT 1...). Using the EXISTS predicate, the subquery does not form a result set per se, but rather causes EXISTS to returns true or false. The use of SELECT * in the inner query is common among SQL programmers. However, from an "internal" standpoint, SELECT * causes the SQL engine to check the data dictionary unnecessarily. As the actual result of the inner query is not important, it is strongly suggested that you use SELECT 'X' (or SELECT 1 . ..) instead of SELECT * ... so that a constant is SELECTed instead of some "sensible" entry. The SELECT 'X' .. or SELECT 1 ... is simply more efficient.

In the EXISTS case, we do not specify any columns to be SELECTed in the inner query's result set; rather, we use a dummy result—SELECT 'X' (or we could use SELECT 1). If the subquery WHERE is satisfied, it returns true, and if the inner query is not satisfied, it selects nothing, then the subquery returns false. The EXISTS predicate forces us to correlate the query. To illustrate that correlation is usually necessary with EXISTS, consider the following query:

```
SELECT    s.sname
FROM      Student s
WHERE EXISTS
   (SELECT 'X' FROM Grade_report gr, Section t
    WHERE    t.section_id = gr.section_id
    AND      t.course_num LIKE 'COSC%'
    AND      gr.grade = 'B')
```

This query produces 48 rows of output (of which we show the first 20 rows):

```
sname
--------------------
Lineas
Mary
Zelda
Ken
Mario
```

```
Brenda
Romona
Richard
Kelly
Lujack
Reva
Elainie
Harley
Donald
Chris
Jake
Lynette
Susan
Monica
Bill.
    .
    .
```

(48 row(s) affected)

This query uses EXISTS, but has no correlation. This syntax infers that for each student row, we test the joined Grade_report and Section tables to see whether there is a course number like COSC and a grade of B (which, of course, there is). We unnecessarily ask the subquery question over and over again. The result from this latter, uncorrelated EXISTS query is the same as the following:

```
SELECT   s.sname
FROM     Student s
```

The point is that the correlation is usually necessary when we use EXISTS.

Consider another example in which a correlation could be used. Suppose that we want to find the names of all students who have three or more Bs. A first pass at a query might be something like this:

```
SELECT   s.sname
FROM     Student s WHERE "something" IN
  (SELECT "something"
   FROM     Grade_report
   WHERE   "count of grade = 'B'" > 2)
```

This query can be done with a HAVING clause, as you saw previously (Chapter 9), but we want to show how to do this in yet another way. Suppose we arrange the subquery to use the student number (stno) from the Student table as a filter and count in the subquery only when a row in the Grade_report table correlates to that student. The query (this time with an implied EXISTS) looks like this:

```
SELECT   s.sname
FROM     Student s
WHERE 2 < (SELECT COUNT(*)
           FROM     Grade_report gr
           WHERE    gr.student_number = s.stno
           AND      gr.grade = 'B')
```

which results in the following output (8 rows):

```
sname
--------------------
Lineas
Mary
Lujack
Reva
Chris
Hillary
Phoebe
Holly

(8 row(s) affected)
```

Although there is no EXISTS in this query, it is implied. The syntax of the query does not allow an EXISTS, but the sense of the query is "WHERE EXISTS a COUNT of 2 which is less than..." In this correlated subquery, we have to examine the Grade_report table for each member of the Student table to see whether the student has more than two Bs. We test the entire Grade_report table for each student row in the outer query.

If it were possible, a subquery without the correlation would be more desirable, because it would appear simpler to understand. The overall query might be as follows:

```
SELECT   s.sname
FROM     Student s
WHERE    s.stno IN
  (subquery that defines a set of students who have made 3 Bs)
```

Therefore, we might attempt to write the following query:

```
SELECT   s.sname
FROM     Student s
WHERE    s.stno IN
  (SELECT   gr.student_number
     FROM   Grade_report gr
    WHERE   gr.grade = 'B')
```

However, as the following output (27 rows) shows, this query would give us only students who earned at least one B:

```
sname
--------------------
Lineas
Mary
Zelda
Ken
Mario
Brenda
Kelly
Lujack
Reva
Harley
Chris
```

Lynette
Hillary
Phoebe
Holly
Sadie
Jessica
Steve
Cedric
George
Cramer
Fraiser
Francis
Smithly
Sebastian
Lindsay
Stephanie

```
(27 row(s) affected)
```

To get a list of students who have earned at least three Bs, we could try the following query:

```
SELECT    s.sname
FROM      Student s
WHERE     s.stno IN
  (SELECT    gr.student_number, COUNT(*)
   FROM      Grade_report gr
   WHERE     gr.grade = 'B'
   GROUP BY  gr.student_number
   HAVING    COUNT(*) > 2)
```

However, this approach does not work, because the subquery cannot have two columns in its result set unless the main query has two columns in the WHERE .. IN.

Here, the subquery must have only gr.student_number to match s.stno. So, we might try to construct an inline view, as shown in the following query:

```
SELECT  s.sname
FROM    Student s
WHERE   s.stno IN
  (SELECT vi.student_number
   FROM (SELECT    student_number, ct = COUNT(*)
            FROM      Grade_report gr
            WHERE     gr.grade = 'B'
            GROUP BY student_number
            HAVING COUNT(*) > 2) AS vi)
```

This is an example of the inline view, discussed in Chapter 6. This query succeeds in SQL Server 2005, producing the following output (8 rows):

```
sname
--------------------
Lineas
Mary
Lujack
Reva
```

```
Chris
Hillary
Phoebe
Holly

(8 row(s) affected)
```

 This query also works in Oracle, but it may fail in other SQL languages.

As you can see, several ways exist to query the database with SQL. In this case, the correlated subquery may be the easiest to see and perhaps the most efficient.

From IN to EXISTS

A simple example of converting from IN to EXISTS—uncorrelated to correlated (or vice versa)—would be to move the set test in the WHERE .. IN of the uncorrelated subquery to the WHERE of the EXISTS in the correlated query.

As an example, consider the following uncorrelated subquery:

```
SELECT *
FROM   Student s
WHERE  s.stno  IN
  (SELECT  g.student_number
   FROM    Grade_report g
   WHERE   grade = 'B')
```

The following is the same query written as a correlated subquery:

```
SELECT *
FROM   Student s
WHERE EXISTS
  (SELECT  g.student_number
   FROM    Grade_report g
   WHERE   grade = 'B'
   AND     s.stno = g.student_number)
```

This query produces 27 rows of output (of which we show the first 15 rows):

```
STNO   SNAME                 MAJOR CLASS  BDATE
------ --------------------- ----- ------ -----------------------
  2    Lineas                ENGL  1      1980-04-15 00:00:00
  3    Mary                  COSC  4      1978-07-16 00:00:00
  5    Zelda                 COSC  NULL   1978-02-12 00:00:00
  6    Ken                   POLY  NULL   1980-07-15 00:00:00
  7    Mario                 MATH  NULL   1980-08-12 00:00:00
  8    Brenda                COSC  2      1977-08-13 00:00:00
 13    Kelly                 MATH  4      1980-08-12 00:00:00
 14    Lujack                COSC  1      1977-02-12 00:00:00
 15    Reva                  MATH  2      1980-06-10 00:00:00
 19    Harley                POLY  2      1981-04-16 00:00:00
```

```
24      Chris           ACCT  4       1978-02-12 00:00:00
34      Lynette         POLY  1       1981-07-16 00:00:00
121     Hillary         COSC  1       1977-07-16 00:00:00
122     Phoebe          ENGL  3       1980-04-15 00:00:00
123         Holly             POLY  4       1981-01-15 00:00:00.
.
.
```

```
(27 row(s) affected)
```

This example gives you a pattern to move from one kind of query to the other kind and to test the efficiency of both kinds of queries. Both of the preceding queries should produce the same output.

NOT EXISTS

As with the IN predicate, which has a NOT IN compliment, EXISTS may also be used with NOT. In some situations, the predicates EXISTS and NOT EXISTS are vital. For example, if we ask a "for all" question, it must be answered by "existence"—actually, the lack thereof (that is, "not existence"). In logic, the statement, "find x for all y" is logically equivalent to "do not find x where there does not exist a y." Or, there is no x for no y. Or, you cannot find an x when there is no y.

In SQL, there is no "for all" predicate. Instead, SQL uses the idea of "for all" logic with NOT EXISTS. (A word of caution, however—SQL is not simply a logic exercise, as you will see.) In this section, we look at how EXISTS and NOT EXISTS work in SQL. In the following section, we address the "for all" problem.

Consider the following query:

```
SELECT    s.sname
FROM      Student s
WHERE EXISTS
  (SELECT 'X'
   FROM        Grade_report gr
   WHERE       s.stno = gr.student_number
   AND         gr.grade = 'C')
```

which produces the following output (24 rows):

```
sname
--------------------
Zelda
Ken
Mario
Brenda
Richard
Reva
Donald
Jake
Susan
Monica
```

```
Bill
Sadie
Jessica
Steve
Alan
Rachel
Smithly
Sebastian
Losmith
Genevieve
Thornton
Gus
Benny
Lionel

(24 row(s) affected)
```

For this correlated subquery, "student names" are SELECTed when:

- The student is enrolled in a section (WHERE s.stno = gr.student_number)
- The same student has a grade of C (note the correlation in the WHERE clause in the inner query)

Both statements must be true for the student row to be SELECTed. Recall that we use SELECT 1 or SELECT 'X' in our inner query, because we want the subquery to return something if the subquery is true. The actual value of the "something" does not matter. true means something is returned; false means nothing was returned from the subquery. Therefore, SELECT .. EXISTS "says" SELECT .. WHERE true. The inner query is true if any row is SELECTed in the inner query.

Now consider the preceding query with a NOT EXISTS in it instead of EXISTS for students who do not have a grade of C:

```
SELECT s.sname
FROM    Student s
WHERE NOT EXISTS
   (SELECT 'X'
    FROM    Grade_report gr
    WHERE   s.stno = gr.student_number
    AND     gr.grade = 'C')
```

This query produces the following output (24 rows):

```
sname
--------------------
Lineas
Mary
Romona
Kelly
Lujack
Elainie
Harley
Chris
Lynette
```

Smith
Hillary
Phoebe
Holly
Brad
Cedric
George
Jerry
Cramer
Fraiser
Harrison
Francis
Lindsay
Stephanie
Jake

(24 row(s) affected)

In this query, we are still SELECTing with the pattern SELECT .. WHERE true because all SELECTs with EXISTS work that way. But, the twist is that the subquery has to be false to be SELECTed with NOT EXISTS. If the subquery is false, then NOT EXISTS is true and the outer row is SELECTed.

Now, logic implies that if either s.stno <> gr.student_number or gr.grade <> 'C', then the subquery "fails"—that is, it is false for that student row. As the subquery is false, the NOT EXISTS would return a true for that row. Unfortunately, this logic is not quite what happens. Recall that we characterized the correlated subquery as follows:

```
LOOP1: For each row in Student  s  DO
    LOOP2: For each row in Grade_report DO
           IF (gr.student_number = s.stno) THEN
                    IF (gr.grade = 'C') THEN TRUE
    END LOOP2;
       IF TRUE, THEN student row is SELECTed
END LOOP1
```

Note that LOOP2 is completed before the next student is tested. In other words, just because a student number exists that is not equal, it will not cause the subquery to be false. Rather, the entire subquery table is parsed and the logic is more like this:

For the case .. WHERE EXISTS s.stno = gr.student_number ..., is there a gr.grade = 'C'? If, when the student numbers are equal, no C can be found, then the subquery returns no rows—it is false for that student row. So, with NOT EXISTS, we will SELECT students who have student numbers equal in the Grade_report and Student tables, but who have no C in the Grade_report table. The point about "no C in the Grade_report table" can be answered true only by looking at all the rows in the inner query and finding no C for that student.

SQL Universal and Existential Qualifiers

In SQL, "for all" and "for each" are the universal qualifiers, whereas "there exists" is the existential qualifier. As mentioned in the preceding section, SQL does not have a "for all" predicate; however, logically, the following relationship exists:

For all x, WHERE P(x) is true …

which is logically the same as the following:

There does not exist an x, WHERE P(x) is not true.

A "for all" type SQL query is less straightforward than the other queries we have used, because it involves a double-nested, correlated subquery using the NOT EXISTS predicate. The next section shows an example.

Example 1

To show a "for all" type SQL query, we will use another table in our Student_course database—a table called Cap (for "capability"). This table has names of students who have multiple foreign-language capabilities. We begin by looking at the table by typing the following query:

```
SELECT *
FROM    Cap
ORDER BY name
```

This query produces the following output (18 rows):

```
NAME        LANGU
---------   -------
BRENDA      FRENCH
BRENDA      CHINESE
BRENDA      SPANISH
JOE         CHINESE
KENT        CHINESE
LUJACK      SPANISH
LUJACK      FRENCH
LUJACK      GERMAN
LUJACK      CHINESE
MARY JO     FRENCH
MARY JO     GERMAN
MARY JO     CHINESE
MELANIE     FRENCH
MELANIE     CHINESE
RICHARD     SPANISH
RICHARD     FRENCH
RICHARD     CHINESE
RICHARD     GERMAN

(18 row(s) affected)
```

Suppose that we want to find out which languages are spoken by all students (for which we would ask the question, "For each language, does it occur with all students?"). Although this manual exercise would be very difficult for a large table, for our practice table, we can answer the question by displaying and manually counting in the table ordered by language.

To see how to answer a question of the type—"Which languages are spoken by all students?"—for a much larger table where sorting and examining the result would be tedious, we will construct a query. After showing the query, we will dissect the result. Following is the query to answer our question:

```
SELECT  name, langu
FROM    Cap x
WHERE NOT EXISTS
            (SELECT 'X'
            FROM Cap y
            WHERE NOT EXISTS
                    (SELECT 'X'
                    FROM Cap z
                    WHERE x.langu = z.langu
                    AND y.name = z.name))
```

 As you will see, all the for all/for each questions follow this double-nested, correlated NOT EXISTS pattern.

This query produces the following output (7 rows):

```
name        langu
---------   -------
BRENDA      CHINESE
RICHARD     CHINESE
LUJACK      CHINESE
MARY JO     CHINESE
MELANIE     CHINESE
JOE         CHINESE
KENT        CHINESE

(7 row(s) affected)
```

The way the query works

To SELECT a "language" spoken by all students, the query proceeds as follows:

1. SELECT a row in Cap (x) (outer query).

2. For that row, begin SELECTing each row again in Cap (y) (middle query).

3. For each of the middle query rows, we want the inner query (Cap z) to be true for all cases of the middle query (remember that true is translated to false by the NOT EXISTS). As each inner query is satisfied (it is true), it forces the middle query to continue looking for a match—to look at all cases and eventually

conclude false (evaluate to false overall). If the middle query is false, the outer query sees true because of its NOT EXISTS.

To make the middle query (y) find false, all the inner query (z) occurrences must be true; that is, the languages from the outer query must exist with all names from the middle one (y) in the inner one (z). For an eventual "match," every row in the middle query for an outer query row must be false (that is, every row in the inner query is true).

These steps are explained in further detail in the next example, in which we use a smaller table, so that the explanation is easier to understand.

Example 2

Suppose that we have the simpler table Cap1 (see Table 10-1) when attempting to answer the question "Which languages are spoken by all students?"

Table 10-1. Cap1

```
Name          Language
-----------   ------------
Joe           Hindi
Mary          Hindi
Mary          French

(3 row(s) affected)
```

 The table Cap1 does not exist in the Student_course database. You will have to create it. Keep the column names and types similar to the table Cap.

The query will be similar to the one used in the previous section:

```
SELECT name, language
FROM   Cap1 x
WHERE NOT EXISTS
     (SELECT 'X'
       FROM Cap1 y
      WHERE NOT EXISTS
        (SELECT 'X'
            FROM   Cap1 z
            WHERE  x.language = z. language
            AND    y.name = z.name))
ORDER BY language
```

This query produces the following output:

```
name          language
-----------   ------------
Joe           Hindi
Mary          Hind

(2 row(s) affected)
```

The way this query works

The following is a step-by-step explanation of how this query would work in Table 10-1 (Cap1):

1. The row <Joe, Hindi> is SELECTed by the outer query (x).

2. The row <Joe, Hindi> is SELECTed by the middle query (y).

3. The row <Joe, Hindi> is SELECTed by the inner query (z).

4. The inner query is true:

   ```
   X.LANGUAGE = Hindi
   Z.LANGUAGE = Hindi
   Y.NAME = Joe
   Z.NAME = Joe
   ```

5. Because the inner query returns a row (is true), the NOT EXISTS of the middle query translates this to false and continues with the next row in the middle query. The middle query SELECTs <Mary, Hindi> and the inner query begins again with <Joe, Hindi> seeing:

   ```
   X.LANGUAGE = Hindi
   Z.LANGUAGE = Hindi
   Y.NAME = Mary
   Z.NAME = Joe
   ```

   This is false, so the inner query SELECTs a second row <Mary, Hindi>:

   ```
   X.LANGUAGE = Hindi
   Z.LANGUAGE = Hindi
   Y.NAME = Mary
   Z.NAME = Mary
   ```

   This is true, so the inner query is true. (Notice that the X.LANGUAGE has not changed yet; the outer query [X] is still on the first row.)

6. Because the inner query returns a row (is true), the NOT EXISTS of the middle query translates this to false and continues with the next row in the middle query.

   The middle query now SELECTs <Mary, French> and the inner query begins again with <Joe, Hindi> seeing:

   ```
   X.LANGUAGE = Hindi
   Z.LANGUAGE = Hindi
   Y.NAME     = Mary
   Z.NAME     = Joe
   ```

   This is false, so the inner query SELECTs a second row <Mary, Hindi>:

   ```
   X.LANGUAGE = Hindi
   Z.LANGUAGE = Hindi
   Y.NAME     = Mary
   Z.NAME     = Mary
   ```

   This is true, so the inner query is true.

7. Because the inner query is true, the NOT EXISTS of the middle query again converts this true to false and wants to continue, but the middle query is out of rows. Thus the middle query is false.

8. Because the middle query is false, and because we are testing

```
"SELECT distinct name, language
 FROM Cap1 x
 WHERE NOT EXISTS
     (SELECT 'X' FROM Cap1 y ...",
```

the false from the middle query is translated to true for the outer query and the row <Joe, Hindi> is SELECTed for the result set. Note that "Hindi" occurs with both "Joe" and "Mary."

9. The second row in the outer query will repeat the previous steps for <Mary, Hindi>. The value "Hindi" will be seen to occur with both "Joe" and "Mary" as <Mary, Hindi> is added to the result set.

10. The third row in the outer query begins with <Mary, French>. The middle query SELECTS <Joe, Hindi> and the inner query SELECTs <Joe, Hindi>. The inner query sees the following:

```
X.LANGUAGE = French
Z.LANGUAGE = Hindi
Y.NAME     = Joe
Z.NAME     = Mary
```

This is false, so the inner query SELECTs a second row, <Mary, Hindi>:

```
X.LANGUAGE = French
Z.LANGUAGE = Hindi
Y.NAME     = Joe
Z.NAME     = Mary
```

This is false, so the inner query SELECTs a third row, <Mary, French>:

```
X.LANGUAGE = French
Z.LANGUAGE = French
Y.NAME     = Joe
Z.NAME     = Mary
```

This is also false. The inner query returns no rows (fails). The inner query evaluates to false, which causes the middle query to returns rows (see true) because of the NOT EXISTS. Because the middle query sees true, it is finished and evaluated to true. Because the middle query evaluates to true, the NOT EXISTS in the outer query changes this to false and X.LANGUAGE = French fails because X.LANGUAGE = French did not occur with all the values of NAME.

Consider again the "for all" query presented in Example 2:

```
SELECT name, language
FROM   Cap1 x
WHERE NOT EXISTS
     (SELECT 'X'
       FROM Cap1 y
       WHERE NOT EXISTS
```

```
(SELECT 'X'
        FROM    Cap1 z
        WHERE   x.language = z. language
        AND     y.name = z.name))
ORDER BY language
```

A clue as to what a query of this kind means can be found in the inner query where the outer query is tested. In the phrase that says WHERE *x.language = z. language*..., the *x.language* is where the query is testing which *language occurs for all* names.

This query is a SQL realization of a relational division exercise. Relational division is a "for all" operation just like that illustrated earlier. In relational algebra, the query must be set up into a divisor, dividend, and quotient in this pattern:

Quotient (B) ← Dividend(A, B) divided by Divisor (A).

If the question is "What language for *all* names?" then the Divisor, A, is names, and the Quotient, B, is language. It is most prudent to set up SQL like relational algebra with a two-column table (like Cap or Cap1) for the Dividend and then treat the Divisor and the Quotient appropriately. Our query will have the column for language, x.language, in the inner query, as language will be the quotient. We have chosen to also report name in the result set.

Example 3

Note that the preceding query is completely different from the following query, which asks, "Which *students* speak all languages?":

```
SELECT DISTINCT name, language
FROM    Cap1 x
WHERE NOT EXISTS
            (SELECT 'X'
            FROM Cap1 y
            WHERE NOT EXISTS
                    (SELECT 'X'
                            FROM    Cap1 z
                            WHERE   y.language = z.language
                            AND     x.name = z.name))
ORDER BY language
```

This query produces the following output:

```
name          language
------------  ------------
Mary          French
Mary          Hindi

(2 row(s) affected)
```

Note that the inner query contains x.name, which means the question was "Which names occur for *all* languages?" or, put another way, "Which students speak all languages?" The "all" goes with languages for x.name.

Summary

In this chapter, we discussed the correlated subquery, noncorrelated subquery, EXISTS, and NOT EXISTS. We described situations where the correlation of a subquery is necessary and can be written with the EXISTS predicate, and other times when EXISTS can be used, even with no correlation. We also introduced loops and discussed how the "for all" and "for each" are used in SQL.

Review Questions

1. What is a noncorrelated subquery?
2. Which type of subquery can be executed on its own?
3. Which part of a query is evaluated first, the query or the subquery?
4. What are correlated subqueries?
5. What does the EXISTS predicate do?
6. What are considered universal qualifiers?
7. Is correlation necessary when we use EXISTS? Why?
8. Explain how the "for all" type SQL query involves a double-nested correlated subquery using the NOT EXISTS predicate.

Exercises

Unless specified otherwise, use the Student_course database to answer the following questions. Also, use appropriate column headings when displaying your output.

1. List the names of students who have received Cs. Do this in three ways: (a) as a join, (b) as an uncorrelated subquery, and (c) as a correlated subquery. Show both results and account for any differences.

2. In section "Existence Queries and Correlation," you were asked to find the names of students who have taken a computer science class and earned a grade of B. We noted that it could be done in several ways. One query could look like this:

```
SELECT   s.sname
FROM     Student s
WHERE    s.stno IN
   (SELECT  gr.student_number
    FROM    Grade_report gr, Section
    WHERE   Section.section_id = gr.section_id
    AND         Section.course_num LIKE 'COSC___'
    AND         gr.grade = 'B')
```

Redo this query, putting the finding of the COSC course in a correlated subquery. The query should be as follows:

The Student table uncorrelated subquery to the Grade_report table, correlated EXISTS to the Section table.

3. In the section "SQL Universal and Existential Qualifiers," we illustrated both an existence query:

```
SELECT   s.sname
FROM     Student s
WHERE EXISTS
  (SELECT 'X'
    FROM     Grade_report gr
    WHERE    Student.stno = gr.student_number
    AND      gr.grade = 'C')
```

and a NOT EXISTS version:

```
SELECT   s.sname
FROM     Student s
WHERE NOT EXISTS
  (SELECT 'X'
    FROM     Grade_report gr
    WHERE    Student.stno = gr.student_number
    AND      gr.grade = 'C')
```

Show that the EXISTS version is the complement of the NOT EXISTS version—count the rows in the EXISTS result, the rows in the NOT EXISTS result, and the rows in the Student table. Also, devise a query to give the same result with IN and NOT..IN.

4. Discover whether all students take courses by counting the students, and then count those students whose student numbers are in the Grade_report table and those whose student numbers are not in the table. Use IN and then NOT..IN, and then use EXISTS and NOT EXISTS. How many students take courses and how many students do not?

    a. Find out which students have taken courses but who have not taken COSC courses. Create a set of student names and courses from the Student, Grade_report, and Section tables (use the prefix COSC to indicate computer science courses). Then, use NOT..IN to "subtract" from that set another set of student names of students (who take courses) who have taken COSC courses. For this set difference, use NOT..IN.

    b. Change NOT..IN to NOT EXISTS (with other appropriate changes) and explain the result. The "other appropriate changes" include adding the correlation and the change of the result column in the subquery set.

5. There exists a table called Plants. List the table and then find out what company or companies have plants in all cities. Verify your result manually.

6. Run the following query and print the result:

```
SELECT distinct name, langu
FROM Cap x
WHERE NOT EXISTS
            (SELECT 'X'
            FROM Cap y
            WHERE NOT EXISTS
                        (SELECT 'X'
                        FROM Cap z
                        WHERE X.langu =Z.langu
                        AND Y.name=Z.name))
```

Save the query (e.g., save forall) and hand in the result.

- a. Recreate the Cap table (e.g., call it some other name, such as LANG1). To do this, first create the table and then use the INSERT statement with the sub select option (INSERT INTO LANG1 AS SELECT * FROM Cap).

- b. Add a new person to your table who speaks only BENG.

- c. Recall your previous SELECT (get for all).

- d. CHANGE the table from CAP to LANG1 (for all occurrences, use CHANGE/Cap/lang1/ repeatedly, assuming that you called your table LANG1).

- e. Start the new query (the one you just created with LANG1 in it).

- f. How is this result different from the situation in which Newperson was not in LANG1? Provide an explanation of why the query did what it did.

7. The Department_to_major table is a list of four-letter department codes with the department names. In Chapter 8, Exercise 7 (hereafter referred to as Exercise 8-7), you created a table called Secretary, which should now have data like this:

Secretary	
dCode	Name
ACCT	Beryl
COSC	Kaitlyn
ENGL	David
HIST	Christina
BENG	Fred
Null	Brenda

In Exercise 8-7, you did the following:

- a. Create a query that lists the names of departments that have secretaries (use IN and the Secretary table in a subquery). Save this query as q8_7a.

- b. Create a query that lists the names of departments that do not have secretaries (use NOT..IN). Save this query as q8_7b.

- c. Add one more row to the Secretary table that contains <null,'Brenda'>. (This could be a situation in which you have hired Brenda but have not yet assigned her to a department.)

d. Recall q8_7a and rerun it.

e. Recall q8_7b and rerun it.

We remarked in Exercise 8-7 that the NOT..IN predicate has problems with nulls: the behavior of NOT..IN when nulls exist may surprise you. If nulls may exist in the subquery, then NOT..IN should not be used. If you use NOT..IN in a subquery, you must ensure that nulls will not occur in the subquery or you must use some other predicate, such as NOT EXISTS. Perhaps the best advice is to avoid NOT..IN.

Here, we repeat Exercise 8-7 using NOT EXISTS:

f. Reword query q8_7a to use EXISTS. You will have to correlate the inner and outer queries. Save this query as q10_7aa.

g. Reword query q8_7b to use NOT EXISTS. You will have to correlate the inner and outer queries. Save this query as q10_7bb. You should *not* have a phrase IS NOT NULL in your NOT EXISTS query.

h. Rerun q8_9a with and without <null, Brenda>.

i. Rerun q8_9b with and without <null, Brenda>.

Note the difference in behavior versus the original question. List the names of those departments that do or do not have secretaries. The point here is to encourage you to use NOT EXISTS in a correlated subquery, rather than NOT..IN.

CHAPTER 11

Indexes and Constraints on Tables

In previous chapters, we concentrated primarily on retrieving information from existing tables. This chapter revisits the creation of tables, but focuses on how indexes and constraints can be added to tables to make the tables more efficient and to increase the integrity of the data in the tables (and hence in the database). Referential integrity constraints and other constraints are also discussed.

SQL Server 2005 does not need indexes to successfully retrieve results for a SELECT statement. But, an *index* may speed up queries and searches on the indexed columns and may facilitate sorting and grouping operations. As tables get larger, the value of using proper indexes becomes more of an issue. Indexes can be used to find data quickly that satisfy conditions in a WHERE clause, find matching rows in a JOIN clause, or to efficiently maintain *uniqueness* of the key columns during INSERTs and UPDATEs.

Constraints are a very powerful ways to increase the data integrity in a database. Integrity implies believability and correctness. Any data that destroys the sense of correctness is said to lack integrity. For example, a constraint is used to establish relationships with other tables. A violation of integrity would be, for instance, if a nonexistent referenced row were included in the relationship. The CONSTRAINT clause can be used with the CREATE TABLE and the ALTER TABLE statements to create constraints or delete constraints, respectively.

The "Simple" CREATE TABLE

You have seen a "simple" CREATE TABLE statement in Chapter 3. To refresh your memory, here is an example:

```
CREATE TABLE Test1
   (name          VARCHAR(20),
    ssn           CHAR(9),
    dept_number   INT,
    acct_balance  SMALLMONEY)
```

The following are the elements of this CREATE TABLE command:

- We created a table called Test1.
- name is a variable-length character string with maximum length of 20
- ssn (Social Security number) is a fixed-length character string of length 9
- dept_number is an integer (which in SQL Server 2005 simply means no decimals allowed)
- acct_balance is a currency column

Beyond choosing data types for columns in tables, you may need to make other choices to create an effective database. You can create indexes on tables, which then can be used to aid in the enforcement of certain validation rules. You also can use other "add-ons" called CONSTRAINTs, which make you enter *good* data (or, prevents you from entering invalid data into the database) and hence maintain the integrity of a database. In the following sections, we explore indexes and then CONSTRAINTs.

Indexes

SQL Server 2005 allows you to create several indexes on a table. In SQL Server 2005, it is the job of the query optimizer to determine which indexes will be the most useful in processing a specific query. Although indexes may speed up queries in large tables, indexes will slow update operations (insert, delete, update), because every update causes a rebuild of the index. We begin by introducing the "simple" CREATE INDEX statement.

 Discussing the query optimizer is beyond the scope of this book.

The "Simple" CREATE INDEX

The CREATE INDEX statement is used to create a new index on some column in an existing table. The following is the general syntax for the CREATE INDEX statement:

```
CREATE INDEX index_name
ON Tablename (column [ASC | DESC])
```

For example, if we wanted to create an index called ssn_ndx on the ssn column, in descending order of ssn, for the Test1 table, we would type the following:

```
CREATE INDEX ssn_ndx
ON Test1 (ssn DESC)
```

You will get:

```
Command(s) completed successfully.
```

This result means that the index was successfully created. Although the user has the option of setting the column in ascending (ASC) or descending (DESC) order, if DESC is not included, the index will be created in ascending order, because ASC is the default order for indexes.

To view the index that you just created, click on the + sign beside the newly created table, Test1, and then click on the + sign beside the Indexes node, and you will be able to see that index that we just created, ssn_ndx, and you will get Figure 11-1.

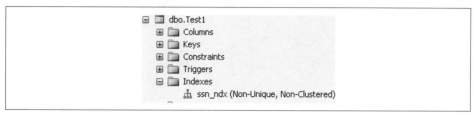

Figure 11-1. Viewing the index

Now, to see if this index, ssn_ndx, is in ascending order or descending order, right-click on the index, ssn_ndx and select Properties, and you will get Figure 11-2. Figure 11-2 shows that this index, ssn_ndx, is in descending order, indexed by the ssn column.

Also from Figure 11-2, to add more columns to the index key, we can click Add; to remove columns from the index key, we can select the key and then click Remove.

To prevent duplicate values in indexed columns, you must use the UNIQUE option in the CREATE INDEX statement, as follows:

```
CREATE UNIQUE INDEX ssn_ndx1
ON Test1 (ssn DESC)
```

This query will create the unique index, ssn_ndx1, as shown in Figure 11-3.

The UNIQUE option can be used on columns that will not be a primary key in a table. A primary key is a key or field that uniquely identifies a row in a table.

The UNIQUE option will disallow duplicate entries for a column even though the column is not a primary key in a table. NULLs are allowed in nonprimary key indexes.

Deleting Indexes Using SQL

You can use a DROP INDEX statement to delete an index in SQL. The general format of the DROP INDEX statement is as follows:

```
DROP INDEX Table_name.index_name
```

For example, to delete the index ssn_ndx1 created on Test1, you would type the following:

```
DROP INDEX Test1.ssn_ndx1
```

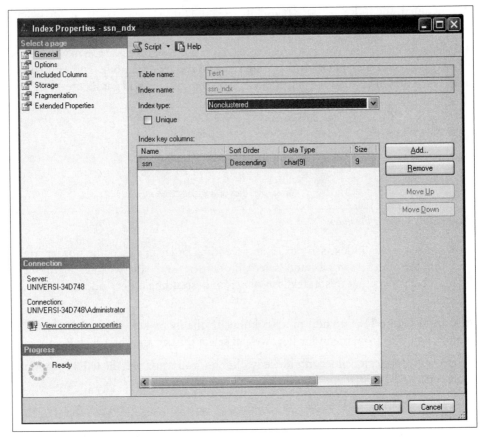

Figure 11-2. Index properties

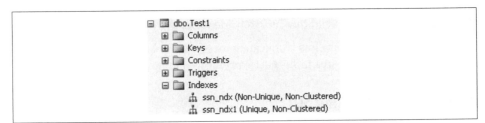

Figure 11-3. Showing the UNIQUE index

Unused indexes slow data modification without helping retrieval. So, if you have indexes that are not being used, you should delete (drop) them. All indexes will automatically get deleted (dropped) if the table is deleted.

Indexes cannot be created on all column types in SQL Server 2005. For example, you cannot create an index on a column of TEXT, NTEXT, or IMAGE data type.

Constraints

As with indexes, constraints can be added to tables. As explained previously, constraints are added to give tables more integrity. In this section, we discuss some of the constraints available in SQL Server 2005: the NOT NULL constraint, the PRIMARY KEY constraint, the UNIQUE constraint, the CHECK constraint, and a few referential constraints.

The NOT NULL Constraint

The NOT NULL constraint is an integrity CONSTRAINT that allows the database creator to deny the creation of a row where a column would have a null value. Usually, a null signifies a missing data item. As discussed in previous chapters, nulls in databases present an interpretation problem—do they mean not applicable, not available, unknown, or what? If a situation in which a null is present could affect the integrity of the database, then the table creator can deny anyone the ability to insert nulls into the table for that column. To deny nulls, we can create a table with the NOT NULL constraint on a column(s) after the data type. The following example shows how to include the NOT NULL constraint using a CREATE TABLE statement:

```
CREATE TABLE Test2
   (name            VARCHAR(20),
    ssn             CHAR(9),
    dept_number     INT NOT NULL,
    acct_balance    SMALLMONEY)
```

In this newly created table, Test2, the dept_number column, now has a NOT NULL constraint included (and the Allow Nulls option is unchecked, as shown in Figure 11-4).

Table - dbo.Test2	UNIVERSI-34D...QLQuery1.sql*	Summai
Column Name	Data Type	Allow Nulls
name	varchar(20)	☑
ssn	char(9)	☑
dept_number	int	☐
▶ acct_balance	smallmoney	☑

Figure 11-4. Table definition of Test2

The NOT NULL constraint can also be added to the column after the table has been created. You can check the Allow Nulls option of the dept_number column in Figure 11-4, or you can use SQL to do this. To do this in SQL, you will have to use the ALTER TABLE command, as we illustrate in the following example.

Suppose that we created the Test2 table as follows:

```
CREATE TABLE Test2
   (name            VARCHAR(20),
    ssn             CHAR(9),
    dept_number     INT,
    acct_balance    SMALLMONEY)
```

Now, we want to add a NOT NULL constraint (using SQL) after the table has been created. To do so, we must use the ALTER COLUMN option within the ALTER TABLE statement, with the following general syntax:

```
ALTER TABLE Tablename
ALTER COLUMN column_name column_type(size) NOT NULL
```

So, to set the dept_number column in the Test2 table to NOT NULL, we would type the following:

```
ALTER table Test2
ALTER COLUMN dept_number INTEGER NOT NULL
```

This query will give us the same table definition that we got in Figure 11-4.

But you need to understand the following three things about the ALTER COLUMN extension of the ALTER TABLE statement:

- The column *type* and *size* must *always* be typed after the column *name*. For example, the following statement will cause SQL Server 2005 to announce a syntax error:

```
ALTER TABLE Test2
ALTER COLUMN name NOT NULL
```

You will get following error message:

```
Msg 156, Level 15, State 1, Line 2
Incorrect syntax near the keyword 'NOT'.
```

- If you type only the column *type*, without the column *size*, the column *size* will reset to the default maximum size of the data type.
- You cannot put a NOT NULL constraint on a column that already contains nulls.

The PRIMARY KEY Constraint

When creating a table, a PRIMARY KEY constraint will prevent duplicate values for the column(s) defined as a primary key. Internally, the designation of a primary key also creates a primary key index.

Designation of a primary key will be necessary for the referential integrity constraints that follow. The designation of a primary key also automatically puts the NOT NULL constraint in the definition of the column(s), as you will see in an example later in the chapter. A fundamental rule of relational database is that primary keys cannot be null.

One of the following three options can be used to set the primary key.

Option 1

The first option is to declare the primary key while creating the table, in the CREATE TABLE statement. Here, the PRIMARY KEY constraint is added to the column upon creation:

```
CREATE TABLE Test2a
  (ssn    CHAR(9)        CONSTRAINT ssn_pk PRIMARY KEY,
   name   VARCHAR2(20),  etc.
```

ssn_pk is the name of the PRIMARY KEY constraint for the ssn column. It is conventional to name all CONSTRAINTs (although most people often do not bother to name NOT NULL constraints).

The following two options of setting the primary key are preferable because they provide greater flexibility.

Option 2

The second option available to create a primary key is called the *table format*, in which the CREATE TABLE looks like the following:

```
CREATE TABLE Test2a
  (ssn              CHAR(9),
   blah blah .. ,
   acct_balance     NUMBER,
   CONSTRAINT ssn_pk PRIMARY KEY (ssn))
```

Option 3

The third option available to create a primary key is to add the stipulation of the PRIMARY KEY post hoc by using the ALTER TABLE command. The syntax for the PRIMARY KEY in the ALTER TABLE command would be as follows:

```
ALTER TABLE Tablename
ADD CONSTRAINT constraint_name PRIMARY KEY (column_name(s))
```

So, to make ssn a primary key column in Test2, we could type the following:

```
ALTER TABLE Test2
ADD CONSTRAINT ssn_pk PRIMARY KEY (ssn)
```

But, once you type in that syntax, you will receive the following error message:

```
Msg 8111, Level 16, State 1, Line 1
Cannot define PRIMARY KEY constraint on nullable column in table 'Test2'.
Msg 1750, Level 16, State 0, Line 1
Could not create constraint. See previous errors.
```

This error occurs because SQL Server 2005 does not allow you to define a primary key on a column that has not been specified as NOT NULL. So, we need to first make ssn a column that will not accept nulls as follows:

```
ALTER TABLE Test2
ALTER COLUMN ssn CHAR(9) NOT NULL
```

The design of the Test2 table will now be as in shown in Figure 11-5.

Column Name	Data Type	Allow Nulls
name	varchar(20)	☑
ssn	char(9)	☐
dept_number	int	☐
acct_balance	smallmoney	☑

Figure 11-5. New table definition of Test2

Now we can type the following command to create the primary key:

```
ALTER TABLE Test2
ADD CONSTRAINT ssn_pk PRIMARY KEY (ssn)
```

Figure 11-6 shows the primary key constraint that we just created (note the key icon on the left of the ssn column).

Column Name	Data Type	Allow Nulls
name	varchar(20)	☑
⚷ ssn	char(9)	☐
dept_number	int	☐
acct_balance	smallmoney	☑

Figure 11-6. Primary key constraint

You can view this ssn_pk constraint by clicking the + sign beside Test2, and then clicking the + sign beside the Keys node. You will get the results shown in Figure 11-7.

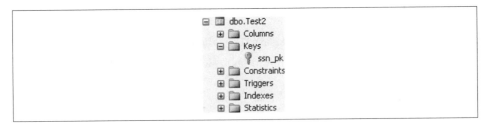

Figure 11-7. The ssn_pk constraint

You can modify, rename, delete, or refresh this ssn_pk constraint by right-clicking ssn_pk, as shown in Figure 11-8.

Concatenated primary keys

In relational databases, it is sometimes necessary to define more than one column as the primary key. When more than one column makes up a primary key, it is called a

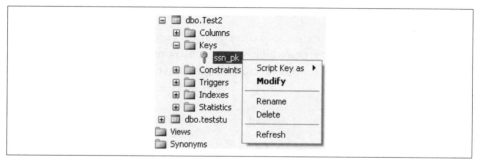

Figure 11-8. Changing constraint properties

concatenated primary key. In SQL Server 2005, however, you cannot directly designate a concatenated primary key with a statement like the following:

```
CREATE TABLE Test2a
  (ssn      CHAR(9)       PRIMARY KEY,
   salary   INT           PRIMARY KEY)
```

This query will give the following error message:

```
Msg 8110, Level 16, State 0, Line 1
Cannot add multiple PRIMARY KEY constraints to table 'Test2a'.
```

In SQL Server 2005, you can define the concatenated primary key in the following way:

```
CREATE TABLE Test2a
  (ssn      CHAR(9),
   salary   INT,
   CONSTRAINT ssn_salary_pk      PRIMARY KEY  (ssn, salary))
```

The table definition of the Test2a table will now be as shown in Figure 11-9.

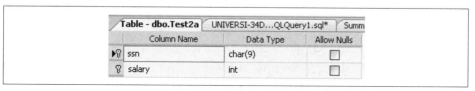

Figure 11-9. Table definition of Test2a

Or, you can create the concatenated primary key in two separate statements, first with a CREATE TABLE:

```
CREATE TABLE Test2b
  (ssn      CHAR(9)       NOT NULL,
   salary   INT           NOT NULL)
```

Then, with an ALTER TABLE:

```
ALTER TABLE Test2b
ADD CONSTRAINT ssn_salary_pk1 PRIMARY KEY (ssn, salary)
```

This query will produce the same table definition as was shown in Figure 11-9.

We called this latter constraint ssn_salary_pk1, because you cannot have another constraint called ssn_salary_pk (which was a constraint created for table Test2a). Figure 11-10 shows the constraints created for table Test2b. Note that the constraint shows up not only as a key constraint, but also as an index.

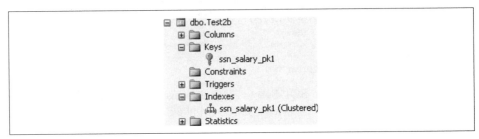

Figure 11-10. Viewing the constraints

Another example of a concatenated primary key. Suppose that we have a new table in our database, Grade1, which has columns student_number, section_id, and grade. Further suppose that a grade cannot be determined by either the student_number or section_id alone. Because both these columns (together) are required to uniquely identify a grade, the student_number and section_id will have to be the concatenated primary key of the Grade1 table.

The CREATE TABLE and ALTER TABLE sequence for creating the Grade1 table with the concatenated primary key as is shown next. First we create the Grade1 table:

```
CREATE TABLE Grade1
   (student_number    CHAR(9) NOT NULL,
    section_id        CHAR(9) NOT NULL,
    grade             CHAR(1))
```

Then we define the concatenated primary key:

```
ALTER TABLE Grade1 ADD CONSTRAINT snum_section_pk
    PRIMARY KEY (student_number, section_id)
```

Figure 11-11 gives the table definition of table Grade1.

| Table - dbo.Grade1 | UNIVERSI-34D...QLQuery1.sql* | Sumr |
Column Name	Data Type	Allow Nulls
▶🔑 student_number	char(9)	☐
🔑 section_id	char(9)	☐
grade	char(1)	☑

Figure 11-11. Table definition of Grade1

Figure 11-12 shows the constraint snum_section_pk.

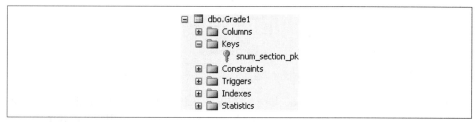

Figure 11-12. The snum_section_pk constraint

The UNIQUE Constraint

Like PRIMARY KEY, UNIQUE is another column integrity constraint. UNIQUE is different from PRIMARY KEY in three ways:

- UNIQUE keys can exist in addition to (or without) the PRIMARY KEY.
- UNIQUE does *not* necessitate NOT NULL, whereas PRIMARY KEY does.
- There can be more than one UNIQUE key, but only one PRIMARY KEY.

As an example of using the UNIQUE constraint, suppose that we created a table of names and occupational titles in which everyone was supposed to have a unique title. Further suppose that the table had an employee number as a primary key. The statement to create the table might look like the following:

```
CREATE TABLE Emp
  (empno      INT,
   name       VARCHAR(20),
   title      VARCHAR(20),
   CONSTRAINT  empno_pk    PRIMARY KEY (empno),
   CONSTRAINT  title_uk    UNIQUE (title))
```

Figure 11-13 shows the table definition of the newly created Emp table.

Column Name	Data Type	Allow Nulls
empno	int	☐
name	varchar(20)	☑
title	varchar(20)	☑

Figure 11-13. Table definition of Emp

From Figure 11-13, we can see that both the empno and title fields will not allow nulls, as empno is defined as a primary key and title is defined as unique.

Figure 11-14 shows the empno_pk and title_uk constraints of the Emp table.

Figure 11-14. Showing the empno_pk and title_uk constraints

In SQL Server 2005, when you declare a PRIMARY KEY or UNIQUE constraint, internally a unique index is created just as if you had used the CREATE INDEX command. In terms of internal storage and maintenance of indexes in SQL Server 2005, there is no difference between unique indexes created using the CREATE INDEX command and indexes created using the UNIQUE constraint. In fact, an index is a type of a constraint. When it comes to the query optimizer, how the index was created is irrelevant to the query optimizer. The query optimizer makes decisions based on the presence of a unique index.

 Discussing the query optimizer is beyond the scope of this book.

The CHECK Constraint

In addition to the NOT NULL, PRIMARY KEY and UNIQUE constraints, we can also include a CHECK constraint on our column definitions in SQL Server 2005. A CHECK constraint will disallow a value that is outside the bounds of the CHECK. Consider the following example:

```
CREATE TABLE StudentA
  (ssn        CHAR(9),
   class      INT
     CONSTRAINT class_ck CHECK (class BETWEEN 1 AND 4),
   name       VARCHAR(20))
```

This query will give the table definition of table StudentA as shown in Figure 11-15.

Column Name	Data Type	Allow Nulls
ssn	char(9)	☑
class	int	☑
name	varchar(20)	☑

Figure 11-15. Table definition of StudentA

To view the CHECK constraint, click the + sign beside table StudentA, and then click the + sign beside Constraints, and you will get Figure 11-16.

Figure 11-16. The CHECK constraint

Once the CHECK constraint has been added, we could not, for example, successfully execute the following INSERT:

```
INSERT INTO StudentA VALUES ('123456789', 5, 'Smith')
```

We would get the following error message:

```
Msg 547, Level 16, State 0, Line 1
The INSERT statement conflicted with the CHECK constraint "class_ck". The conflict
occurred in database "Student_course", table "dbo.StudentA", column 'class'.
The statement has been terminated.
```

This error occurs because the values of the column class have to be between 1 and 4 (and we tried to insert 5). We could however, enter a null value for class, which technically does not violate the integrity constraint (unless we specify so by making class also NOT NULL).

Deleting a Constraint

The following is the general SQL syntax to delete any named constraint:

```
ALTER TABLE Tablename
DROP CONSTRAINT constraint_name
```

For example, in table Test2a we created a constraint called ssn_salary_pk, which made both the ssn and salary columns primary keys of Test2a. If we want to delete this constraint, which means making both the ssn and salary columns just regular columns (and not primary keys), we would type the following:

```
ALTER TABLE Test2a
DROP CONSTRAINT ssn_salary_pk
```

Now the table definition of table Test2a will appear as shown in Figure 11-17. As can be seen from Figure 11-17, the primary keys are no longer marked, as was shown in Figure 11-9.

Table - dbo.Test2a	UNIVERSI-34D...QLQuery1.sql*	Sumn
Column Name	Data Type	Allow Nulls
ssn	char(9)	☐
salary	int	☐

Figure 11-17. Primary keys no longer marked

Figure 11-18 also shows no constraints for table Test2a.

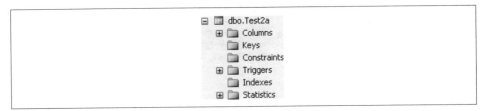

Figure 11-18. Constraint deleted

Referential Integrity Constraints

A relational database consists of relations (tables) and relationships between tables. To define a relationship between two tables, we create a referential integrity constraint. A referential integrity constraint is one in which a row in one table (with a foreign key) cannot exist unless a value (column) in that row refers to a primary key value (column) in another table. This is a primary key–foreign key relationship between two tables. For example, suppose we have the following two tables:

 A foreign key is a column in one table that is used to link that table to another table in which that column is a primary key. Relationships are implemented in relational databases through foreign keys/primary key relationships.

Table 11-1. Department table

Deptno	Deptname
1	Accounting
2	Personnel
3	Development

Table 11-2. Employee table

empno	Empname	Dept
100	Jones	2
101	Smith	1
102	Adams	1
104	Harris	3

To maintain referential integrity, it would be inappropriate to enter a row (tuple) in the Employee table that did not have an existing department number already defined in the Department table. To try to insert the following row into the Employee table would be a violation of the integrity of the database, because department number 4 does not exist (that is, it has no integrity):

```
<105,'Walsh',4>
```

Likewise, it would be invalid to try to change a value in an existing row (that is, perform an UPDATE) to make it equal to a value that does not exist. If, for example, we tried to change:

```
<100,'Jones',2>
```

to:

```
<100,'Jones',5>
```

This operation would violate database integrity, because there is no department 5.

Finally, it would be invalid to delete a row in the Department table that contains a value for a department number that is already in the Employee table. For example, if:

```
<2,'Personnel'>
```

were deleted from the Department table, then the row:

```
<100,'Jones',2>
```

would refer to a nonexistent department. It therefore would be a reference or relationship with no integrity.

In each case (INSERT, UPDATE, and DELETE), we say that there needs to be a referential integrity constraint on the dept column in the Employee table referencing deptno in the Department table. When this primary key (deptno in the Department table)–foreign key (dept in the Employee table) relationship is defined, we have defined the relationship of the Employee table to the Department table.

In the INSERT and UPDATE cases discussed earlier, you would expect (correctly) that the usual action of the system would be to deny the action. In SQL Server 2005, in the case of the DELETE and UPDATE commands, there is an option available that will allow us to CASCADE the DELETE or UPDATE operations respectively. Whereas an "ordinary" referential integrity constraint would simply disallow the deletion of a row where the referenced row would be orphaned, a CASCADEd delete would delete the referencing row as well. If, for example, in the previous data we deleted department 3, in a CASCADEd delete situation, the referencing row in the Employee table, <104,Harris,3>, would be deleted as well.

Defining the referential integrity constraint

To enable a referential integrity constraint, it is necessary for the column that is being referenced to be first defined as a primary key. In the preceding Employee-Department example, we have to first create the Department table with a primary key. The CREATE TABLE statement for the Department table (the *referenced* table) could look like this:

```
CREATE TABLE Department
  (deptno      INT,
   deptname    VARCHAR(20),
   CONSTRAINT  deptno_pk   PRIMARY KEY (deptno))
```

The table definition of the Department table would then be as shown in Figure 11-19.

Table - dbo.Department	UNIVERSI-34D...QLQuery1.sql*	
Column Name	Data Type	Allow Nulls
deptno	int	☐
deptname	varchar(20)	☑

Figure 11-19. Table definition of Department table

The constraints for the Department table would be as shown in Figure 11-20.

Figure 11-20. Constraint of the Department table

The Employee table (the *referencing* table containing the foreign key) would then be created using this statement:

```
CREATE TABLE Employee
    (empno    INT CONSTRAINT    empno_pk1 PRIMARY KEY,
     empname VARCHAR(20),
     dept    INT CONSTRAINT    dept_fk    REFERENCES  Department(deptno))
```

The table definition of the Employee table would then be as shown in Figure 11-21.

Table - dbo.Employee	UNIVERSI-34D...QLQuery1.sql*	Su
Column Name	Data Type	Allow Nulls
empno	int	☐
empname	varchar(20)	☑
dept	int	☑

Figure 11-21. Table definition of the Employee table

Now, to view the referential integrity constraints of the Employee table, click the + sign beside Employee and then click the + sign beside Keys, you will get Figure 11-22.

To modify the foreign key, right-click dept_fk and select Modify, as shown in Figure 11-23.

You will get the results shown in Figure 11-24. You can expand the Table And Columns Specification option (under General), and you will be able to see what the foreign key base table is (that is, the table with the foreign key, which in this case is the Employee table), what the foreign key columns are (in this case, dept), what the pri-

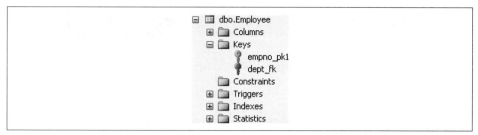

Figure 11-22. Viewing the referential integrity constraints of the Employee table

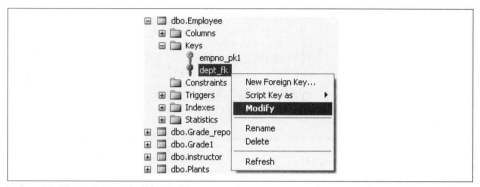

Figure 11-23. Modifying the foreign key

mary/unique key base table is (that is, the table with the primary key, which in this case is Department), the primary/unique key column (which in this case is deptno). You can change these options by clicking on the ... icon on the right of General.

The CREATE TABLE Employee... statement defines a column, dept, to be of type INT, but the statement goes further in defining dept to be a *foreign* key that references another table, Department. Again, within the Department table, the referenced column, deptno, has to be an already-defined primary key.

Also note that the Department table has to be created first. If we tried to create the Employee table before the Department table with the referential CONSTRAINT, we would be trying to reference a nonexistent table and this would also cause an error.

Adding the foreign key after tables are created

As we have seen with other constraints, the foreign key can be added after tables are created. To do so, we must first have set up the primary key of the referenced table. The syntax of the ALTER TABLE command to add a foreign key to a referencing table would look like this:

```
ALTER TABLE xxx
    ADD CONSTRAINT dept_fk
    FOREIGN KEY (dept)
    REFERENCES Department(deptno)
```

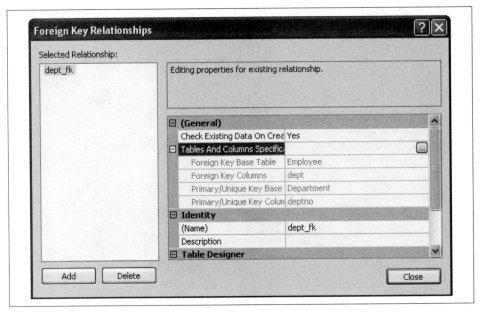

Figure 11-24. The dept_fk foreign key

The (optional) name of the CONSTRAINT is dept_fk. Note that the column's data types in the references clause must agree with the column's data types in the referenced table.

DELETE and the referential CONSTRAINT

There are a couple of options in the DELETE option of a foreign key referential constraint in SQL Server 2005—CASCADE and NO ACTION. Both of these options specify what action takes place on a row if that row has a referential relationship and the referenced row is deleted from the parent table. First we discuss the default, which is NO ACTION, and then we look at the CASCADE option.

ON DELETE NO ACTION. If the NO ACTION alternative is used in the ON DELETE option of the CREATE TABLE command, and we try to delete a row from the parent table (in this case, the Department table) that has a referencing row in the dependent table (in this case, the Employee table), then SQL Server 2005 will raise an error and the delete action on the row in the parent table will be undone. The NO ACTION option on the ON DELETE option is the default.

The ON DELETE NO ACTION option is added after the REFERENCES clause of a CREATE TABLE command. The CREATE TABLE command with the ON DELETE NO ACTION would be as shown in the next example.

In order to create the following Employee table, you will need to delete the previous one.

```
CREATE TABLE Employee
  (empno      INT     CONSTRAINT    empno_pk2 PRIMARY KEY,
   empname    VARCHAR(20),
   dept       INT     REFERENCES    Department(deptno)
              ON DELETE NO ACTION)
```

 Make sure that you have created the Department table first before you attempt to create this Employee table.

The design of the Employee table will now be as shown in Figure 11-25.

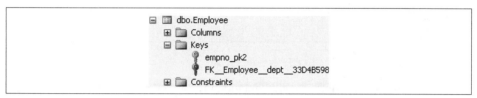

Figure 11-25. Viewing the referential integrity constraints of the Employee table

Then, to view the ON DELETE NO ACTION, from Figure 11-25, right-click on EFK_ Employee_dept_33D4B598 and select Modify, similar to what is shown in Figure 11-23. You will get Figure 11-26, the Foreign Key Relationships screen. On this screen, under Table Designer, expand the "INSERT And UPDATE Specification" option, and you will see the Delete Rule as No Action, shown in Figure 11-26.

ON DELETE CASCADE. The ON DELETE CASCADE option may be added after the REFERENCES clause of a CREATE TABLE command, as shown here:

 In order to create the following Employee table, you will need to delete the previous one.

```
CREATE TABLE Employee
  (empno      INT     CONSTRAINT    empno_pk3 PRIMARY KEY,
   empname    VARCHAR(20),
   dept       INT     REFERENCES    Department(deptno)
              ON DELETE CASCADE)
```

The table definition of the Employee table will be similar to what was shown in Figure 11-21.

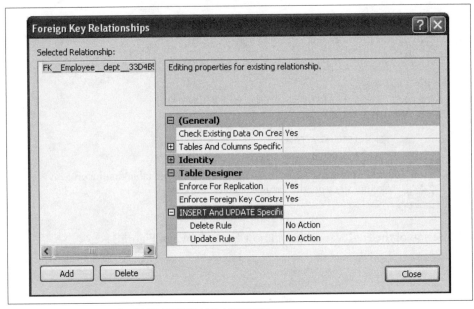

Figure 11-26. Viewing the ON DELETE NO ACTION

The ON DELETE CASCADE option will be included in the referential integrity constraint. To view the ON DELETE CASCADE, from the Foreign Key Relationships screen, once again expand the "INSERT And UPDATE Specification" option, and you will see the Delete Rule as Cascade, shown in Figure 11-27.

CASCADE will allow the deletions in the dependent table (in this case, the Employee table) that are affected by the deletions of the tuples in the referenced table (in this case, the Department table). Suppose, for example, that we had deptno = 3 in the Department table. Also suppose that we had employees in department 3. If we deleted department 3 in the Department table, then with CASCADE we would also delete all employees in the Employee table with dept = 3.

UPDATE and the referential CONSTRAINT

Both the CASCADE and NO ACTION options are also available with the ON UPDATE option of a foreign key referential constraint enforcement in SQL Server 2005. Both these options specify what action takes place on a row if that row has a referential relationship and the referenced row is updated in the parent table. In the following discussion, we show the syntax of these two options.

ON UPDATE NO ACTION. Just as with the ON DELETE option, if the NO ACTION option is used with the ON UPDATE option of the CREATE TABLE command, and we try to update a row from the parent table (in this case, the Department table) that has a referencing row in the dependent table (in this case, the Employee table), then SQL Server 2005

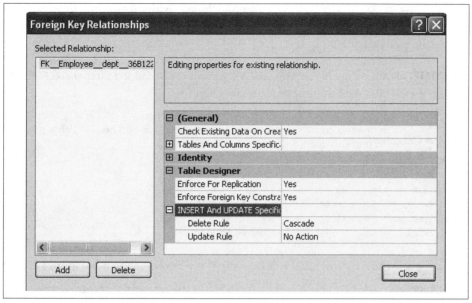

Figure 11-27. Viewing the ON DELETE CASCADE option

will raise an error and the update action on the row in the parent table will be rolled back. The NO ACTION option on the ON UPDATE option is the default.

Just as in the ON DELETE NO ACTION option, the ON UPDATE NO ACTION option is added after the REFERENCES clause of a CREATE TABLE command. The CREATE TABLE command with the ON UPDATE NO ACTION would be as shown here:

In order to create the following Employee table, you will need to delete the previous one.

```
CREATE TABLE Employee
  (empno      INT      CONSTRAINT    empno_pk4 PRIMARY KEY,
   empname    VARCHAR(20),
   dept       INT      REFERENCES    Department(deptno)
              ON UPDATE NO ACTION)
```

Make sure you have created the Department table first before you attempt to create this Employee table.

Once again, the design of the Employee table will be similar to what was shown in Figure 11-21.

The ON UPDATE NO ACTION option will be included in the referential integrity constraint. View the ON UPDATE NO ACTION as shown in Figure 11-27. Figure 11-27 also shows the Update Rule.

ON UPDATE CASCADE. The ON UPDATE CASCADE option is also added after the REFERENCES clause of a CREATE TABLE command, as shown here:

 In order to create the following Employee table, you will need to delete the previous one.

```
CREATE TABLE Employee
  (empno     INT      CONSTRAINT   empno_pk5 PRIMARY KEY,
   empname   VARCHAR(20),
   dept      INT      REFERENCES   Department(deptno)
             ON UPDATE CASCADE)
```

The design of the Employee table will be similar to what was shown in Figure 11-21.

The ON UPDATE CASCADE option will be included in the referential integrity constraint. To view the ON UPDATE CASCADE, from the Foreign Key Relationships screen, once again expand the "INSERT And UPDATE Specification" option, and you will see the Update Rule as Cascade, shown in Figure 11-28.

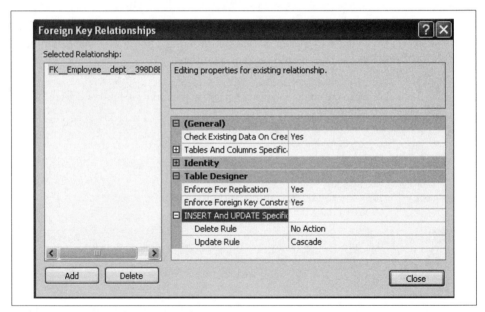

Figure 11-28. Viewing the ON UPDATE CASCADE

When CASCADE is included in the ON UPDATE option, the row is updated in the referencing table (in this case, the Employee table) if that row is updated in the parent table (in this case, the Department table).

Using the ON DELETE and ON UPDATE together

You can also use the ON DELETE and ON UPDATE options together if needed. Both the ON DELETE and ON UPDATE do not necessarily have to be set to the same option. That is, both of them do not have to be set to NO ACTION or CASCADE at the same time. You can have a NO ACTION option set for one option and a CASCADE set for the other option. For example, you may create the Employee table as follows:

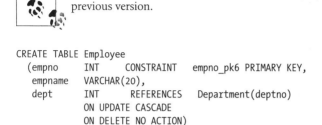 Once again, note that before you create this Employee table, delete the previous version.

```
CREATE TABLE Employee
   (empno      INT     CONSTRAINT    empno_pk6 PRIMARY KEY,
    empname    VARCHAR(20),
    dept       INT     REFERENCES    Department(deptno)
               ON UPDATE CASCADE
               ON DELETE NO ACTION)
```

Once again, the table definition of the Employee table would then be as shown in Figure 11-21.

Both the ON UPDATE CASCADE option and the ON DELETE NO ACTION option will be included in the referential integrity constraint. Once again, from the Foreign Key Relationships screen, expand the "INSERT And UPDATE Specification" option, and you will see the Delete Rule as well as Update Rule.

The foreign key relationships figure will be as shown in Figure 11-29.

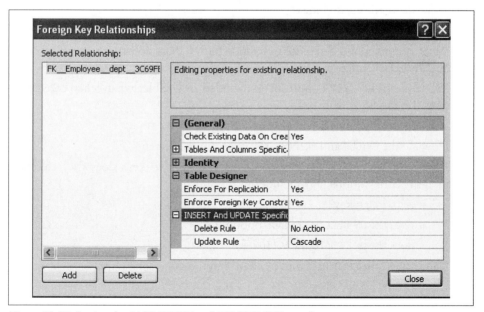

Figure 11-29. Setting the ON DELETE and ON UPDATE together

So, in summary, SQL Server 2005 gives you quite a bit of flexibility in setting up your referential integrity constraints.

Summary

In this chapter, we showed you how to create indexes and constraints using different options. We also showed you how to view, edit, and delete indexes and constraints. We explained referential integrity constraints, and also showed you how to create, view and edit them.

Review Questions

1. What is an index?
2. Does an index slow down updates on indexed columns?
3. What is a constraint?
4. How many indexes does SQL Server 2005 allow you to have on a table?
5. What command would you use to create an index?
6. Is there a difference between an index and a constraint?
7. What is the default ordering that will be created by an index (ascending or descending)?
8. When can the UNIQUE option be used?
9. What does the IGNORE NULL option do?
10. How do you delete an index?
11. What does the NOT NULL constraint do?
12. What command must you use to include the NOT NULL constraint after a table has already been created?
13. When a PRIMARY KEY constraint is included in a table, what other constraints does this imply?
14. What is a concatenated primary key?
15. How are the UNIQUE and PRIMARY KEY constraints different?
16. What is a referential integrity constraint? What two keys does the referential integrity constraint usually include?
17. What is a foreign key?
18. What does the ON DELETE CASCADE option do?
19. What does the ON UPDATE NO ACTION do?
20. Can you use the ON DELETE and ON UPDATE in the same constraint?

Exercises

Unless specified otherwise, use the Student_course database to answer the following questions. Unless otherwise directed, name all CONSTRAINTs.

1. To test choices of data types, create a table with various data types like this:

   ```
   CREATE TABLE Test3
     (name            VARCHAR(20),
      ssn             CHAR(9),
      dept_number     INTEGER,
      acct_balance    SMALLMONEY)
   ```

   Then insert values into the table to see what will and will not be accepted. The following data may or may not be acceptable. You are welcome to try other choices.

   ```
   'xx','yy',2,5
   'xx','yyy',2000000000,5
   'xx','yyyy',2,1234567.89
   ```

2. Create an index of ssn in ascending order of ssn. Try to insert some new data in the ssn column. Does your ssn column take nulls?

   a. Does your ssn column take duplicates? If so, how can you prevent this column from taking duplicates?

   b. Include a NOT NULL constraint on the ssn column. Now try to insert some new data in the ssn column with nulls in the ssn column. What happens?

   c. With this NOT NULL constraint, is it necessary to include the PRIMARY KEY constraint? Why or why not? Now include the PRIMARY KEY constraint and see whether there is any difference in the types of values it accepts.

   d. Include some data with null values in the dept_number and acct_balance columns. Now include the NOT NULL constraint in the acct_balance column. What happens?

   e. Include the NOT NULL constraint in the acct_balance column. What happens?

   Delete Test3.

3. To test the errors generated when NOT NULL is used, create a table called Test4, which looks like this:

   ```
   CREATE TABLE Test4
     (a    CHAR(2)    NOT NULL,
      b    CHAR(3))
   ```

   Input some data and try to enter a null value for A. Acceptable input data for a null is "null."

4. Create or recreate, if necessary, Test3, which does not specify a primary key. Populate the table with at least one duplicate ssn. Then, try to impose the PRIMARY KEY constraint with an ALTER TABLE command. What happens?

a. Recreate the Test3 table, but this time add a primary key of ssn. If you still have the Test3 table from Exercise 4, you may be able to delete *offending* rows and add the PRIMARY KEY constraint. Enter two more rows to your table—one containing a new ssn and one with a duplicate ssn. What happens?

5. Create the Department and Employee tables, as per the examples earlier in the chapter, with all the constraints (PRIMARY KEYs, referential and UNIQUE constraints). You can add the constraints at create time or you can use ALTER TABLE to add the constraints. Populate the Department table first with departments 1, 2, and 3. Then populate the Employee table.

Note: before doing the next few exercises, it is prudent to create two tables, called Deptbak and Empbak, to contain the data you load, because you will be deleting, inserting, dropping, recreating, and so on. You can create Deptbak and Empbak tables (as temporary tables) with the data we have been using with a query like:

```
SELECT *
INTO Deptbak
FROM Dept
```

Then, when you have added, deleted, updated, and so on and you want the original table from the start of this problem, you simply run the following commands:

```
DROP TABLE Dept
SELECT *
INTO Dept
FROM  Deptbak
```

a. Create a violation of insertion integrity by adding an employee to a nonexistent department. What happens?

b. Create an UPDATE violation by trying to change an existing employee to a nonexistent department, and then by trying to change a referenced department number.

c. Try to delete a department for which there is an employee. What happens? What happens if you try to DELETE a department to which no employee has yet been assigned?

d. Redo this entire experiment (starting with Exercise 5a), except that this time create the Employee table with the ON DELETE CASCADE. View the table definition of the Employee table.

e. Redo exercises 5a–5c, except that this time, create the Employee table with the ON DELETE NO ACTION.

f. Redo exercises 5a–5c, except that this time, create the Employee table with the ON UPDATE CASCADE.

g. Redo exercises 5a–5c, except that this time, create the Employee table with the ON UPDATE NO ACTION.

h. Redo exercises 5a–5c, except that this time, create the Employee table with the ON UPDATE NO ACTION and ON DELETE CASCADE together.

6. Create a table (your choice) with a PRIMARY KEY and a UNIQUE constraint. Insert data into the table and, as you do, enter a *good* row and a *bad* row (the *bad* row violates a constraint). Demonstrate a violation of each of your constraints one at a time. Show the successes and the errors as you receive them.

7. In this chapter, the Employee table was referenced to (depended on) the Department table. Suppose that there were another table that depended on the Employee table, such as Dependent, where the Dependent table contained the columns name and empnum. Create the Dependent table. Then add the referential constraint where empnum references the Employee table, with ON DELETE CASCADE (and note that the Employee table also has an ON DELETE CASCADE option). You are creating a situation in which the Dependent table references the Employee table, which references the Department table. Will SQL Server let you do this? If so, and if you delete a tuple from the Department table, will it cascade through the Employee table and on to the Dependent table?

The Student Database and Other Tables Used in This Book

Table A-1. *Table definitions of the tables in the Student_course database*

```
STUDENT
    STNO        NOT NULL    SMALLINT        PRIMARY KEY
    SNAME                   NVARCHAR(20)
    MAJOR                   NVARCHAR(4)
    CLASS                   SMALLINT
    BDATE                   SMALLDATETIME

DEPENDENT
    PNO                         SMALLINT
    DNAME                       NVARCHAR(20)
    RELATIONSHIP                NVARCHAR(8)
    SEX                         CHAR(1)
    AGE                         SMALLINT

GRADE_REPORT
    STUDENT_NUMBER    NOT NULL    SMALLINT
    SECTION_ID        NOT NULL    SMALLINT
    GRADE                         CHAR(1)
    PRIMARY KEY(STUDENT_NUMBER, SECTION_ID)

SECTION
    SECTION_ID      NOT NULL    SMALLINT        PRIMARY KEY
    COURSE_NUM                  NVARCHAR(8)
    SEMESTER                    NVARCHAR(6)
    YEAR                        CHAR(2)
    INSTRUCTOR                  NVARCHAR(10)
    BLDG                        SMALLINT
    ROOM                        SMALLINT

DEPARTMENT_TO_MAJOR
    DCODE           NOT NULL    NVARCHAR(4)     PRIMARY KEY
    DNAME                       NVARCHAR(20)

COURSE
    COURSE_NAME                 NVARCHAR(20)
    COURSE_NUMBER   NOT NULL    NVARCHAR(8)     PRIMARY KEY     NOT NULL
```

```
    CREDIT_HOURS                        SMALLINT
    OFFERING_DEPT                       NVARCHAR(4)

ROOM
    BLDG            NOT NULL            SMALLINT
    ROOM            NOT NULL            SMALLINT
    CAPACITY                            SMALLINT
    OHEAD                               NVARCHAR(1)
    PRIMARY KEY(BLDG, ROOM)

PREREQ
    COURSE_NUMBER                       NVARCHAR(8)
    PREREQU                             NVARCHAR(8)
    PRIMARY KEY (COURSE_NUMBER, PREREQ)
```

A. ER Diagram for the Student_course Database

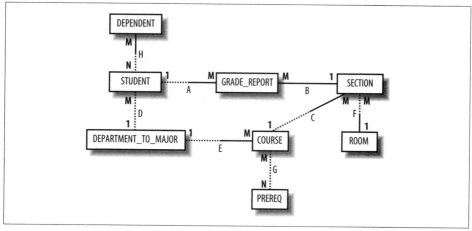

Figure A-1. Diagram for the Student_course database

Brief English Description of the ER Diagram

A. Student *may* be registered in one or more (M) Grade_Reports (Grade_report is for a specific course).

A Grade_Report *must* relate to one and only one (1) Student.

(Students may be in the database and not registered for any courses, but if a course is recorded in the Grade_report table, it must be related to one and only one student).

B. A Section *must* have one or more (M) Grade_Reports (Sections only exist if they have students in them).

A Grade_Report *must* relate to one and only one (1) Section.

C. A Section *must* relate to one and only one (1) Course.

A Course *may* be offered as one or more (M) Sections.

(Courses may exist where they are not offered in a section, but a section, if offered, must relate to one and only one course).

D. A Student *may* be related to one and only one (1) `Department_to_major` (A student may or may not have declared a major).

A `Department_to_major` *may* have one or more (M) `Students` (A department may or may not have student-majors).

E. A Course *must* be related to one and only one (1) `Department_to_major`.

A `Department_to_major` *may* offer one or more (M) `Courses`.

F. A Section *must* be offered in one and only one (1) `Room`.

A Room *may* host one or more (M) `Sections`.

G. A Course *may* have one or more (M) `Prereq` (A course may have one or more prerequisites).

A `Prereq` *may* be a prerequisite for one or more (M) `Courses`.

H. A Student *may* have one or more (M) `Dependents`.

A Dependent *must* be related to one or more (N) `Students`.

Table A-2. Table definition of other tables that have been used in this book

PLANTS
```
    COMPANY                 NVARCHAR(20)
    PLANTLO                 NVARCHAR(15)
    PRIMARY KEY(COMPANY, PLANTLO)
```

CAP
```
    NAME                    NVARCHAR(9)
    LANGU                   NVARCHAR(7)
    PRIMARY KEY(NAME, LANGU)
```

Script Used to Create the Student_course Database

Here we present the actual script used to create the Student_Course database.

```
drop table student;
drop table grade_report;
drop table section;
drop table department_to_major;
drop table plants;
drop table prereq;
drop table course;
drop table cap;
drop table room;
drop table teststu;
create table Student
(STNO SMALLINT PRIMARY KEY NOT NULL,
 SNAME NVARCHAR(20) NULL,
 MAJOR NVARCHAR(4) NULL,
 CLASS SMALLINT NULL,
 BDATE SMALLDATETIME NULL)
;
create table Grade_report
(STUDENT_NUMBER SMALLINT NOT NULL,
 SECTION_ID SMALLINT NOT NULL,
 GRADE CHAR(1),
 CONSTRAINT stno_secid PRIMARY KEY (STUDENT_NUMBER, SECTION_ID))
;
create table Section
(SECTION_ID SMALLINT PRIMARY KEY NOT NULL,
 COURSE_NUM NVARCHAR(8),
 SEMESTER NVARCHAR(6),
 YEAR CHAR(2),
 INSTRUCTOR NVARCHAR(10),
 BLDG SMALLINT,
 ROOM SMALLINT)
;
create table Department_to_major
(Dcode NVARCHAR(4) PRIMARY KEY NOT NULL,
 DNAME NVARCHAR(20))
;
```

```
create table Plants
(COMPANY NVARCHAR(20),
 PLANTLO NVARCHAR(15))
;
create table Prereq
(COURSE_NUMBER NVARCHAR(8),
 PREREQ NVARCHAR(8),
 CONSTRAINT couno_pre PRIMARY KEY(COURSE_NUMBER, PREREQ))
;
create table Course
(COURSE_NAME NVARCHAR(20),
 COURSE_NUMBER NVARCHAR(8) PRIMARY KEY NOT NULL,
 CREDIT_HOURS SMALLINT,
 OFFERING_DEPT NVARCHAR(4))
;
create table Cap
(NAME NVARCHAR(9),
 LANGU NVARCHAR(7))
;
create table Room
 (BLDG SMALLINT NOT NULL,
 ROOM SMALLINT NOT NULL,
 CAPACITY SMALLINT,
 OHEAD NVARCHAR(1),
 CONSTRAINT bldg_room PRIMARY KEY(BLDG, ROOM))
;
create table Dependent
(PNO SMALLINT NOT NULL,
 DNAME NVARCHAR(20) NULL,
 RELATIONSHIP NVARCHAR(8) NULL,
 SEX CHAR(1) NULL,
 AGE SMALLINT NULL)
;
insert into cap values('BRENDA','FRENCH');
insert into cap values('BRENDA','CHINESE');
insert into cap values('RICHARD','CHINESE');
insert into cap values('RICHARD','GERMAN');
insert into cap values('MARY JO','FRENCH');
insert into cap values('RICHARD','FRENCH');
insert into cap values('LUJACK','GERMAN');
insert into cap values('LUJACK','CHINESE');
insert into cap values('MARY JO','GERMAN');
insert into cap values('MARY JO','CHINESE');
insert into cap values('MELANIE','FRENCH');
insert into cap values('LUJACK','FRENCH');
insert into cap values('MELANIE','CHINESE');
insert into cap values('BRENDA','SPANISH');
insert into cap values('RICHARD','SPANISH');
insert into cap values('JOE','CHINESE');
insert into cap values('LUJACK','SPANISH');
insert into cap values('KENT','CHINESE');
insert into course values('ACCOUNTING I','ACCT2020',3,'ACCT');
insert into course values('ACCOUNTING II ','ACCT2220',3,'ACCT');
insert into course values('MANAGERIAL FINANCE','ACCT3333',3,'ACCT');
```

```
insert into course values('ACCOUNTING INFO SYST','ACCT3464',3,'ACCT');
insert into course values('INTRO TO COMPUTER SC','COSC1310',4,'COSC');
insert into course values('TURBO PASCAL','COSC2025',3,'COSC');
insert into course values('ADVANCED COBOL','COSC2303',3,'COSC');
insert into course values('DATA STRUCTURES ','COSC3320',4,'COSC');
insert into course values('DATABASE','COSC3380',3,'COSC');
insert into course values('OPERATIONS RESEARCH ','COSC3701',3,'COSC');
insert into course values('ADVANCED ASSEMBLER','COSC4301',3,'COSC');
insert into course values('SYSTEM PROJECT','COSC4309',3,'COSC');
insert into course values('ADA - INTRODUCTION','COSC5234',4,'COSC');
insert into course values('NETWORKS','COSC5920',3,'COSC');
insert into course values('ENGLISH COMP I','ENGL1010',3,'ENGL');
insert into course values('ENGLISH COMP II ','ENGL1011',3,'ENGL');
insert into course values('WRITING FOR NON MAJO','ENGL3520',2,'ENGL');
insert into course values('ALGEBRA ','MATH2333',3,'MATH');
insert into course values('DISCRETE MATHEMATICS','MATH2410',3,'MATH');
insert into course values('CALCULUS 1','MATH1501',4,'MATH');
insert into course values('AMERICAN CONSTITUTIO','POLY1201',1,'POLY');
insert into course values('INTRO TO POLITICAL S','POLY2001',3,'POLY');
insert into course values('AMERICAN GOVERNMENT ','POLY2103',2,'POLY');
insert into course values('SOCIALISM AND COMMUN','POLY4103',4,'POLY');
insert into course values('POLITICS OF CUBA','POLY5501',4,'POLY');
insert into course values('TECHNICAL WRITING ','ENGL3402',2,'ENGL');
insert into course values('FUND. TECH. WRITING ','ENGL3401',3,'ENGL');
insert into course values('INTRO TO CHEMISTRY','CHEM2001',3,'CHEM');
insert into course values('ORGANIC CHEMISTRY ','CHEM3001',3,'CHEM');
insert into course values('CALCULUS 2','MATH1502',3,'MATH');
insert into course values('CALCULUS 3','MATH1503',3,'MATH');
insert into course values('MATH ANALYSIS','MATH5501',3,'MATH');
insert into department_to_major values('ACCT','Accounting');
insert into department_to_major values('ART','Art');
insert into department_to_major values('COSC','Computer Science');
insert into department_to_major values('ENGL','English');
insert into department_to_major values('MATH','Mathematics');
insert into department_to_major values('POLY','Political Science');
insert into department_to_major values('UNKN',null);
insert into department_to_major values('CHEM','Chemistry');
insert into grade_report values(2,85,'D');
insert into grade_report values(2,102,'B');
insert into grade_report values(2,126,'B');
insert into grade_report values(2,127,'A');
insert into grade_report values(2,145,'B');
insert into grade_report values(3,85,'A');
insert into grade_report values(3,87,'B');
insert into grade_report values(3,90,'B');
insert into grade_report values(3,91,'B');
insert into grade_report values(3,92,'B');
insert into grade_report values(3,96,'B');
insert into grade_report values(3,101,null);
insert into grade_report values(3,133,null);
insert into grade_report values(3,134,null);
insert into grade_report values(3,135,null);
insert into grade_report values(8,85,'A');
insert into grade_report values(8,92,'A');
```

```
insert into grade_report values(8,96,'C');
insert into grade_report values(8,102,'B');
insert into grade_report values(8,133,null);
insert into grade_report values(8,134,null);
insert into grade_report values(8,135,null);
insert into grade_report values(10,101,null);
insert into grade_report values(10,112,null);
insert into grade_report values(10,119,null);
insert into grade_report values(10,126,'C');
insert into grade_report values(10,127,'A');
insert into grade_report values(10,145,'C');
insert into grade_report values(13,85,'B');
insert into grade_report values(13,95,'B');
insert into grade_report values(13,99,null);
insert into grade_report values(13,109,null);
insert into grade_report values(13,119,null);
insert into grade_report values(13,133,null);
insert into grade_report values(13,134,null);
insert into grade_report values(13,135,null);
insert into grade_report values(14,102,'B');
insert into grade_report values(14,112,null);
insert into grade_report values(14,91,'A');
insert into grade_report values(14,135,null);
insert into grade_report values(14,145,'B');
insert into grade_report values(14,158,'B');
insert into grade_report values(15,85,'F');
insert into grade_report values(15,92,'B');
insert into grade_report values(15,99,null);
insert into grade_report values(15,102,'B');
insert into grade_report values(15,135,null);
insert into grade_report values(15,145,'B');
insert into grade_report values(15,158,'C');
insert into grade_report values(17,112,null);
insert into grade_report values(17,119,null);
insert into grade_report values(17,135,null);
insert into grade_report values(19,102,'B');
insert into grade_report values(19,119,null);
insert into grade_report values(19,133,null);
insert into grade_report values(19,158,'D');
insert into grade_report values(20,87,'A');
insert into grade_report values(20,94,'C');
insert into grade_report values(6,201,null);
insert into grade_report values(8,201,null);
insert into grade_report values(24,90,'B');
insert into grade_report values(34,90,'B');
insert into grade_report values(49,90,'C');
insert into grade_report values(62,90,'C');
insert into grade_report values(70,90,'C');
insert into grade_report values(121,90,'B');
insert into grade_report values(122,90,'B');
insert into grade_report values(123,90,'B');
insert into grade_report values(125,90,'C');
insert into grade_report values(126,90,'C');
insert into grade_report values(127,90,'C');
```

```
insert into grade_report values(128,90,'F');
insert into grade_report values(129,90,'A');
insert into grade_report values(130,90,'C');
insert into grade_report values(131,90,'C');
insert into grade_report values(132,90,'B');
insert into grade_report values(142,90,'A');
insert into grade_report values(143,90,'B');
insert into grade_report values(144,90,'B');
insert into grade_report values(145,90,'F');
insert into grade_report values(146,90,'B');
insert into grade_report values(147,90,'C');
insert into grade_report values(148,90,'C');
insert into grade_report values(31,90,'C');
insert into grade_report values(151,90,'C');
insert into grade_report values(153,90,'C');
insert into grade_report values(155,90,'B');
insert into grade_report values(157,90,'B');
insert into grade_report values(158,90,'C');
insert into grade_report values(163,90,'C');
insert into grade_report values(161,90,'C');
insert into grade_report values(160,90,'C');
insert into grade_report values(5,90,'C');
insert into grade_report values(7,90,'C');
insert into grade_report values(9,90,'F');
insert into grade_report values(62,94,'C');
insert into grade_report values(70,94,'C');
insert into grade_report values(49,94,'C');
insert into grade_report values(5,94,'C');
insert into grade_report values(6,94,'C');
insert into grade_report values(7,94,'C');
insert into grade_report values(8,94,'C');
insert into grade_report values(9,94,'F');
insert into grade_report values(5,95,'B');
insert into grade_report values(6,95,'B');
insert into grade_report values(7,95,'B');
insert into grade_report values(8,95,'B');
insert into grade_report values(9,95,'F');
insert into grade_report values(121,95,'B');
insert into grade_report values(122,95,'B');
insert into grade_report values(123,95,'B');
insert into grade_report values(125,95,'B');
insert into grade_report values(126,95,'B');
insert into grade_report values(127,95,'B');
insert into grade_report values(128,95,'F');
insert into grade_report values(129,95,'B');
insert into grade_report values(130,95,'C');
insert into grade_report values(121,94,'B');
insert into grade_report values(122,94,'B');
insert into grade_report values(123,94,'B');
insert into grade_report values(125,94,'C');
insert into grade_report values(126,94,'C');
insert into grade_report values(127,94,'C');
insert into grade_report values(128,94,'F');
insert into grade_report values(129,94,'A');
```

```
insert into grade_report values(130,94,'C');
insert into grade_report values(24,95,'B');
insert into grade_report values(24,96,'B');
insert into grade_report values(24,97,null);
insert into grade_report values(24,98,null);
insert into grade_report values(24,99,null);
insert into grade_report values(24,100,null);
insert into grade_report values(34,98,null);
insert into grade_report values(34,97,null);
insert into grade_report values(34,93,'A');
insert into grade_report values(49,98,null);
insert into grade_report values(49,97,null);
insert into grade_report values(49,93,'A');
insert into grade_report values(123,98,null);
insert into grade_report values(123,97,null);
insert into grade_report values(123,93,'A');
insert into grade_report values(125,98,null);
insert into grade_report values(125,97,null);
insert into grade_report values(125,93,'A');
insert into grade_report values(126,98,null);
insert into grade_report values(126,97,null);
insert into grade_report values(126,93,'A');
insert into grade_report values(127,98,null);
insert into grade_report values(127,97,null);
insert into grade_report values(127,93,'A');
insert into grade_report values(142,100,null);
insert into grade_report values(143,100,null);
insert into grade_report values(144,100,null);
insert into grade_report values(145,100,null);
insert into grade_report values(146,100,null);
insert into grade_report values(147,100,null);
insert into grade_report values(148,100,null);
insert into grade_report values(142,107,null);
insert into grade_report values(143,107,null);
insert into grade_report values(144,107,null);
insert into grade_report values(145,107,null);
insert into grade_report values(146,107,null);
insert into grade_report values(147,107,null);
insert into grade_report values(148,107,null);
insert into grade_report values(142,202,null);
insert into grade_report values(143,202,null);
insert into grade_report values(144,202,null);
insert into grade_report values(145,202,null);
insert into grade_report values(146,202,null);
insert into grade_report values(147,202,null);
insert into grade_report values(148,202,null);
insert into grade_report values(142,88,null);
insert into grade_report values(143,88,null);
insert into grade_report values(144,88,null);
insert into grade_report values(145,88,null);
insert into grade_report values(146,88,null);
insert into grade_report values(147,88,null);
insert into grade_report values(148,88,null);
insert into grade_report values(142,89,'A');
```

```
insert into grade_report values(143,89,'B');
insert into grade_report values(144,89,'B');
insert into grade_report values(145,89,'F');
insert into grade_report values(146,89,'B');
insert into grade_report values(147,89,'B');
insert into grade_report values(148,89,'B');
insert into grade_report values(151,97,null);
insert into grade_report values(153,97,null);
insert into grade_report values(155,97,null);
insert into grade_report values(157,97,null);
insert into grade_report values(158,97,null);
insert into grade_report values(160,97,null);
insert into grade_report values(161,97,null);
insert into grade_report values(163,97,null);
insert into grade_report values(151,109,null);
insert into grade_report values(153,109,null);
insert into grade_report values(155,109,null);
insert into grade_report values(157,109,null);
insert into grade_report values(158,109,null);
insert into grade_report values(160,109,null);
insert into grade_report values(161,109,null);
insert into grade_report values(163,109,null);
insert into grade_report values(151,201,null);
insert into grade_report values(153,201,null);
insert into grade_report values(155,201,null);
insert into grade_report values(157,201,null);
insert into grade_report values(158,201,null);
insert into grade_report values(160,201,null);
insert into grade_report values(161,201,null);
insert into grade_report values(163,201,null);
insert into plants values('GULP OIL','PITTSBURGH');
insert into plants values('GULP OIL','GULF BREEZE');
insert into plants values('GULP OIL','MOBILE');
insert into plants values('GULP OIL','SAN FRANCISCO');
insert into plants values('GULP OIL','HONOLULU');
insert into plants values('GULP OIL','BINGHAMTON');
insert into plants values('IBN COMPUTERS','PITTSBURGH');
insert into plants values('IBN COMPUTERS','GULF BREEZE');
insert into plants values('IBN COMPUTERS','MOBILE');
insert into plants values('IBN COMPUTERS','SAN FRANCISCO');
insert into plants values('IBN COMPUTERS','HONOLULU');
insert into plants values('IBN COMPUTERS','BINGHAMTON');
insert into plants values('BO$S TIRES','PITTSBURGH');
insert into plants values('BO$S TIRES','GULF BREEZE');
insert into plants values('BO$S TIRES','MOBILE');
insert into plants values('BO$S TIRES','SAN FRANCISCO');
insert into plants values('BO$S TIRES','HONOLULU');
insert into plants values('BO$S TIRES','BINGHAMTON');
insert into plants values('BANK D$AMERICER','PITTSBURGH');
insert into plants values('BANK D$AMERICER','GULF BREEZE');
insert into plants values('BANK D$AMERICER','MOBILE');
insert into plants values('BANK D$AMERICER','SAN FRANCISCO');
insert into plants values('BANK D$AMERICER','HONOLULU');
insert into plants values('BANK D$AMERICER','BINGHAMTON');
```

```
insert into plants values('COLONEL MOTORS','PITTSBURGH');
insert into plants values('COLONEL MOTORS','GULF BREEZE');
insert into plants values('COLONEL MOTORS','SAN FRANCISCO');
insert into plants values('COLONEL MOTORS','HONOLULU');
insert into plants values('COLONEL MOTORS','BINGHAMTON');
insert into plants values('COLONEL MOTORS','TUSCALOOSA');
insert into plants values('COKE COLA','PITTSBURGH');
insert into plants values('COKE COLA','GULF BREEZE');
insert into plants values('COKE COLA','MOBILE');
insert into plants values('COKE COLA','SAN FRANCISCO');
insert into plants values('COKE COLA','HONOLULU');
insert into plants values('COKE COLA','BINGHAMTON');
insert into plants values('COKE COLA','TUSCALOOSA');
insert into plants values('WENDIES','PITTSBURGH');
insert into plants values('WENDIES','GULF BREEZE');
insert into plants values('WENDIES','MOBILE');
insert into plants values('WENDIES','SAN FRANCISCO');
insert into plants values('WENDIES','HONOLULU');
insert into plants values('WENDIES','BINGHAMTON');
insert into plants values('WENDIES','TUSCALOOSA');
insert into plants values('CAPTAIN E$S','PITTSBURGH');
insert into plants values('CAPTAIN E$S','GULF BREEZE');
insert into plants values('CAPTAIN E$S','MOBILE');
insert into plants values('CAPTAIN E$S','SAN FRANCISCO');
insert into plants values('CAPTAIN E$S','HONOLULU');
insert into plants values('CAPTAIN E$S','BINGHAMTON');
insert into plants values('CAPTAIN E$S','TUSCALOOSA');
insert into plants values('RADAR SHACK','PITTSBURGH');
insert into plants values('RADAR SHACK','GULF BREEZE');
insert into plants values('RADAR SHACK','SAN FRANCISCO');
insert into plants values('RADAR SHACK','HONOLULU');
insert into plants values('RADAR SHACK','BINGHAMTON');
insert into plants values('RADAR SHACK','TUSCALOOSA');
insert into plants values('PHIL$S BAKE SHOP','PITTSBURGH');
insert into plants values('PHIL$S BAKE SHOP','GULF BREEZE');
insert into plants values('PHIL$S BAKE SHOP','SAN FRANCISCO');
insert into plants values('PHIL$S BAKE SHOP','HONOLULU');
insert into plants values('PHIL$S BAKE SHOP','BINGHAMTON');
insert into plants values('PHIL$S BAKE SHOP','TUSCALOOSA');
insert into plants values('WYATT$S TOMBSTONE','PITTSBURGH');
insert into plants values('WYATT$S TOMBSTONE','GULF BREEZE');
insert into plants values('WYATT$S TOMBSTONE','SAN FRANCISCO');
insert into plants values('WYATT$S TOMBSTONE','HONOLULU');
insert into plants values('WYATT$S TOMBSTONE','BINGHAMTON');
insert into plants values('WYATT$S TOMBSTONE','TUSCALOOSA');
insert into plants values('EAST PUBLISHING','PITTSBURGH');
insert into plants values('EAST PUBLISHING','GULF BREEZE');
insert into plants values('EAST PUBLISHING','SAN FRANCISCO');
insert into plants values('EAST PUBLISHING','HONOLULU');
insert into plants values('EAST PUBLISHING','BINGHAMTON');
insert into plants values('EAST PUBLISHING','TUSCALOOSA');
insert into plants values('UTAH BOB$S','PITTSBURGH');
insert into plants values('UTAH BOB$S','GULF BREEZE');
insert into plants values('UTAH BOB$S','SAN FRANCISCO');
```

```
insert into plants values('UTAH BOB$S','HONOLULU');
insert into plants values('UTAH BOB$S','BINGHAMTON');
update plants set company = replace(company,'$','''');
insert into prereq values('ACCT3333','ACCT2220');
insert into prereq values('COSC3320','COSC1310');
insert into prereq values('COSC3380','COSC3320');
insert into prereq values('COSC3380','MATH2410');
insert into prereq values('COSC5234','COSC3320');
insert into prereq values('ENGL1011','ENGL1010');
insert into prereq values('ENGL3401','ENGL1011');
insert into prereq values('ENGL3520','ENGL1011');
insert into prereq values('MATH5501','MATH2333');
insert into prereq values('POLY2103','POLY1201');
insert into prereq values('POLY5501','POLY4103');
insert into prereq values('CHEM3001','CHEM2001');
insert into room values(13,101,85,'Y');
insert into room values(36,123,35,'N');
insert into room values(58,114,60,null);
insert into room values(79,179,35,'Y');
insert into room values(79,174,22,'Y');
insert into room values(58,112,40,null);
insert into room values(36,122,25,'N');
insert into room values(36,121,25,'N');
insert into room values(36,120,25,'N');
insert into room values(58,110,null,'Y');
insert into section values(85,'MATH2410','FALL','98','KING',36,123);
insert into section values(86,'MATH5501','FALL','98','EMERSON',36,123);
insert into section values(87,'ENGL3401','FALL','98','HILLARY',13,101);
insert into section values(88,'ENGL3520','FALL','99','HILLARY',13,101);
insert into section values(89,'ENGL3520','SPRING','99','HILLARY',13,101);
insert into section values(90,'COSC3380','SPRING','99','HARDESTY',79,179);
insert into section values(91,'COSC3701','FALL','98',null,79,179);
insert into section values(92,'COSC1310','FALL','98','ANDERSON',79,179);
insert into section values(93,'COSC1310','SPRING','99','RAFAELT',79,179);
insert into section values(94,'ACCT3464','FALL','98','RODRIGUEZ',74,null);
insert into section values(95,'ACCT2220','SPRING','99','RODRIQUEZ',74,null);
insert into section values(96,'COSC2025','FALL','98','RAFAELT',79,179);
insert into section values(97,'ACCT3333','FALL','99','RODRIQUEZ',74,null);
insert into section values(98,'COSC3380','FALL','99','HARDESTY',79,179);
insert into section values(99,'ENGL3401','FALL','99','HILLARY',13,101);
insert into section values(102,'COSC3320','SPRING','99','KNUTH',79,179);
insert into section values(107,'MATH2333','SPRING','00','CHANG',36,123);
insert into section values(109,'MATH5501','FALL','99','CHANG',36,123);
insert into section values(112,'MATH2410','FALL','99','CHANG',36,123);
insert into section values(119,'COSC1310','FALL','99','ANDERSON',79,179);
insert into section values(126,'ENGL1010','FALL','98','HERMANO',13,101);
insert into section values(127,'ENGL1011','SPRING','99','HERMANO',13,101);
insert into section values(133,'ENGL1010','FALL','99','HERMANO',13,101);
insert into section values(134,'ENGL1011','SPRING','00','HERMANO',13,101);
insert into section values(135,'COSC3380','FALL','99','STONE',79,179);
insert into section values(145,'COSC1310','SPRING','99','JONES',79,179);
insert into section values(158,'MATH2410','SPRING','98',null,36,123);
insert into section values(201,'CHEM2001','FALL','99',null,58,114);
insert into section values(202,'CHEM3001','SPRING','00','CARNEAU',58,null);
```

```
insert into section values(100,'POLY1201','FALL','99','SCHMIDT',null,null);
insert into section values(101,'POLY2103','SPRING','00','SCHMIDT',null,null);
insert into section values(104,'POLY4103','SPRING','00','SCHMIDT',null,null);
insert into student values(2,'Lineas','ENGL','1','15-APR-80');
insert into student values(3,'Mary','COSC','4','16-JUL-78');
insert into student values(8,'Brenda','COSC','2','13-AUG-77');
insert into student values(10,'Richard','ENGL','1','13-MAY-80');
insert into student values(13,'Kelly','MATH','4','12-AUG-80');
insert into student values(14,'Lujack','COSC','1','12-FEB-77');
insert into student values(15,'Reva','MATH','2','10-JUN-80');
insert into student values(17,'Elainie','COSC','1','12-AUG-76');
insert into student values(19,'Harley','POLY','2','16-APR-81');
insert into student values(20,'Donald','ACCT','4','15-OCT-77');
insert into student values(24,'Chris','ACCT','4','12-FEB-78');
insert into student values(34,'Lynette','POLY','1','16-JUL-81');
insert into student values(49,'Susan','ENGL','3','11-MAR-80');
insert into student values(62,'Monica','MATH','3','14-OCT-80');
insert into student values(70,'Bill','POLY',null,'14-OCT-80');
insert into student values(121,'Hillary','COSC','1','16-JUL-77');
insert into student values(122,'Phoebe','ENGL','3','15-APR-80');
insert into student values(123,'Holly','POLY','4','15-JAN-81');
insert into student values(125,'Sadie','MATH','2','12-AUG-80');
insert into student values(126,'Jessica','POLY','2','16-JUL-81');
insert into student values(127,'Steve','ENGL','1','11-MAR-80');
insert into student values(128,'Brad','COSC','1','10-SEP-77');
insert into student values(129,'Cedric','ENGL','2','15-APR-80');
insert into student values(130,'Alan','COSC','2','16-JUL-77');
insert into student values(131,'Rachel','ENGL','3','15-APR-80');
insert into student values(132,'George','POLY','1','16-APR-81');
insert into student values(142,'Jerry','COSC','4','12-MAR-78');
insert into student values(143,'Cramer','ENGL','3','15-APR-80');
insert into student values(144,'Fraiser','POLY','1','16-JUL-81');
insert into student values(145,'Harrison','ACCT','4','12-FEB-77');
insert into student values(146,'Francis','ACCT','4','11-JUN-77');
insert into student values(147,'Smithly','ENGL','2','13-MAY-80');
insert into student values(148,'Sebastian','ACCT','2','14-OCT-76');
insert into student values(31,'Jake','COSC','4','12-FEB-78');
insert into student values(151,'Losmith','CHEM','3','15-JAN-81');
insert into student values(153,'Genevieve','UNKN',null,'15-OCT-79');
insert into student values(155,'Lindsay','UNKN','1','15-OCT-79');
insert into student values(157,'Stephanie','MATH',null,'16-APR-81');
insert into student values(158,'Thornton',null,null,'15-OCT-79');
insert into student values(163,'Lionel',null,null,'15-OCT-79');
insert into student values(161,'Benny','CHEM','4','10-JUN-80');
insert into student values(160,'Gus','ART ','3','15-OCT-78');
insert into student values(5,'Zelda','COSC',null,'12-FEB-78');
insert into student values(7,'Mario','MATH',null,'12-AUG-80');
insert into student values(9,'Romona','ENGL',null,'15-APR-80');
insert into student values(6,'Ken','POLY',null,'15-JUL-80');
insert into student values(88,'Smith',null,null,'15-OCT-79');
insert into student values(191,'Jake','MATH','2','10-JUN-80');
insert into dependent values(2,'Matt','Son','M',8);
insert into dependent values(2,'Mary','Daughter','F',9);
insert into dependent values(2,'Beena','Spouse','F',31);
```

```
insert into dependent values(10,'Amit','Son','M',3);
insert into dependent values(10,'Shantu','Daughter','F',5);
insert into dependent values(14,'Raju','Son','M',1);
insert into dependent values(14,'Rani',' ','F',3);
insert into dependent values(17,'Susan','Daughter','F',4);
insert into dependent values(17,'Sam','Son','M',1);
insert into dependent values(20,'Donald II','Son','M',Null);
insert into dependent values(20,'Chris','Son','M',6);
insert into dependent values(34,'Susan','Daughter','F',5);
insert into dependent values(34,'Monica','Daughter','F',1);
insert into dependent values(62,'Tom','Husband','M',45);
insert into dependent values(62,'James','Son','M',14);
insert into dependent values(62,'Hillary','Daughter','F',16);
insert into dependent values(62,'Phoebe','Daughter','F',12);
insert into dependent values(123,'James','Son','M',5);
insert into dependent values(123,'Jon','Son','M',2);
insert into dependent values(126,'Om','Son','M',6);
insert into dependent values(126,'Prakash','Son','M',1);
insert into dependent values(128,'Mithu','Son','M',1);
insert into dependent values(128,'Mita','Daughter','F',Null);
insert into dependent values(128,'Nita','Daughter','F',2);
insert into dependent values(128,'Barbara','Wife','F',26);
insert into dependent values(132,'Rekha','Daughter','F',6);
insert into dependent values(142,'Rakhi','Daughter','F',2);
insert into dependent values(143,'Mona','Daughter','F',7);
insert into dependent values(144,'Susan','Wife','F',22);
insert into dependent values(145,'Susie','Wife','F',22);
insert into dependent values(146,'Xi du','Wife','F',22);
insert into dependent values(147,'Barbara','Wife','F',23);
insert into dependent values(147,'Sebastian','Son','M',4);
insert into dependent values(147,'Jake','Son','M',2);
insert into dependent values(147,'Losmith','Son','M',Null);
insert into dependent values(153,'Madhu','Daughter','F',5);
insert into dependent values(153,'Mamta','Daughter','F',4);
insert into dependent values(153,'Mahesh','Son','M',2);
insert into dependent values(158,'Sally','wife', 'F',22);

select top 6 sname, major, class into teststu from student;
```

Glossary of Terms

Aggregate Function

A function that returns a result based on values of some attributes in multiple rows.

Alias

A temporary intra-query substitute for a table name or column name.

Alphanumeric

A data type that will accept a combination of characters as well as numbers.

Anomaly

An undesirable consequence of a data modification.

Attribute

Column in a table.

Binary Intersection

An operation on two sets that generates unique values in common between two sets.

Binary Set Difference

An operation on two sets that generates values in one set less those contained in another.

Binary Union

An operation on two sets that generates all unique elements of both sets.

Byte

A storage unit consisting of 8 bits.

Candidate Key

A column (attribute, or group of columns) that identifies a unique row in a table. One of the candidate keys is chosen to be the primary key.

Cartesian Product

A binary operation resulting in the combination of all rows of one table with all rows of another table.

CHAR(*size*)

Data type that stores fixed-length character data, *size* characters long.

Columns

Vertical slices of a table. Columns are defined to be one data type.

Column Alias

A temporary column name within a query.

Comments

Nonexecutable words included in SQL queries for documentation.

Constant

An unvarying value used in a query.

Constraint

A restriction placed on a value in a database used to increase data integrity.

Correlated Subquery

A subquery in which the information in the subquery is referenced by the outer, main query. A correlated subquery cannot stand alone; it depends on the outer query.

Data

Recorded facts pertaining to entities.

Database

A collection of logically associated or related data.

Database Administrator (DBA)
See DBA.

DBA (Database Administrator)
A person who has all system privileges and the ability to grant all privileges to other users. The DBA creates and drops users and space in a database.

DDL (Data Definition Language)
A language used to define the internal schema and conceptual schema in a database.

DML (Data Manipulation Language)
A language used to manipulate data (INSERT, UPDATE, and DELETE).

Default
A value assigned to data when no value is supplied.

Domain
The set of all possible values that a column value can have.

Entity
An object about which data is recorded

Entity Relationship (ER) Diagram
A visual tool to describe how data in a database is arranged.

Equi-Join
A join condition with equality comparisons only.

Execute
Run a query to get an output of the task requested.

Field
An attribute or column in a table. A field is defined to be of one data type.

Float
A data type that accepts numbers with decimals.

Foreign Key
An attribute that is a primary key of another table. Relationships are implemented with the use of foreign keys in relational databases.

Full Outer Join
Used to designate the union of the left and right outer joins.

Functionally Dependent
A relationship between two attributes in a relation. Attribute Y is functionally dependent on attribute X if attribute X identifies attribute Y.

Global Temporary Table
Temporary tables that can be accessed by anyone signed on while the table exists.

Group Function
A function that returns a result based on multiple rows. Also known as an aggregate function.

Index
An internal table created to speed up queries and searches in database.

Inline View
A view that exists only during the execution of a query.

Inner Query
A subquery.

Integer
A data type that accepts only whole numbers and no decimals.

Join
An operation used to combine related rows from two tables into one table based on a logical comparison of column values.

Key
A column value that uniquely identifies a row in a table.

Large Object Data Type (LOB)
LOBs are data types that can store large amounts (up to four gigabytes) of raw data, binary data (such as images) or character text data.

Local Temporary Tables
Temporary tables that are local to the session in which they are created.

Noncorrelated Subquery
A subquery that is independent of the outer query.

Non-Equi Join
Joins that do not test for equality.

Null
A value given to a data item when the result is unknown.

Outer Join

A join condition where all the rows from one table (for example, the left table) are kept in the result set even though those rows do not have matching rows in the other table (the right table).

Outer Query

The part of the query that will return the result set. Outer queries are usually designated when a query has one or more subqueries (inner queries).

Primary Key

A candidate key selected to be the key of a table. The primary key will uniquely identify a row in a table.

Qualifier

A prefix used to identify a column of a particular table. For example, in "Student.sname," Student is the table qualifier.

Query

A SQL instruction used to retrieve data from one or more tables or views. Queries begin with the SQL keyword SELECT.

Record

A named collection of data items. In a relational model, a record is a physical realization of a row.

Referential Integrity

The property that guarantees that values from one column that depend on values from another column are present in the "other column."

Relation

A two-dimensional table containing single-value entries and no duplicate rows. The data type of the columns is the same in every row. The order of the rows is immaterial as the table is considered a set of rows. Often a relation is defined as a populated table. See also Table.

Relational Database

A database consisting of relations (tables).

Relationship

An association between two tables.

Result Set

Output of a SQL statement.

Row

A horizontal slice of a table. A row is also known as a "tuple" and at times is called a "record"; however, a "record" usually refers to a physical representation of data and a row refers to a logical representation.

Row Filter

A criterion that is used to select rows based on certain criteria.

Row Function

A function that is performed on a single row of a table.

Schema

A design of the database typically using an entity relationship diagram.

Script

A sequence of SQL statements.

Self Join

A join condition where a table is joined with itself.

Set

A data structure that represents a collection of rows with no order and no duplicate rows.

Set Compatibility

For two sets (or tables) to be set compatible, both sets must match in number of items and must have compatible data types. Set compatibility is also referred to as union compatibility.

SQL (Structured Query Language)

A language for defining the structure and processing of a relational database.

SQL Statements

Used to issue commands to a database.

String

A mixture of letters, numbers, spaces, and other symbols where one byte is assigned to a symbol.

String Function

A row function used to manipulate string data.

Subquery

The inner query within the outer (main) query; usually one SELECT query within another SELECT query.

Subset

Some group of objects taken from a set.

Synonym

External names of objects in the data that are intended to allow the object to be addressed in more than one way.

Table

Consists of rows of information, each of which contains the same kind of values (columns). It is also referred to as a relation in the relational model.

Table Alias

A temporary name given to a table within a query.

Table Qualifiers

A query mechanism used to define where a column comes from. Qualifiers are often needed when more than one table is being used in a query.

Temporary Table

A table in which the result of a SELECT is temporarily saved and then used in other SELECT statements - see Global Temporary Tables and Local Temporary Tables.

Tuple

A row in a table.

Union Compatibility

When working with sets (tables), for two sets to have union compatibility, both sets must match in number of items and must have compatible data types.

View

A query that is stored in the data dictionary and is rerun when called for. A view appears to a user to be a table.

XML

A universal language used to generically identify data that will be shared.

Important Commands and Functions

ABS
Row-level function that returns an absolute value.

ALTER COLUMN
Command used to change a column's size or type in a table.

ALTER TABLE
Command used to modify a table's definition.

AND
Logical operator that, when used in a WHERE clause, means that both criteria have to be met for a row to be included in the result set.

ASC
Function used in ORDER BY to put a SQL result set in ascending order.

AVG
Aggregate function used to average a group of row values.

BETWEEN
An operator used to determine whether a value occurs within a given range of values (inclusive); used with a WHERE clause.

BIGINT
Integer data type that can store numbers from −263 to 263 − 1.

BINARY
Data type used to store strings of bits.

BIT
Data type that consumes only a single bit of storage.

CAST
Conversion function used to change a data type of a column within a query.

CEILING
Row-level function that returns the next larger integer.

CHAR(size)
Character data type used when the column length is known and unvarying.

CHARACTER
Data type used to store any combination of letters, numbers, and symbols.

CHARINDEX
String function that returns the starting position of a specified pattern.

CHECK
Integrity constraint used to create bounds for a column value.

CONSTRAINTS
Restrictions that can be placed on values when creating database objects such as tables and views.

CONVERT
Conversion function used to explicitly convert to a given data type within in a query.

COUNT(*)
Function used to count the total number of rows in a result set.

COUNT(attribute)
Group function that counts the number of rows where *attribute* is not NULL.

CREATE INDEX
Command used to create an index.

CREATE DATABASE
Command used to create a database.

CREATE SYNONYM
Command used to create a synonym.

CREATE TABLE
Command used to create a table.

CREATE VIEW
Command used to create a view.

CROSS JOIN
A query option used to generate a Cartesian product.

DATE
Oracle equivalent of DATETIME.

DATEADD
Date function that adds to a specified part of a date.

DATEDIFF
Date function that returns the difference between two dates.

DATEFORMAT
Date function that controls how SQL Server interprets date constants that are entered for dates.

DATEPART
Date function that returns the specified part of the date requested.

DATETIME
Data type that can be used for dates.

DAY
Date function that extracts a day from a date.

DEC
Data type; synonym for DECIMAL data type.

DECIMAL
Numeric data type whose storage type varies based on a specified precision.

DECLARE
Command used to create variables on the fly within a script.

DELETE FROM
Command that deletes rows in a table that may satisfy a given condition.

DESC
Function used in ORDER BY to put a SQL result set into descending order.

DISTINCT
Result set function that omits rows that contain duplicate data.

DROP COLUMN
Command used to delete a column in a table.

DROP CONSTRAINT
Command used to delete a named constraint.

DROP INDEX
Command used to delete an index.

DROP SYNONYM
Command used to delete a synonym.

DROP TABLE
Command used to delete a table.

DROP VIEW
Command used to delete a view.

EXISTS
A keyword in a SQL statement that returns true in a WHERE clause if the subquery following it returns at least one row.

FLOAT
Decimal data type that has a precision of 15 digits.

FLOOR
Row-level function which returns the next lower integer value when a number contains decimal places.

GETDATE
Date function that returns the current system date and time.

GROUP BY
Produces one summary row for the aggregate value of all values for a given column.

GUID
Global unique identifier; UNIQUEIDENTIFIER data type guarantees worldwide uniqueness, even among unconnected computers.

HAVING
Part of a SQL statement that is used to determine which groups of a GROUP BY will be included in the result set.

IMAGE

Large object binary data type; used to store pictures.

IN

Logical operator for a WHERE clause that tests for inclusion in a named set.

INT

Integer data type that can store numbers from −231 to 231 − 1.

INDEX BY

Command used to create an index on a table by a certain column value.

INNER JOIN

Command used to combine two tables in an equi-join operation.

INSERT INTO.. SELECT

A way to insert many rows into a new table at one time.

INSERT INTO..VALUES

A way to insert values into a table one row at a time.

INSERT

Command that allows for the addition of new rows to a table.

INTEGER

Numeric data type that has no digits after the decimal point.

INTERSECT

Set operation that combines two queries such that it returns all rows that are the same in both result sets.

IS NOT NULL

Function that tests for the NOT NULL condition.

ISNULL

Function that returns a true value if a data item contains a null.

JOIN

Command used to join two tables; synonymous with INNER JOIN.

LEFT

String function that returns the left portion of a string up to a given number of characters.

LEFT JOIN

Same as LEFT OUTER JOIN.

LEFT OUTER JOIN

A join where all the rows from the first (left) table are kept in the result set, regardless of whether they have matching rows in the second (right) table.

LEN

String function that returns the length of a string.

LIKE

A WHERE clause option that matches a particular pattern.

LONG

Oracle equivalent of TEXT data type.

LOWER

String function used to convert a string to lowercase.

LTRIM

String function that removes blanks or other named character from the beginning of a string.

MAX

Aggregate function that returns the highest of all values from a column in a set of rows.

MIN

Aggregate function that returns the lowest of all values from a column in a set of rows.

MINUS

Set operation that returns only those rows from the result of the first query that are not in the result of the second query; not available in SQL Server.

MONEY

Data type used with currency data.

MONTH

Date function that extracts the month from a date.

NATIONAL CHARACTER

A data type; synonym for NCHAR data type.

NCHAR

Fixed-length Unicode character data type.

NOT

Operator that reverses the effect of any logical operator such as IN, LIKE, and EXISTS.

NOT BETWEEN
Operator that allows you to determine whether a value does not occur within a given range of values.

NOT EXISTS
Operator that returns true in a WHERE clause if the subquery following it returns no rows.

NOT NULL
Operator that returns true if an attribute has a non-null value.

NOT NULL Constraint
Integrity constraint that denies the creation of a row when an attribute has a null value.

NULL
Value that is unknown.

NULLIF
Function that returns a NULL if a certain condition is met in an expression.

NUMERIC
Synonym for DECIMAL data type.

NVARCHAR
Variable-length Unicode character data type.

OR
Binary logical operator that returns a true value if either one of the expressions is true.

ORDER BY
Clause that sorts the results of a query before they are displayed.

OUTER JOIN
Join where rows from a table are kept in the result set although there is no matching row in the other table used in the join.

PERCENT
Function that is used to return a certain percentage of records that fall at the top of a range specified.

PRIMARY KEY
Constraint used to create a primary key in a table; used in CREATE TABLE and ALTER TABLE commands.

REAL
Decimal data type that has a precision of seven digits.

REFERENCES
Constraint part that defines the table name and key used to reference another table.

RIGHT
String function that returns the right portion of a string.

RIGHT JOIN
Same as RIGHT OUTER JOIN.

RIGHT OUTER JOIN
Join where all the rows from the second (right) relation are kept whether matched or not in a join operation.

ROUND
Function used to round numbers to a specified number of decimal places.

ROWCOUNT(n)
Function that returns the first n rows.

RTRIM
String function that removes blanks from the right end of a string.

SELECT
Command that allows you to retrieve rows from tables (or views) in a database.

SET
Command used to assign values to variables.

SET DATEFORMAT
Date function used to change the format in which SQL Server reads in dates.

SMALLDATETIME
Data type used to store dates.

SMALLINT
Integer data type that can store numbers between −215 to 215 − 1.

SMALLMONEY
Data type that can be used with currency data.

SQUARE
Row-level function that returns the square of a number.

SQL_VARIANT

Data type used to store values of any data type except TEXT or IMAGE.

SQRT

Row-level function that returns the square root of positive numeric values.

STR

Conversion function that always converts from a number to a character data type.

SUBSTRING

String function that returns part of a string.

SUM

Group function that adds up all the values for a column value in a set of rows.

TABLE

A two-dimensional (row by column) arrangement of data.

TEXT

Character large object data type.

TINYINT

Integer data type that can store numbers between 0 and 255.

TOP

Function that returns a specified number of records from the top of a result set.

UNION

Set operation that combines two queries such that it returns all distinct rows for the result sets of both queries. The two queries must have union-compatible result sets.

UNION ALL

Set operation that combines two queries and returns all rows from both the SELECT statements (queries). A UNION ALL also includes duplicate rows. The two queries must have union-compatible result sets.

UNIQUE

Integrity constraint that disallows duplicate entries for an attribute even though the column is not a primary key.

UNIQUEIDENTIFIER

Data type that guarantees uniqueness of the identifier, even among unconnected computers.

UPDATE

Command that changes values in specified columns in specified tables.

UPPER

String function used to display all output in uppercase.

USE

Command used to open a database.

UUID

Universal unique identifier; the UNIQUEIDENTIFIER data type that guarantees uniqueness, even among unconnected computers.

VARBINARY

Data type used to store variable-length binary data.

VARCHAR

Character data type used when the field length is varying.

VARCHAR2

Oracle equivalent of VARCHAR.

WHERE

Row filter part of a SQL statement that allows you to specify criteria on column values for rows that are being selected from a table.

WITH TIES

Clause used with the TOP function to retrieve rows that are ties.

XML

A new SQL Server data type used to model complex data.

YEAR

Date function that extracts the year from a date.

Index

We'd like to hear your suggestions for improving our indexes. Send email to *index@oreilly.com*.

columns, tables
    adding, ALTER TABLE command, 75
    aliases, 161
    arithmetic operations, 110
    data types, ALTER TABLE command, 75
    deleting, ALTER TABLE command, 77
    displaying, 28–32
    selecting, 28–32
commands
    ALTER COLUMN, 311
    ALTER TABLE, 75, 77, 311
    CREATE DATABASE, 312
    CREATE INDEX, 312
    CREATE SYNONYM, 312
    CREATE TABLE, 65, 312
    CREATE VIEW, 312
    DECLARE, 312
    DELETE, 78, 79
    DELETE FROM, 312
    DROP COLUMN, 312
    DROP CONSTRAINT, 312
    DROP INDEX, 312
    DROP SYNONYM, 312
    DROP TABLE, 312
    DROP VIEW, 312
    INDEX BY, 313
    INNER JOIN, 313
    INSERT, 313
    INSERT INTO...SELECT, 70–73
    INSERT...INTO, 67–70
    JOIN, 313
    SELECT, 314
    SET, 314
    UPDATE, 73–74, 315
    USE, 315
comments, statements, 53–54
concatenation, string functions, 121
constants, UNION operation, 182
constraints, 311
    CHECK, 276–277
    deleting, 277
    NOT NULL, 269
    PRIMARY KEY, 270–275, 276
    referential integrity, 278–288
    UNIQUE, 275
conversion functions
    CAST, 134, 311
    CONVERT, 136
    STR, 135
CONVERT function, 136, 311
correlated queries, 245–254

correlated subqueries, 242, 243–245
    EXISTS predicate, 246–251
    IN predicate, 251–252
    NOT EXISTS predicate, 252–254
COUNT function, 44–46, 106, 311
    IS NOT NULL condition, 45
    IS NULL condition, 45
CREATE DATABASE command, 312
CREATE INDEX command, 312
CREATE INDEX statement, 266
CREATE SYNONYM command, 312
CREATE TABLE command, 65, 312
CREATE TABLE statement, 265
CREATE VIEW command, 312
CROSS JOIN, 91
CROSS JOIN query option, 312

D

data in views, 162
data type precedence, parentheses, 156
data types, 58
    BIGINT, 311
    BINARY, 311
    BIT, 311
    CHAR, 311
    CHARACTER, 311
    character data types
        CHAR data type, 60
        NCHAR data type, 61
        NVARCHAR data type, 61
        selecting, 61
        TEXT data type, 61
        Unicode character strings, 61
        VARCHAR data type, 60
    date and time data types, 62
    DATETIME, 312
    DEC, 312
    DECIMAL, 312
    FLOAT, 312
    IMAGE, 313
    INT, 313
    INTEGER, 313
    LONG, 313
    miscellaneous data types
        BINARY data type, 62
        BIT data type, 63
        IMAGE data type, 63
        monetary data types, 63
        SQL_VARIANT data type, 63
        TABLE data type, 63
        UNIQUEIDENTIFIER data type, 64
        XML data type, 64

tables, 315
  columns
    adding, 75
    aliases, 161
    data types, 75
    deleting, 77
    displaying, 28–32
    selecting, 28–32
  creating, 65–67
    Load script, 12–13
  data, viewing, 16
  deleting, 18
    DELETE command, 79
  joins, multiple, 95
  rows
    displaying, 38–44
    selecting, 38–44
  Student_course database, 292
    default, 5
  temporary, 165–168
  tuples, 38–44
tempdb database, 8
terms, glossary of, 307–310
TEXT data type, 61, 315
Text Editor tab, 24
text form, query results, 22
TINYINT data type, 315
TOP function, 116, 315
  PERCENT and, 118
T-SQL (Transact-SQL), 19
tuples, 38–44

U

Unicode character strings, 61
UNION ALL set operation, 183, 315
  columns and, 183
union compatibility, 179
UNION set operation, 180–182, 315
  columns and, 183
  JOIN and, 197–203
UNIQUE constraint, 275

UNIQUE IDENTIFIER data type, 315
UNIQUE integrity constraint, 315
UNIQUEIDENTIFIER data type, 64
universal qualifiers, 255–260
UPDATE command, 73–74, 315
UPPER function, 128, 315
USE command, 315
USE, opening databases, 11
UUID (Universal unique identifier), 315

V

VARBINARY data type, 315
VARCHAR data type, 60, 315
VARCHAR2 data type, 315
views, 157
  column alises, 161
  creating, 158
  data in, 162
  ORDER BY clause, 160
  SELECT INTO statement, 160
  using, 159

W

WHERE clause
  JOIN and, 88
  SELECT statement, 38
    AND operator, 40
    BETWEEN operator, 42, 43
    OR operator, 41
WHERE row filter, 315
WITH TIES clause, 315
writing statements, 54

X

XM Ldata type, 64
XML data type, 315

Y

YEAR function, 140, 315

About the Authors

Dr. Sikha Bagui is an Assistant Professor in the Department of Computer Science at the University of West Florida in Pensacola. She teaches a variety of computer science courses and database courses, and her research areas are database design, data mining, pattern recognition, and statistical computing. Dr. Bagui has published many journal articles and co-authored several books with Dr. Earp. Books co-authored with Dr. Earp are *Learning SQL: A Step-by-Step Guide using Oracle* and *Learning SQL: A Step-by-Step Guide using Access*, both published by Addison Wesley; *Database Design Using ER Diagrams*, published by CRC Press, and *Advanced SQL Functions in Oracle 10g*, published by Wordware Publishing.

Dr. Richard Walsh Earp is the former Chair of and a former Associate Professor in the Department of Computer Science at the University of West Florida in Pensacola, Florida. He also served at Dean of the College of Science and Technology at that institution. He has taught a variety of computer science courses, including database systems and advanced database systems. Dr. Earp has authored and co-authored several papers and has co-authored several books with Dr. Bagui. Dr. Earp was also an instructor with Learning Tree International for several years and worked for Computer Sciences Corporation at the Naval Air Station in Pensacola, Florida as a database consultant after his retirement from academia.

Colophon

The animal on the cover of *Learning SQL on SQL Server 2005* is a Spanish ribbed newt (*Pleurodeles waltl*). This salamander inhabits the ponds, lakes, and calm brooks of the Iberian Peninsula and Morocco. The ribbed newt is an amphibian, but is rarely found on land; if its watery habitat dries out, the newt burrows into mud and waits for rain.

The ribbed newt gets its name from the pointed ribs that can often be seen poking through its skin. This feature protects the newts from some enemies—their obviously sharp bones discourage predators in search of tender prey. When attacked, the newt can force the ribs through its own skin, presenting a pointed defense. The ribs also resemble warts, common in more poisonous newt species. Although the ribbed newt is not as toxic as others, their similarities give predators pause.

The ribbed newt is an able swimmer and voracious predator. It consumes most attainable moving prey, including aquatic insects, other invertebrates or amphibians, and small fish.

The cover image is from the *Dover Pictoral Archive*. The cover font is Adobe ITC Garamond. The text font is Linotype Birka; the heading font is Adobe Myriad Condensed; and the code font is LucasFont's TheSans Mono Condensed.

Better than e-books

Try it Free! Sign up today
and get your first 14 days free.
Go to *safari.oreilly.com*

Search
thousands of
top tech books

Download
whole chapters

Cut and Paste
code examples

Find
answers fast

Search Safari! The premier electronic reference
library for programmers and IT professionals.

Related Titles from O'Reilly

Windows Administration

Active Directory Cookbook

Active Directory, *3rd Edition*

DNS on Windows Server 2003

Essential Microsoft Operations Manager

Essential SharePoint

Exchange Server Cookbook

Learning Windows Server 2003, *2nd Edition*

MCSE Core Required Exams in a Nutshell, *3rd Edition*

Monad

Securing Windows Server 2003

SharePoint Office Pocket Guide

SharePoint User's Guide

Windows Server 2003 in a Nutshell

Windows Server 2003 Network Administration

Windows Server 2003 Security Cookbook

Windows Server Cookbook

Windows Server Hacks

Windows XP Cookbook